The Fall of Fortress Europe
1943-1945

THE FALL OF FORTRESS EUROPE 1943-1945

Albert Seaton

HM

HOLMES & MEIER PUBLISHERS, INC.

NEW YORK

First published in the United States of America 1981 by
HOLMES & MEIER PUBLISHERS, INC.
30 Irving Place, New York, N.Y. 10003

© Albert Seaton 1981

Library of Congress Catalog Card Number: 81-81959

ISBN 0-8419-0722-6

PRINTED IN GREAT BRITAIN

Contents

List of Illustrations

19 A Nazi press photo showing Rommel inspecting coastal gun emplacements (1944)

20 German beach obstacles in Normandy, photographed on 7 June 1944, the day after the invasion

21 German Army cycle mobility in the west

22 Part of the invasion fleet shortly bound for South France (August 1944)

23 American and French airborne troops landing behind Nice and Marseilles (August 1944)

24 Railway sidings at Vire, Normandy, after Allied bombing (June 1944)

25 A German dual-purpose 88mm gun used hastily in an anti-tank role

26 A V-1 pilotless winged jet missile photographed in flight (1944)

27 A V-2 rocket leaving its launching pad (1944)

28 United States tanks passing through part of the West Wall near Aachen (September 1944)

29 A Captured German Panther (Mk V) tank with a British crew on the 2 (Br) Army sector (January 1945)

30 Red Army Troops attacking near Königsberg in East Prussia (February 1945)

31 The city of Kiel after Allied air bombing (May 1945)

List of Maps

Acknowledgments

I am much indebted to the authors, editors and publishers of General Müller-Hillebrand's three volume work *Das Heer* and of the four volume *Kriegstagebuch des Oberkommandos der Wehrmacht 1940-1945*, edited by Professors Jacobsen, Hillgruber, Hubatsch and Schramm, and in particular for the information in the editorial notes furnished by Professors Hubatsch and Schramm for the period 1943-1945. The use of the materials included in *Das Heer* and the *KTB, OKW* has been of outstanding value. I am also grateful to the Keeper of the Department of Documents of the Imperial War Museum in London, to the Militär-Archiv and the Militärgeschichtliches Forschungsamt in Freiburg, and to the Stato Maggiore dell' Esercito (Ufficio Storico) in Rome, for most helpful assistance with queries on documentary material.

I acknowledge my very grateful thanks to the Commandant of the Royal Military College of Canada for his generous permission to use printed material from the collections of the Massey Library, R.M.C., Kingston, and I thank, most wholeheartedly, Mr R.K.C. Crouch, the Chief Librarian, and Mr C.R. Watt, the Assistant Librarian and Head of Special Collections. I am also grateful indeed to the Robarts Library, the University of Toronto, and to the Chief Librarian and to the Librarian in charge of the Library's Historical Section of the Ministry of Defence Library (Central and Army), London, for the use of the material held by them.

I should like to thank both of my publishers, Weidenfeld and Nicolson and B.T. Batsford, for their kind agreement that I should reproduce a number of paragraphs that have appeared in my earlier books, *The Russo-German War 1941-45* (Arthur Barker 1970), and *Stalin as Warlord* (Batsford 1976).

My very thankful acknowledgment is due to the following authors and publishers for kind permission to quote from their works:

Das Heer 1933-1945 by General B. Müller-Hillebrand—published by E.S. Mittler und Sohn GmbH, Steintorwall 17, 4900 Herford, and Bonngasse 3, 5300 Bonn: *Das Kriegstagebuch des Oberkommandos der Wehrmacht 1940-1945*, edited by Professors Jacobsen, Hillgruber, Hubatsch and Schramm—published by Bernard und Graefe Verlag, Hubertusstrasse 5, 8000 Munich: *Hitler's Last Days* by Gerhardt Boldt—published by Arthur Barker (Weidenfeld), 91 Clapham High Street, London SW4: *The Goebbels Diaries*, edited by Louis P. Lochner—copyright 1948 by The Fireside Press, Inc. and reprinted by permission of Doubleday & Company Inc., 245 Park Avenue, New York 10017: *The Final Entries—The Diaries of Joseph Goebbels*, edited by Professor Trevor-Roper and translated by

General Barry—published by Secker and Warburg, 54 Poland Street, London
W 11: *Victory in the West—History of the Second World War*, Volume 1 by
L. F. Ellis—published by HMSO, London.

Lastly I should like to thank my wife for typing the manuscript and for her
constant support and valuable assistance in the research, the reading and the
compilation.

Sources of the photographs were: Popperfoto, nos. 2, 3, 7, 9, 11, 13-24, 26-29 and
31; BBC Hulton Picture Library, nos. 1, 4, 5, 8, 10 and 25; no. 6 is by courtesy of
the Trustees of the Imperial War Museum.

The maps are by Patrick Leeson.

Introduction

German generals came in all guises, sometimes with very different backgrounds and always with widely varying characteristics, and it would be wrong to suppose that they, the general staff or the officer corps, could be cast to type. It is true, of course, that the generals suffered from a lack of a liberal education so that nearly all had what General Faber du Faur, who had lived among them for forty years, called 'a military cadet mentality' in which an exaggerated regard for obedience edged out common-sense. And it is true, too, that the German military system had aimed, and perhaps in part had succeeded, in moulding its officers to a near Prussian pattern—at least to the outward eye—and that its general staff and arms schools had impregnated them with a common doctrine for the waging of war. Yet, inevitably, underneath they remained how their Maker had fashioned them. Keitel was a very different type of general from Guderian; Jodl was poles apart from Model; von Rundstedt differed again from von Kluge; and Zeitzler had little affinity with Krebs. The single common factor amongst the high-ranking generals that came to terms with Nazism was that they were eager for advancement and, notwithstanding what any might have said after the war, they had at one time been Nazi supporters and admirers of Hitler; few among them were men of political or strategic perspicacity or of any great strength of character, for ambition or lack of courage blinded most of them to the demands of conscience and moral responsibility.

This defect in the military leadership had, however, little to do with Hitler, for it had already become apparent in the Prussian Army of the new German Empire, under its youthful sovereign Wilhelm II; there was no longer any place in its senior ranks for the individualist or the man of character, for the von Ziethen or the von Blücher of earlier times. Von Schlieffen, the Chief of the Great General Staff, himself unable to withstand the demands of his Kaiser, wanted none but disciplined conformists about him; and this affected the selection, promotion and retirement of general officers and, particularly, the education and standards of the general staff. Von Moltke, the younger, was indecisive and a failure; von Falkenhayn was indecisive and secretive and 'without a single strategic idea in his head': both were personally dependent upon the emperor. Von Hindenburg without Tannenberg (von Ludendorff's victory) 'was nothing', and he was to show at times a lamentable lack of judgement and moral courage: von Ludendorff was something of an exception in that he was sturdily independent of the authority of others, but his lack of vision, moderation and common-sense clouded his great gifts. Groener, the Württemberger, was a moderate and not without character, but his judgement of others was to prove, as he himself afterwards admitted, grievously at fault. Von

Seeckt and von Hammerstein, who were to head the German Army of the Republic, and von Schleicher, his '*Kardinal in politicis*', were all Groener's early protégés.

So it was that the German Army came to be controlled by von Seeckt and the little *Kasino-Klique* made up of the officers of the former Regiment of the Third Imperial Foot Guards—the von Hindenburgs, von Schleicher and von Hammerstein.* Von Seeckt had had a distinguished war career, mainly on the staff as a colonel and major-general, and had proved himself of remarkable ability in these ranks: von Seeckt's weakness, however, was that he was a product of the 'Schlieffen' school, for he appears to have modelled even his personal behaviour on von Schlieffen, with his sphinx-like mask, curt speech and long silences; he was, moreover, inclined to be vain and petty and was intolerant of new ideas unless they came from himself. Like von Schlieffen he looked to the past and not to the future.

It is perhaps extraordinary that von Seeckt and his successors should have deliberately and successfully sought to encourage the use of personal initiative of action at the lower tactical levels, even amongst junior leaders, and yet have stifled the research and development of politico-strategic thought within the *Heeresleitung*. But von Seeckt was a military conformist with a distrust of the unorthodox, a highly efficient organizer of a cadre army trained for the type of war envisaged by von Schlieffen in 1905. Von Seeckt's politico-strategic ability was never put to the test but his subsequent writings indicate that his education and views had advanced little beyond 1914. If Groener's latter-day opinion, written in the thirties, is to be believed, von Seeckt was neither far-sighted nor morally courageous.

Von Hammerstein, the last head of the *Heeresleitung* before Hitler came to power, was opposed to Hitlerism; but he was indolent, almost supine, and his influence was limited, even within the German Army itself. During his tenure there was much discontent. Some army officers, particularly the young, were openly in favour of Hitler; among these Nazi supporters were some who were later to be most active in the 20 July 1944 bomb plot to destroy the dictator, including Beck, at that time commanding an artillery regiment and later brought in, presumably at Hitler's instigation, to be Chief of the Army General Staff. Von Fritsch, who succeeded von Hammerstein, and von Blomberg, who replaced Groener as the Minister for Defence, were both selected by von Hindenburg, and both were unhappy choices.

It was against this military background, so unpromising to Germany, that Hitler came to power.

---

* Two other former members of the Third Foot Guards who later achieved prominence were von Brauchitsch and von Manstein.

CHAPTER ONE

The Feldherr

The Swedish statesman Count Oxenstierna said, in the seventeenth century, that what one learns from history is that mankind learns nothing from history. Professor Schramm, the war diarist of the German high command in Hitler's war years, added to this his own opinion, that world history was a primer from which one could learn much if only it were correctly read. These statements are, of course, so self-evident as to be almost platitudinous, except that the correctness of the reading must depend largely on who presents the history, and largely on the education, experience, discernment and interpretation of those who read it.

The German Army of the Weimar Republic and of the Third Reich was the direct descendant of the German Army of the Empire, its leaders being arrogant, chauvinistic, anti-Semitic, particularly narrow-minded, and poorly read in world—as opposed to German—history and in the realities of politics. This failure in the education of Germany's soldiers was shared by a very large section of the German public in the first three decades of the twentieth century; all of them, the politicians, the soldiers, and the men and women in the street provided the ready prepared ground that was to be the forcing-bed for Hitlerism.

Hitler himself had very much in common with the political and military leaders of the Hohenzollern Empire, because he was a product of his times and because he appears to have been an avid reader of the German political and military histories and treatises of the day. So Hitler and his military men were to display much of the strength and nearly all the weaknesses of the old Empire, showing that they had learned little from the errors of their predecessors as together they prepared to launch, and then Hitler alone led, eighty million people further along the very same path to political, national and existential suicide.

Probably the most important factor underlying the defeat of Germany in the First World War had been the inability of the Kaiser and his political and military leaders to understand the limits of Germany's war potential and, at the same time, appreciate the political, moral and material strength of the enemy coalition that they had so wantonly provoked into the war against them. Nor could they realize the limitations of the use of armed force or the proper place of arms in the exercise of politics. Intoxicated by military pageantry, they let armed force oust diplomacy so that they came to believe that foreign politics and the fate of nations could be decided only by the sword. And so political action came to be based on military thought, on the quicksands of the Great General Staff's appreciations, for all German general staff planning before 1914 had been based on the assumption that had been allowed to develop into an unquestionable premise—*that no nation was capable of conducting a protracted war, and that German troops were superior to all others.* Discounting world opinion and the certainty that Britain would come into the war, Berlin intended to crush the French in a lightning six weeks campaign before throwing its main forces eastwards against Russia. In such a way did the German Empire enter the First World War armed with a plan of campaign (*Feldzugsplan*) instead of a war plan (*Kriegsplan*).

German politicians and soldiers of the post-war years continued to explain away the defeat by causes other than the true one. Some account was, admittedly, taken of the gravity of the British economic blockade that had reduced Germany to hunger, and of the difficulties in the waging of a war on two fronts that had drained away German manpower; but these were, in reality, effects and not causes. Groener and von Seeckt, even fifteen years after the event, still professed to believe, together with a large number of other senior general officers, that the whole war was irretrievably lost for Germany when, in August 1914, the younger von Moltke, the Chief of General Staff, took away a handful of formations badly needed for the flanks of the armies invading France and gave them to the centre.* Von Ludendorff, the German war-lord on the western front, still fondly imagined in 1925 that he had had final victory within his grasp in the late summer of 1918; and von Hindenburg, taking his words from the mouths of others, attributed the defeat to the collapse of the home front and to the stab in the back, for which Germany's right wing and centre politicians, and most of the military, held the communists, socialists, trade unionists and Jews to be to blame. All of these views, entirely unfounded though they might have been, had a profound effect on Hitler and on German military thinking in the nineteen-thirties and nineteen-forties.

Before 1914 von Ludendorff, as head of the operations department of the Great General Staff, had been responsible for enacting the von Schlieffen plan on which the attack against France was based. But after 1918 his personality and many of his ideas had changed. He still had an unshaken faith in the absolute superiority of German arms and of the German soldier, and he continued to believe, together with his fellows, in the primacy of the offensive, so much so that his unbalanced views bordered on the absurd. By 1925 von Ludendorff had become the complete advocate of total war, and some years later he was in close touch with Beck, the Chief of the Army General Staff, where von Ludendorff's works were studied and some of his ideas adopted, even though that body might have been loth to admit it. At an earlier period, before 1924, von Ludendorff had been associated with Hitler, who, it would appear, had been much influenced by the general's philosophy, for it later became obvious that there was a remarkable similarity both in their opinions and in their mentalities. And, although von Ludéndorff might have updated himself to the twentieth century in that he now talked about war potential instead of armed force, his new views on war, total or otherwise, like those of the Great General Staff that had preceded him and of the latter-day German dictator who was to follow him, were unrelated to the reality of power, in that, with that German arrogance first born in 1864, von Ludendorff and Hitler continued to underestimate not only the fighting men, but the political will, the stamina and the resilience, and the industrial and economic might of their adversaries. Nor did they attach much importance to the role of diplomacy, for Hitler, like the Kaiser and his imperial suite, of which von Ludendorff had once formed part, continued

---

* General Groener was at one time von Hindenburg's First Quartermaster-General and later the Defence Minister of the Weimar Republic: General von Seeckt was the Chief of the Weimar *Reichsheer*.

to rely on the *military* solution to Germany's problems, based on the cowing of opposition by the threat of arms or on the single lightning campaign, breathtaking in its effrontery in that it was undertaken with scant attention to the strength of the enemy or of his allies or to the long term and world-wide political and economic consequences. For Hitler, like the German generals and the general staff whose war planning ceased at the water's edge, lacked a sense of world geography. As it had happened in 1914, so it happened again in 1939 and 1941 when Hitler launched Germany into the unknown with nothing but a six weeks' campaign plan in his pocket.

The success of Hitler and his National Socialist Party during the interwar years was a reflection of the failure of the democratic parties of the Weimar Republic to cope with the serious problems that beset Germany at that time, inflation, unemployment, social and industrial unrest and the rapidly growing threat of international communism. But Hitler's meteoric rise was also due to the fact that his mental outlook was that of a 1914 German imperialist imbued with Prussian despotism and anti-Semitism and that his views were shared by what was probably the majority of the German electorate. Hitler intended that Germany should throw off the shackles of Versailles and be restored to what he considered to be its rightful place in Europe and the world, with a parity in armed might; the lands lost in 1919 were to be restored, and Austria, Poland and Czechoslovakia were to disappear from the map of Europe. But this was not the true extent of his foreign ambitions, for he was determined that what he called the mistakes of 1914 should not be repeated, when Germany, together with the Austro-Hungarian Empire, had been closely ringed by its enemies. He wanted room, room to live and to expand, and room for freedom of manoeuvre; and, remembering the effects of the blockade, he wanted the new Germany to be self-sufficient in raw materials and, in particular, in foodstuffs. This aim could best be achieved by expansion in the east at the expense of what he considered to be the richest of Germany's neighbours, the Soviet Union. In the First World War Germany had gained control of the Ukraine too late to be able to organize and exploit it.

Hitler had never accepted, any more than the general staff and officer corps had done, that the German Army had been defeated in 1918. According to the Nazi and the military view, the capitulation had been caused indirectly by the blockade and directly by the internal collapse of morale and order brought about by disunity and the lack of inner firmness on the home front. For this they blamed the loosening of the control of the old imperial autocracy and the growth, during the war years, of some of the features of democracy, that is to say a gradual assumption of power by the *Reichstag*, party politics, the strengthening of the left wing element, trade unions and strikes. Hitler determined on the re-education and unification of the nation under one Führer and one party, with the suppression and, if need be, the physical destruction of all opposing factions and dissident elements. A purged Germany, closely united by will or by ignorance, or by a perverted education, or, in the last extremity, by the fear of the informer, the secret police and the concentration camp, was to provide fleets and armies incapable of mutinying (as those in the First World War had certainly done), and a civilian population that, in the final outcome, was more terrified of its own government than of the fire-bomb holocaust and the Russian hordes that engulfed it. For there can be little doubt that Hitler's dictatorship aimed not merely at the securing and extension of his own personal position and power, but on the forging of an instrument designed for what he believed to be total war.

In 1933 Hitler had been offered and had accepted the chancellorship, although his party did not command a complete majority in the *Reichstag*. The *Reichstag* fire was presented to the nation as the justification for emergency measures, and the Enabling Bill allowed the new chancellor to outlaw the substantial communist opposition and then force out the other political parties, so that Hitler became the dictator at the head of a one party state. Trade unions and ex-servicemen's associations, where they were not broken up, were brought into the party-state organization. Any independence of the federal states ended at this time, and the German National Socialist Workers' Party was actually superimposed on the organs of the national and local government as part of the executive. The police, the security and part of the espionage services became the SS empire of the bureaucrat Himmler, with a staff recruited largely from the party. Party bosses, the *Gauleiter* and the *Kreisleiter*, began to duplicate the organization and usurp the authority of the local government bodies and many enriched themselves at the expense of the German State.

Except insofar as he had already set them out in *Mein Kampf*, Hitler's long term aims and methods were not of course known to his party colleagues, to his government or to the German population at large, for he kept his designs concealed and proceeded towards his goal methodically and, at first, cautiously. In June 1934 he had relied on the tacit support of the German Army while he purged, in a series of murders, the Nazi Party's strong-armed brownshirted SA bodyguard of those elements that appeared to threaten him. Then, since it was not in his interest to rely on the generals to keep him in power, he began to extend his own influence inside the body of the armed forces, paying particular attention to the navy and what was to become the new *Luftwaffe*, and, at the same time, slowly but steadily increasing the size of the armed SS, his own private army. At the beginning of August 1934, on the death of von Hindenburg, the last President, Hitler adopted the title of Führer and Chancellor and Supreme Commander of the Armed Forces, taking over the offices and duties of the former head of state in addition to those he already held as chancellor; without awaiting the result of a national referendum that was retro-actively to legalize this change of constitution, all troops were *ordered* to take the oath of loyalty not to the head of the republic or to its elected government but to the person of Adolf Hitler. Then, in 1935, a secret defence law was passed in the *Reichstag* conferring upon Hitler powers of emergency, mobilization and the declaration of war, powers greater than those ever possessed by the Hohenzollern Kaisers. These developments had far-reaching effects on Germany's fortunes in the Second World War.

Hitler had inherited a high command organization bequeathed to him by the victors of Versailles after they had attempted to destroy the monolithic military strength of what had been the old Empire. The Weimar high command was, however, suited to Hitler's purpose in that, after a few changes, it enabled him personally to assume the supreme command over all the armed forces without the necessity of having to share power or knowledge with a deputy or with a centralized staff. Mistrustful and suspicious, he wanted to divide and rule, using executives who were often nonentities and on whose unquestioning obedience and loyalty he could rely. Hitler was to find no shortage of these in a general staff founded on von Schlieffen principles, from which von Seeckt, with what Faber du Faur called 'his 100,000 bandbox army', had done his utmost to exclude officers of breadth of vision and independence of character and thought.

Under the German republic the powerful and prestigious Great General Staff that had previously planned and executed all land and air war measures on behalf of the Kaiser and Supreme Commander, had disappeared, and defence had become the responsibility of a civilian defence minister. The chiefs of the army and of the navy formed part of the defence ministry with their own naval and army general staffs. Groener, a retired lieutenant-general of the old imperial army and the last civilian defence minister, was replaced in January 1933, at von Hindenburg's instigation, by von Blomberg, a serving general. This thrusting and energetic officer was entirely suited to Hitler's purpose in that he was an ardent supporter of the Nazi Party and strongly favoured a centralized high command organization that would control the army, the navy and the air force. In this way the armed forces or *Wehrmacht* office within the defence ministry was eventually developed into a planning and executive organ of command, its two principal staff officers being a Major-General Keitel and a Colonel Jodl. Von Blomberg, profiting by the passivity of the army chief von Hammerstein and of his successor von Fritsch, succeeded in diminishing the powers of the army department, a process that was to be continued by Jodl over the next twelve years. Von Blomberg was unable, however, to exercise command over the navy, since the sea was an element that was alien to him, and its commanding admiral, Raeder, the head of the naval department, was on good terms with Hitler and dealt directly with him. With air matters it was much the same story since Göring, the Commander-in-Chief of the new *Luftwaffe* command, as Hitler's party confidant, enjoyed a special relationship with the dictator and, in the early days, a much misplaced trust.*

Hitler's unilateral abrogation of Versailles, his withdrawal of Germany from the League of Nations, his rearmament programme and the law reintroducing conscription had been warmly welcomed by Germany's military leaders, so that it would have appeared that Hitler had their fullest confidence. This confidence was not reciprocal, however, for Hitler had been unpleasantly surprised at what he regarded as von Blomberg's loss of nerve at the time of the re-entry of German troops into the demilitarized zone of the Rhine in 1935, and he had been further disillusioned by von Blomberg's and von Fritsch's lack of enthusiasm, and the written objections of Beck, when the dictator had revealed his earliest plans for expansion into Central Europe. Yet, in truth, these army generals were in agreement with Hitler's aims; their reservations stemmed from nervousness at what they considered to be the rash tempo of his programme of conquest, for they feared that Germany would be attacked from all sides before the rearmament and military expansion had been completed and consolidated.

Hitler, however, was not to be deterred. Confident of Göring's *Luftwaffe* and, presumably, of Raeder's navy, the only armed service that remained to be purged of doubters was the army; von Fritsch and Beck had to go since they were apparently incapable of that unquestioning obedience expected of them. Von Blomberg was in any event superfluous to the organization of the high command since Göring and Raeder already dealt directly with Hitler. Von Blomberg, as war minister, had admittedly succeeded in gaining some personal control over the army, but his influence was not exactly that wanted by the Führer. Von Blomberg was prevailed upon to resign on account of the scandal of his remarriage, and, in

---

* From 1935 the army, naval and air force departments became *Oberkommandos des Heeres (OKH), der Marine (OKM) und der Luftwaffe (OKL)*.

February 1938, Hitler, at von Blomberg's suggestion, proclaimed himself as the actual (as distinct from the titular) Commander-in-Chief of the Armed Forces. The war ministry with its *Wehrmacht* office was transformed into a single Armed Forces High Command (OKW), with Keitel at its head. Although Keitel had been named by Hitler as his military deputy, with the standing and most of the powers of the former war minister and, eventually, the rank of field-marshal, he was in fact to exercise no powers of command at all; he was an ardent Nazi supporter, entirely loyal and obedient to Hitler, a man of weak character and moderate abilities who acted merely as the OKW *chef de bureau*; his opinions and advice counted for nothing since his function was that of Hitler's aide and staff officer administration. Keitel's limitations were well known to the dictator, who spoke of him behind his back with amused contempt. Hitler had found the very type of officer that he was after.*

According to Hitler's understanding of the future that he had plotted out for the Third Reich, his own fate and that of the nation must depend largely on the effectiveness of the German Army and its loyalty to him and the National Socialist Party. On the other hand he intended to create numerous safeguards and checks on the army in order to ensure the security of his own person and position. The navy and the *Luftwaffe* were to act as counterweights to the army in that they were to be kept entirely independent of it, and only in very exceptional circumstances were air or naval detachments put under army command. Normally they acted only in support, taking their orders from Hitler through Raeder's OKM and Göring's OKL.

Although Hitler had promised his generals in 1934 that the German Army 'should be the only bearer of arms', by which he meant the only ground force in the armed services, this of course was not his intention. In 1935 all anti-aircraft artillery and in 1938 all parachute troops were transferred to Göring's air force, the anti-aircraft formations, after being equipped with dual purpose 88mm guns, reappearing in air force uniforms and under *Luftwaffe* officers, even though they formed an essential part of the framework of the German Army's anti-tank and anti-aircraft defence. The armed SS, originally the Nazi Party's praetorian guard, was rapidly expanded from the size of a detachment to that of a regiment and then began to form its own divisions; and in order to ensure its political purity and keep it isolated from other loyalties, the armed SS was forbidden to accept volunteers that had formerly served in the German Army.** From 1942 onwards air force personnel, both officers and other ranks, were formed into panzer and infantry divisions, under their own generals, having been provided, like the armed SS, with their own artillery and tank arm. In all, two *Luftwaffe* panzer formations, twenty-two *Luftwaffe* field divisions, eleven parachute light infantry divisions and forty-

---

* One of the few personalities on whom most were agreed was that of Keitel. Hitler, though praising him for his loyalty '*treu wie ein Hund*', said that he had the brains of a cinema commissionaire, Göring that he was the absolute zero, and Mussolini, that Keitel was a man who was pleased he was Keitel. By 1945 the young staff officers called him 'the nodding jack-ass' since he merely agreed with everything the dictator said, or 'the Reich garage attendant' because his main function appeared to be the rationing of motor fuels. Hitler found it useful to drag Keitel round in his retinue to impress foreign heads of state by his arrogant bearing and field-marshal's uniform.

**An exception was, however, made in the case of some officers: Hausser, Steiner, Gille and a number of others had been army officers who joined the *Waffen SS* at its inception. Similarly, towards the end of the war, a number of serving army officers were transferred into the SS, usually to fill specialist vacancies.

three armed SS divisions were to be raised by 1945, often being grouped together to form *Luftwaffe* field corps and parachute and SS armies. Although these *Luftwaffe* and SS formations were put under the operational control of higher German Army headquarters, they were allotted and withdrawn, disciplined and administered by the *Luftwaffe* and the SS, owing allegiance not to the German Army but to the Führer, through Göring and Himmler. Before the end of the war the armed SS was to take over and control the entire German Army.

By the end of 1938 the principal actors had taken their places and the political and military organization had been evolved that, except in one important particular, was to continue in being throughout most of the Second World War. Adolf Hitler was firmly in control of the state machine and the armed forces for life. He offered the German people what appeared to be the only alternative to unemployment, inflation and the communist threat from which they had suffered in the post-war years. The proscribing and imprisonment of communists, trade unionists, free-masons and some clergy and socialists appeared to many to be a small price to pay, although presumably the national conscience had some qualms in recon-ciling itself to the treatment of its Jews. Generally speaking, the great mass of people were united in their support of the National Socialist Party, and were to remain so until the very end, and for Hitler they showed a sickly adulation. Yet there is little doubt that the support was not entirely spontaneous. Much of it was inspired by fear, much of it was indoctrinated by propaganda; for schools were hotbeds of political education from the earliest age, and this was intensified even in the infant organizations, the Hitler Youth, the compulsory labour service, and finally in the armed services. All were encouraged to join the Nazi Party or one of its associate organizations, and towns and villages were divided into cells and blocks so that the civil police and party officials could keep a close check on the activities and views of each household.

Hitler's character was a complexity of contradictions. Although poorly edu-cated, he was both able and astute. An adventurer and an opportunist, he had a keen eye for assessing the strength and frailties of others and could use both to his own advantage. His own brain was very quick but disorderly and his memory was extraordinarily retentive but clogged with useless trivia. On matters of minor importance he could quickly discern the essentials and could be logical and far-sighted. On the major decisions concerning the Reich he was swayed by emotion and ideology and could be totally irrational. Much of the basis of his political faith was insane. Intensely interested in technicalities that were not his concern, too often he could not see the wood for the trees and saw the details but not the grand design. He was a gambler, convinced that boldness always paid; but his boldness had no basis on intelligence or on sober estimate, but rather on sudden impulse. He was volatile, and having given rein to impetuosity he was prone to bouts of nervousness from which he learned nothing, for having regained his composure he became both overbearing and over-confident and rushed on to new excesses. When in difficulty he often refused to face up to threatening situations and he pretended that they did not exist. He was an untidy improviser and a man of snap decisions. He could become violently excited over unimportant matters, yet he could hear out the news of disasters with the calmest detachment.

The dictator was entirely unscrupulous and ruthless and despised anything but that which he judged as strength. He was mean and vindictive and his close associates lived in great fear of him, for he had a long memory and did not fail to repay old scores. The people around him, and indeed the whole German nation, merely served as the instruments of his ambition and will. His powers eventually became so complete that he was able to order arbitrarily, without any form of trial, removal from office and forfeiture of pension and property. Later were to be added imprisonment in concentration camps, torture and execution. These punishments were visited not only upon those who had displeased him, but were extended to their families.

He was not truthful. Some lies were told for effect. Some were self-delusion and wishful thinking. Some were for the furtherance of his Machiavellian schemes. He was secretive and kept the right hand in ignorance of the activities of the left. He believed in the dispersal and limitation of authority, all authority and knowledge being centralized in himself. According to his Basic Order No. 1, issued in January 1940, the need for security dictated that no one should know more than was necessary for the performance of his duties, and this meant that Hitler alone was the all powerful co-ordinator and director not only of the armed services but of all government and political activities within the Reich. He was a paranoiac with a deep-rooted pathological distrust, and there were few who enjoyed his complete confidence for long; in his dark suspicious mind he saw everywhere conspirators intent on misleading or deceiving him. His own circle, his *chauffereska*, was of a mean intellect and very narrow, and he disliked admitting new faces to it, possibly because he feared assassination. Urged on by his inordinate vanity, his restless ambition and his strength of will, he was determined on a path of conquest in his own short lifetime, and he was resolved to stop at nothing. This megalomaniac, particularly as the stress and strain of war took its toll of his nervous system, was to become increasingly immoderate and unbalanced.

At some time subsequent to 1943 the dictator was to show symptoms of a nervous affliction or disease, which has been described variously as Parkinson's Disease, as a nervous breakdown brought on by strain and hysteria, or as a condition resulting from the administration of drugs. Since Hitler relied almost exclusively on the advice and drugs given to him by Dr Morell, his personal physician, and would not submit to other medical examination, the true nature of the disability has never been proved. Consequently no deductions can be drawn as to the effect that his illness may have had on his mind. Until his death his mental powers seemed unimpaired. Rages were more frequent and his views became even more extreme, but these tendencies were strong in the days of his health. Before his death he certainly became completely divorced from reality, but this trait was common throughout the whole of the Nazi hierarchy.

Hitler had of course an obverse side to his character. No dictator can indulge in a sense of humour at his own expense, and his wit was earthy and used others as its butt. Except to those who incurred his displeasure or distrust he made some attempts at courtesy. He could be gay and even charming, if he so wished, and to many who talked to him, even in his later days, he could give the impression of being a rational being whose views were logical and moderate. Yet this same man was responsible for the murder of millions of innocents, the majority of whom were women and children. No man of the twentieth century, except Stalin, can more richly have deserved hanging.

Hitler's qualifications and experience in military matters were limited to his four years' service in the First World War on the western front, in which theatre he had served in the capacity of an orderly with the rank of *Gefreiter*, something between that of a first-class private and a lance-corporal. In the Second World War he never ceased to impress upon his generals that he had been a front line soldier and knew what war really meant. Yet his previous service, commendable though it might have been, was certainly a very inadequate preparation for the post of a Commander-in-Chief. But, by attending military manoeuvres, exercises and presentations, he rapidly acquired the necessary vocabulary, and, by lending an attentive ear to the opinions and criticism of subordinate officers and ambitious military specialists with *avant-garde* views, he soon had at his disposal a store of tactical and technical detail with which to confound his own military chiefs. With the egoism of the politician he produced this information as his own. This practice proved so effective in disconcerting opposition that he extended it to using as part of his arguments a great wealth of statistical and technical information that could not be refuted on the spot, since the subject matter was entirely outside his opponents' province. Nor indeed was he above fabricating evidence to win his point. In this way it was a relatively simple matter to manipulate the weaker of his generals, the more naive of whom soon began to regard him as a military genius. The Führer was quick, too, to sense any opposition or schism within the body of the officer corps, and he was expert in using one faction as a counter to, or check upon, the other.

Hitler's function as the Commander-in-Chief of the Armed Forces was very real and he did not hesitate, firstly to interfere with, and then, eventually, to instigate and control the planning and conduct of operations. This did not result, however, in widespread resignations of the generals in protest. Indeed some of them were to compete in prostituting themselves before this man in their scramble for advancement, power, grants of landed estates and even gifts of money from his privy purse; for this they plotted and intrigued against each other, earning in return the dictator's scorn, which, as the war progressed, he did not bother to conceal.

By 1938 the Rhineland and Austria had already been occupied in bloodless *coups*. Originally faltering, Hitler gained confidence with each step, and his political and military advisers, whose forecasts of disaster had so often proved wrong in the past, became more hesitant in restraining him. In September he precipitated the Munich crisis. It was believed by a substantial body of world opinion that the dictator's threats were both blackmail and bluff, and that a determined stand by Britain and France would have changed the course of history and averted the Second World War. In the light of subsequent evidence concerning Hitler's mentality this is by no means certain, for Hitler had already started on his career of conquest and probably preferred war to a major political check that might have been fatal to his personal position. By the late summer of 1939 Hitler, already determined to have *military* solutions to Germany's foreign aspirations, was fearful only that some mediator might prevent *his* war against Poland.

When Germany went to war Hitler had counted on the Nazi-Soviet Pact of 23 August 1939 (by which Poland was to be attacked and partitioned by both Germany and Russia) deterring France and Britain from honouring their defence agreements with Poland; in this way the dictator expected to escape, for the time being, a war on two fronts. The defeat of Poland by the sudden, powerful and crushing blow based on the mobility of motorized troops and hard-marching infantry, together with the fire power of massed tanks and of the supporting *Luftwaffe*, was a resounding victory. But the price of this military success had been a diplomatic disaster, in that it had lighted a fire that Hitler had been at first unwilling, and then unable, to extinguish, a fire that was to spread rapidly into the world-wide conflagration that eventually destroyed Germany.

Germany had gone to war with the equivalent of about 104 divisions, of which roughly sixty had been used against Poland, the remainder being deployed for defence against the west. During that four week campaign the artillery ammunition fired off had been twice the rate of monthly production, so that an eighth of all gun and a quarter of all mortar ammunition had been used up; the stock was so low that, if any more fighting had taken place, only one third of all the field formations in the German Army could have been maintained at sustained battle usage rates. And if the French and British forces in Western Europe had launched a determined and immediate offensive across the Rhine, the German Army would have run out of artillery ammunition within two months.

If he had been left to his own devices, von Brauchitsch, the Commander-in-Chief of the Army, would have remained on the defensive, if not indefinitely, then at least until he had reorganized his troops and improved the precarious munition position.* But, on 27 September, Hitler told von Brauchitsch that he intended to attack France and overrun Belgium and Holland before the onset of winter—in spite of the Reich declaration made only a month before that the neutrality and sovereignty of Luxembourg, Belgium, the Netherlands and Switzerland were held to be inviolable. Von Brauchitsch complied with the dictator's order that the army was to be made ready for the new war by 10 November 1939, and the troops remained at virtual stand-to waiting for an improvement of weather conditions until 16 January when the final close down of winter made it impossible to start the campaign. By then, as a result of Raeder's prompting, a suggested new war into Scandinavia had taken hold in Hitler's mind.

On 30 November the Soviet Union attacked Finland and Hitler began to fear that British or French aid to Finland might involve allied intervention in Norway, so threatening Germany's northern flank and its Swedish source of iron ores. Fourteen days later Hitler ordered Jodl's OKW staff—not von Brauchitsch's OKH—to begin the study of a lightning occupation of Denmark and Norway. At the end of January a small all arms planning staff was added to Jodl's office and an army corps was given the task of invading Norway, this group being under Adolf Hitler's direct command. The OKH was divorced from this activity so that it might continue to prepare for the war against France undisturbed by the necessity to plan other operations.

It was in this way that Hitler got his first experience of direct command over army formations, and that the first of the so-called OKW theatres was born. In Jodl the Führer had found the second man he had been seeking, an army officer of ability who could do all the work translating and transmitting the dictator's orders in a militarily understandable form, and from whom he could exact implicit obedience—in fact an alternative chief of army general staff prepared to serve

---

* Von Brauchitsch, recommended to Hitler by Keitel and von Rundstedt, had replaced von Fritsch in 1938 as the Commander-in-Chief of the Army.

Hitler in his new role as the alternative Commander-in-Chief of the Army. For Hitler, presumably influenced by von Ludendorff's book *Der totale Krieg*, wanted above all to be not merely a *Kriegsherr*, but a *Feldherr*, which is neither a rank nor a title but is a quality attributed to a war-lord, a quality that can be proved only by military genius and by strategic and tactical success in the large-scale handling of armed forces in the field. True *Feldherrn*, according to the German usage, were rarely encountered in the course of centuries. But von Ludendorff believed that the *Feldherr*, whom von Ludendorff saw as a serving general, must also be the real and only head of state to ensure the unity of direction and control necessary for total war.* Hitler intended merely to reverse the sequence, for the real and only head of state was about to become the general and the *Feldherr*.

Jodl became closer to Hitler than any other military officer since, throughout the course of the whole war, he personally briefed the Führer daily and discussed with him the plans and operation orders that he was responsible for drafting in the Führer's name. It was in this way that Jodl may have unconsciously served in the early days as one of Hitler's military tutors. Jodl was able but his views were extraordinarily narrow, and he was one of those that came to regard the Führer as a military genius. But it is not impossible that Hitler, who knew how to use subordinates, merely acquired ideas with which Jodl, not unnaturally, found himself in complete agreement. At the critical time of the invasion of Norway in 1940, Jodl's judgement and nerves, prompted apparently by the O K W army staff officer, von Lossberg, were sounder than those of Hitler, and this the dictator readily recognized. From then onwards Jodl was obliged to sit next to the Führer at meals, which practice continued until Jodl fell temporarily from grace three years later when he dared to side with the opinions of the recalcitrant List against Hitler, shortly before Stalingrad. Yet even then Jodl chose to remain at his desk. The most serious flaw in Jodl's character was his reluctance or inability to judge and condemn the Führer for what he was, for he was as submissive to Hitler as was Keitel, and he followed the Führer obediently right to the very end. The dictator's somewhat patronizing opinion of Jodl, given to Goebbels in 1943, saw in him only 'a very good and solid worker with an excellent general staff training'.

Jodl's appointment as chief of the *Wehrmacht* office (later *Chef des Wehrmacht-führungsstabs*) might be translated as chief of the defence staff. Yet the name is entirely misleading, since Jodl had no knowledge of, and virtually no responsibility for, naval and air matters, and enjoyed little standing in the army because of his lack of rank and experience; for although he was rapidly advanced in grade from colonel to colonel-general, a rank immediately below that of field-marshal, this was without change to his appointment or function. Although Jodl pretended that his own department within the O K W was a supreme joint service staff, it was in fact nothing of the kind since it merely duplicated the general staff of the O K H; and Jodl's efforts to divorce the O K H from the operational control of ground troops estranged him from many of his fellows, including the successive heads of the army general staff. He interfered with army matters that were not his concern, busying himself, like his master, both with strategy and tactics; but since he was merely Hitler's executive, his activity did not match any ability that he might have had and he was unable to rise above the level of routine. Moreover, Jodl had

* Von Ludendorff said: 'The man who is the *Feldherr*, must be the real head [of the state]. Any other position would be unworkable and wrong. Only if he is in control can he, and he alone, centralize all efforts so that they might effectively preserve the state and defeat the enemy.'

no experience of command since the Führer refused to release him, and, except for a short break before the war, he was employed for nearly seven years in the offices of the OKW and at the Führer headquarters. Lacking any breadth of vision, it is doubtful whether he had more understanding than Hitler of the effect on the troops of some of the orders that he caused to be issued, and, as Germany began to lose the war, Jodl's influence on Hitler, such as it was, became malignant, in that agreeing with his chief in most matters, he added fuel to the flames and fortified Hitler's obstinacy.

The dictator's original design of the offensive to be made against France was very similar to the von Schlieffen plan of 1905, with the weight of the attack in the north. It was superseded, however, by a second plan suggested by von Manstein, the chief of staff to von Rundstedt's Army Group A. This differed from von Brauchitsch's plan in that the enemy was no longer to be outflanked from the north; instead the weight of the attack was to be launched further to the south in the area of the Ardennes, and once the French line had been pierced and freedom of manoeuvre gained, panzer and motorized troops would leave the marching infantry divisions behind and drive north for the Channel coast, encircling and pinning the enemy's northern group of armies against the sea. This battle plan was forced on to a reluctant von Brauchitsch by Hitler.

Once again Berlin entered its new war without a war plan, but armed only with a plan of campaign based on the surprise lightning blow. Had this grand offensive failed Germany would have been committed to a long and bloody war of attrition. Even if the offensive succeeded, Britain with its powerful Commonwealth and Empire, backed by the enormous resources of the United States, still remained undefeated. The history of a quarter of a century before was being repeated: on the high seas U-boats were sinking unarmed passenger liners without warning; neutral states were being invaded and occupied; and the news of the treatment of oppressed peoples, particularly of the Jews and the Poles, and the unprovoked terror bombing of open cities in Holland and elsewhere horrified and alienated world opinion.

France, however, was overcome in six weeks and the British expeditionary force was driven back over the Channel with the loss of the whole of its equipment. From then onwards nothing seemed impossible to the Führer; no task could be too difficult for the German soldier and no risk too high for the German nation to run in the furtherance of the dictator's plans of conquest.

The capitulation of the French Army found both Hitler and the *Wehrmacht* planners at a temporary loss on what to do next, for there was no long term political or military war plan in existence. Müller-Hillebrand, the military aide to Halder, the Chief of the Army General Staff, who shared his office and attended with his chief some hundreds of *Führerlage* daily conferences to brief the dictator, has rightly said, although in retrospect, that even in 1940 it was predestined that Germany, faced with the wealthier and stronger economies of Britain and North America, with their control of the sea and of much of the air space above it, must, in the final outcome, inevitably lose the war, however long the struggle might be prolonged and however many glorious victories the German Army might win on land.* Hitler should, thought Müller-Hillebrand, again with the benefit of hind-

---

* Halder succeeded Beck in 1938 and served until 1942 when he was to be replaced by Zeitzler. These daily briefing sessions by the OKW, OKH, OKL and OKM dragged on for several hours and came to be regarded by the successive chiefs as a great waste of their valuable time.

sight, have sought peace at any price, if the dictator could have found anyone in Britain willing to have treated with him, and he should have relinquished all his conquests, so returning to the *status quo* of 1938. But this, said Müller-Hillebrand, was not Hitler's way. And indeed it ignores the spirit of the times and would have been unthinkable, not only to Hitler, but to the vast majority of the German people. For these, united solidly behind their Führer, were arrogant and drunk with success, fully confident that might was right and must succeed. The German public, together with a large number of its generals, had, like Hitler, lost all sense of reality. And it was Guderian, he who in after years could boast that his own operations always hung by a thread yet at the same time so vehemently condemned the Führer on this very account, who had urged the dictator to delay the signing of the June 1940 armistice with the French so that he (Guderian) could seize Gibraltar with two panzer divisions and, crossing the straits and half the breadth of the North African continent, occupy the French colonial empire there. This suggestion was listened to by the dictator with attentive ears.*

In the years of peace Hitler had attempted to make the German economy independent of imported manufactured and raw materials. Although some progress had certainly been made in the production of substitutes, Germany still depended at the outbreak of war on imported food and textiles and what came to be known as strategic war materials, among them gasolene and mineral oils, iron ores, nickel, lead, copper, tin, bauxite and rubber. Germany lacked, moreover, a developed and up to date motor transport and rail rolling-stock industry and the necessary high quality equipment for casting steel ball-bearings and forged crankshafts and the heavy presses required for armoured plate. The railways had been neglected and the permanent way was poor, and there was a shortage of rolling-stock even for the internal needs of the Reich in 1939, this causing the temporary shutting down of much of German industry in the first winter of the war.

Little effort had been made to mobilize the economy to keep pace even with the initial equipping of the rapidly expanding *Wehrmacht*, let alone meet the attrition rates to be associated with total war, partly because the government was trying to conceal from the German people the seriousness of the war and for this reason was reluctant to restrict consumer production of household and luxury goods. The working population was not directed into essential war industry and raw materials were often misused. In the winter of 1939-1940 the O K W and civil building trades were still using 1.3 million tons of steel a month for construction, leaving only 350,000 tons for armament production.

German industry and the economy at large were controlled by Hitler in a series of directives, for there was at first no single war economy planning body in being; instead the responsibility was shared by a number of competing organizations including the ministries for labour and for the economy, the organization for the Four Years' Plan, Todt's building industry and other plenipotentiaries and commissioners. Priorities changed in rapid succession. A Führer *Erweisung* of 7 September 1939 was entirely reversed by another on 4 October that was superseded

* Guderian, a general of infantry, had commanded a panzer corps in France and was later to command one of the four panzer groups in Russia. Like so many of his fellows he was a tactician of outstanding ability, but no strategist.

only six days later by different overriding priorities. By mid November there was yet another change, and so it went on, this disorder originating from the fact that there existed no long term strategic plan for the conduct of the war. Industrial production could not be organized in this haphazard way, and the situation was all the more impossible since there was no reserve of finished goods or raw materials to hand. The military *Wehrwirtschaftsstab*, which in November 1939 had become the *Wehrwirtschafts und Rüstungsamt* within the OKW, could do little about production except to place its requests and try to relate plans to the availability of materials.* But this was not the fashion in which the Führer worked, for his plans, instead of becoming more modest, became more ambitious and wilder day by day.

The weapons already provided for the *Wehrmacht* under the rearmament plan were of high quality and of the most modern design, but the amount of equipment produced could not keep pace with the expansion of the forces, or make good the heavy wastage rates to be expected in protracted and heavy fighting. The German Army had increased in size by a further fifty divisions in the first six months of 1940, but this had been achieved only by making do on very light scales. The *matériel* situation did not permit the use of a common organization and equipment scale for the infantry divisions, so that these had to be scheduled by categories, those with low numbers having enough modern equipment that would enable them to be committed to the heaviest of fighting, while those with the higher category numbers were on improvised scales and often lived from hand to mouth. No fewer than ten infantry divisions were provided with Czech and Polish arms. The horse was regarded as the natural substitute for the motor vehicle, and all infantry divisions relied on horses for transport and for the movement of their artillery. Even so, the German Army still had on paper a motor vehicle establishment of 120,000. But since the motor industry monthly production was only 1,000 vehicles, this was insufficient to replace even the normal losses through wear and tear. A motley collection of captured vehicles and French civilian lorries had been taken into use, but these gave rise to difficulties in servicing and repair. Throughout the war, from 1941 onwards, there were to be successive purges of motor vehicles from the equipment tables, either because the vehicles did not exist, or because they could not be maintained with parts and gas or be replaced when lost, damaged or worn out.

It was very much the same with the *Luftwaffe*, which was shortly to lose its initial superiority, for, by 1940, the United Kingdom aircraft industry had already outstripped the production in the Reich. The *Wehrmacht* could only undertake campaigns where quick decisive victories were assured, for any large scale and lengthy fighting must inevitably founder in a crisis of munition supply.

The *Wehrmacht* had been given an equipment advantage over the Poles, the British, and, to a lesser extent, over the French. But the high quality range of weapons was only a glittering façade, and it was inevitable that the British and the Americans would in due course outclass them both in quality and in quantity. For the German armament industry was organized in breadth but not in depth and Germany was not equipped to win a long war when pitted against first-class industrial powers, whether this war was waged on a single or on multiple fronts. The acute German equipment shortages were brought to Hitler's attention each month in the OKW secret economic *Lageberichte*, but these left him unmoved

* This was General Thomas's Economic and Armament Department.

because he intended, so he said, to avoid a material-consuming and many-fronted war; he was confident that he would attain his political aims without it.

Even before the end of the war in France, Hitler had ordered the reduction in the size of the German Army by disbandments and the slowing down in the rate of call-up. Then followed a short period of uncertainty within the high command and not until 13 July, and then at Raeder's suggestion, did Hitler order the planning for the invasion of the British Isles. But the English Channel currents and tides and the techniques of sea-borne assaults were as foreign to the German Navy as they were to the German Army, and the planning had hardly commenced when Raeder told Hitler of his doubts as to whether the many difficulties could be overcome.

During that crucial four weeks in July and August 1940 there were constant changes and reversals, not merely of orders, but of basic war aims. At first the German Army was to be reduced from 156 to 120 divisions and the priority in war production was switched to the German Navy and *Luftwaffe* so that these could continue the war against England. By 13 July the landings in Britain had definitely been decided upon. But a week later Hitler astounded von Brauchitsch by ordering him to concentrate 'on the Russian problem' as he intended 'to smash England's hope of Russian help [by destroying Russia] and make Germany's position invulnerable on the continent'. At the same time Hitler said that he had decided on an operation against Gibraltar and that, with Spain's aid, he was going to build a defensive front from the North Cape to Morocco. On 31 July Hitler again spoke of his decision *to destroy the Soviet Union in a spring campaign in 1941* and said that he had decided to *increase* the army strength to 180 divisions. The next day, in his *Weisung Nr. 17*, he ordered the waging of an air and sea war that would 'create the conditions for the final defeat of England'. Then, in the first few days of August, the dictator's attention was directed to the south in that, following up Guderian's suggestion, he decided that he would close the Mediterranean to the British by attacking Gibraltar, and, on 12 August, he ordered a light panzer force to be made ready for Africa to spearhead an Italian advance against the Suez Canal.

The defeat of the *Luftwaffe* and the heavy losses it suffered over the United Kingdom, and Raeder's reluctance to attempt the sea-borne landings, in the end ruled out the possibility of an invasion. That August came the first British air raid on Berlin. Hitler vacillated no longer but decided to strike down the Soviet Union (with which he had only a year before signed a non-aggression pact), before Britain should rearm and attempt to gain another foothold in Europe.

The last successful lightning campaign to be mounted by von Brauchitsch's OKH, at Hitler's direction, was that in April 1941 made into the Balkans against Yugoslavia and Greece and preceded by a heavy terror bombing raid on Belgrade, the capital of a country with which Germany was not at war. But this Balkan campaign was but a prelude to the attack on the Soviet Union and was designed to secure the right flank and safeguard the Rumanian oilfields for Germany. The whole of the Balkans, except for European Turkey, was then occupied by a joint Italo-German-Bulgarian force. South-East Europe was afterwards designated as an OKW theatre, all German Army formations there coming under Hitler's direct command, together with those in North Africa, occupied France, Belgium, Holland

and Scandinavia (including Finland), since it was intended that von Brauchitsch's OKH should be left free for the planning of operations against Russia.

Von Brauchitsch was, of course, to be left anything but free. Hitler had laid down no war aims, or political or economic objectives for the guidance of the OKH in planning the new war, since he himself had no clear idea of what he wanted to do: at first all that was demanded was *the smashing of Russia* in a short summer blitzkrieg campaign. German political, economic and military intelligence covering the Soviet Union was very poor and the OKH itself was in a quandary, for Halder was unable to define a single overriding military mission as a guideline for his own general staff. Control was, however, soon removed from his and von Brauchitsch's hands, for Hitler began to alter military objectives and plans, constantly interjecting random political and economic priorities and demands as they entered his head. Meanwhile he had secretly set Jodl and von Lossberg to work to produce an OKW plan for the invasion of Russia, although this new eastern theatre had nothing to do with the OKW *Führungsstab*; and he used the OKW draft to verify, to amend, to condemn and finally to reject von Brauchitsch's proposals. So Germany went to war on the von Lossberg plan. When the Hitler-Jodl version was finally produced as a war directive it proved to be nothing more than an operational order to take the German Army as far as Smolensk. What was to happen thereafter no one knew, least of all the dictator. Less than three months after Germany had launched itself eastwards in the greatest life and death struggle of its existence, operations were to be brought to a standstill because of fierce disputes as to the true aim of the war.

At the beginning of this new war, heralded as the crusade against Bolshevism, Germany had in all 204 army and four SS divisions of which 145 were used on the eastern front, together with a further force of several German divisions in North Finland that came under the OKW. The German panzer force consisted of about 3,600 tanks, and was supported by 2,000 first line aircraft. In addition Germany's allies provided about fourteen divisions and the Finns a further thirteen. The Red Army had only 150 divisions mobilized and deployed in Central Europe but these could be rapidly increased to a strength of 250 divisions; the total Red Army armoured strength stood at about 15,000 tanks, many of which were, however, of obsolete pattern, and the Red Air Force numbered over 10,000 aircraft of all types, of which probably less than a third were of modern design. Soviet small-arms and artillery were of a high quality and considerable reserve stocks had been amassed, and the new range of tanks that were only just becoming available—the T34 and KV series—were superior to anything that the Germans had as yet developed. The Soviet industrial arms base, unlike the German, had been developed in depth, and much of it had been redeployed in the Urals in Eastern Russia.

The 1941 campaign into Russia was a German political and strategic military failure of the first magnitude, in spite of the great tactical victories and the enormous casualties inflicted on the Red Army and the vast territories overrun; for the *Wehrmacht* failed in that lightning blow to destroy the Soviet government and its armed forces or their will to resist, while the onset of winter found the bulk of the German Army perilously exposed. The primary reason for this was one of geography, for if the Soviet Union had been enclosed by the oceans in an area no greater than that of France, then nothing could have saved it, not its armed and economic strength, nor the ruthlessness of its leaders, nor the dogged determination of its troops. As it was, the German Army and *Luftwaffe* had been unable to

1 Axis occupied territory (Europe and North Africa), 1 November 1942

ARCTIC OCEAN

North Cape

Petsamo

Lofoten Is.

Dietl
20 A

Murmansk

Lapland

Archangel

ATLANTIC

OCEAN

SWEDEN

FINLAND

NORWAY

L. Onega

L. Ladoga

Gulf of Finland

Leningrad

Estonia

v.Küchler
A/Gp North

Moscow

NORTH
SEA

Latvia

DENMARK

BALTIC SEA

Lithuania

GREAT
BRITAIN

East
Prussia

Belo-
russia

v.Kluge
A/Gp Centre

Stalingrad

GERMANY

POLAND

v.Weichs
A/Gp B

v.Rundstedt
OB West

CZECHOSLOVAKIA

Ukraine

v.Kleist
A/Gp A

AUSTRIA

HUNGARY

Unoccupied
France

ITALY

Crimea

Pyrenees

RUMANIA

SPAIN

YUGOSLAVIA

BLACK SEA

BULGARIA

Corsica

Löhr
OB S-E

Sardinia

Dardanelles

TURKEY

Kesselring
OB South

GREECE

Dodecanese

MEDITERRANEAN SEA

Sicily

Peloponnese

SYRIA

ALGERIA

Crete

TUNISIA

Rommel
Pz A

EGYPT

LIBYA

Axis conquered
or controlled

Allies

Neutrals

0   100   500 miles
100   800km

overcome the problems of movement and supply brought about by space, the poorly developed Soviet rail and road system and the effects of the bitter continental winter. Since the bulk of the invading force marched on its feet and relied upon horse drawn waggons, it was no more able to maintain itself in the wintry Russian wastes than Napoleon's *Grande Armée* had been a century and a quarter before.

With the sustained fighting, the effect of other military truisms at last became apparent. The German scale of ammunition for each weapon in June 1941 was the same as that before the 1940 campaign against France except that there was an increase of thirty per cent for the heavier guns, howitzers and mortars; this had been thought sufficient for a short war against the Soviet Union and the manufacture of ammunition had actually been cut back in the early summer of 1941. There was virtually no reserve of armoured fighting vehicles above the monthly factory output, and at the end of two months of campaigning the German tank fighting strength fell rapidly below fifty per cent of establishment. A supply of cold weather clothing had not been provided for the whole invasion army since victory had been forecast for September and it had been intended to leave only a skeleton German occupation force in defeated Russia that winter. For the first time personnel replacements became a problem, for with the heavy and extended fighting came the casualties, with a loss rate twice that at the height of the French campaign. Within eight weeks of the opening of the offensive into Russia the German Army had already lost more men than it had in the first twenty-one months of the war. Then, after the close down of the very early winter, came the really heavy losses, firstly in horses and then in troops, with a fall out through frost-bite and sickness of over half a million men. The unexpected Russian mid winter counter-offensive then threw the German centre near Moscow back for nearly 200 miles. That autumn the German people were warned, for the first time, that they could expect a long war, and priority was given to the air raid defence of the Reich.

In June 1941 Hitler had already forfeited any standing as a statesman and war leader when, wilfully underestimating his enemies and believing that all problems could be resolved by force, he extended the war and began the struggle on two fronts. Then, later that year, he incited Japan to take up arms, not against the Soviet Union but against Great Britain's eastern dependencies; Tokyo, misled by what it believed to be the rapidity of the German advance on Moscow, attacked both United States and British Pacific bases. The Führer's penultimate folly, without reason and without regard for the consequences, was his personal and capricious decision in December 1941 to declare war on the United States.

The final madness was yet to be played out in Russia. For Hitler's overwhelming desire to display his military genius was to have a disastrous effect on the way in which he controlled Germany's destiny in war. He was no longer the statesman, the diplomat or even the *Kriegsherr*. There was no further attempt to formulate or to enact a foreign policy. The dictator wanted only to be the *Feldherr*, and emulate Napoleon and Frederick the Great. His attention became rivetted not merely on the conduct of military operations, but on the technicalities, the details, even the unimportant trivialities of the fighting on the eastern front, so that when the territories in which he had so light-heartedly entered bogged down his panzers and soaked up the blood of his infantry, what was to have become an easily won campaign became, instead, firstly a major war and then an all-consuming struggle for existence against the Bolsheviks, pursued with ever increasing fanatical fury, making the dictator blind to any other considerations.

On 19 December 1941 Hitler dismissed von Brauchitsch as the Commander-in-Chief of the German Army and himself assumed direct command of all army formations in Russia. The OKH was then dismantled, the army general staff alone remaining as Hitler's instrument for command in the east, carrying out the same task as Jodl's *Führungsstab* for the OKW theatres in the west, the north and the south. The Führer had at last arrived at the situation where he was not only the *Supremo* commanding air, naval and ground forces everywhere, but he also personally controlled all field formations in all theatres through two separate chiefs of army general staff, neither of whom was properly responsible for army organization, training, equipment or manning, since a large part of the OKH organization and responsibilities, including Fromm's Replacement Army and the military districts at home, were transferred to the control of Keitel's OKW.

In the autumn of 1942 Hitler removed the Army Personnel Office from Keitel and put it under his military adjutant, Colonel Schmundt, a man on whose implicit obedience and boundless admiration he could rely.* Hitler's control over the German Army and its senior officers was now complete, for, with Keitel nominally responsible for representing the army and for safeguarding its interests, there was no longer any question but that it would be subordinated entirely to the demands of any party adventurer. Even within the OKW and the army, opportunism, nepotism and dishonesty were, from now on, according to Müller-Hillebrand, to become commonplace.

The late winter campaign was to be conducted from Hitler's map board at his headquarters in East Prussia, and, remarkable though it may now seem, faith in the Führer was so boundless that a new wave of optimism spread through the exhausted, filthy and verminous troops on the eastern front. But the Führer order that every formation and unit should stand and fight, without giving a foot of ground and without regard to the threat from the flanks, was found impossible to carry out, for the battle line was steadily forced back. Some commanders thought that the orders for a rigid defence saved the German Army from the panic and rout that had destroyed Napoleon's Grand Army in 1812; others, however, took the opposite view that it caused heavy and needless losses that might have been avoided by a breaking of contact and a rapid withdrawal to Vyazma or Smolensk. Whether Hitler was right or wrong in his standstill order, the Nazi Party propaganda machine soon saw to it that the public and the rank and file of the German Army came to believe that the Führer was the saviour of the army, and this, in itself, did great and permanent damage to the war direction. Hitler became even more convinced of his own military genius and certain that any crisis could be weathered by will-power and rigidity. Throughout the whole war he was to quote what he believed to be his success before Moscow as a justification for his obdurate and senseless attitude towards German withdrawals. This was to be one of the main factors that subsequently brought such heavy defeats to German arms at Stalingrad and in the Ukraine, in the Crimea and in Belorussia, in Africa and in France.

In his arrogance, Hitler, amid the acclaim of the German nation, had openly taken over the command of the German Army. He had previously been the *de facto* commander, but had kept himself in the background, so that as Führer he tended to take the credit for the German Army successes, whereas von Brauchitsch,

* The Army Personnel Office had been headed formerly by Bodewin Keitel, the younger brother of Field-Marshal Wilhelm Keitel, and had come under von Brauchitsch.

particularly during the autumn, had collected a measure of opprobrium and blame for faults that were primarily Hitler's. Such a tactic at least accorded with an accepted practice of government in that the head of state cannot afford to permit himself to be identified with a subordinate post like that of the Commander-in-Chief of the Army, for, while it is a relatively simple matter to replace a senior general, the failure of a head of state in a subordinate and technical capacity puts him in an invidious and almost ludicrous position. But Hitler's conceit had grown to such proportions that he regarded himself first and foremost as a soldier of such genius that no replacement could be found for him. Any failure on the part of the army under his command, however trivial, tended to be regarded as a personal affront. Hitler was suspicious of and disliked the officer corps, particularly, as he called them, the gentlemen of the general staff, and judicial investigations down to divisional level, courts-martial and dismissals were to follow any setback; during 1942 came the first sentencing of a corps commander to death for withdrawing without permission. The dictator's control over operations was paramount and he began to interfere with the remotest detail, his mistrust of his personal military staff assuming such proportions that he was to insist that stenographers should be present to make a shorthand and typescript record of all conversations and meetings. He was soon to rid himself of Halder, but those who followed as chiefs of the army general staff merely filled a subordinate executive post of no great account; all of them were ambitious officers, often lacking status, seniority and experience, selected by Hitler because he believed them to be men whom he could bend to his will.

The summer of 1942 brought the last of the great German offensives of the war. Hitler had by then switched his main strategic objective: Moscow and Leningrad, he said, were no longer of any importance and he now wanted Donets ores and Caucasian oil. The great German victory at Kharkov in June 1942 left a vacuum in the Russian defence of the Ukraine and the Don steppe, so that the German armies swept forward almost unopposed to the Volga and into the Caucasus, covering a massive area that there were not enough German formations to hold or defend. When winter fell, the Russian resistance had stiffened once more both at Stalingrad and in front of the Caspian, and the exhausted German troops could make no further progress. Because of the lack of German manpower, the defence of the north and south flanks of the thousand mile salient was entrusted, by Hitler's order, to Rumanian, Italian and Hungarian troops. Then the great Russian winter counter-offensive of November 1942 destroyed these weaker Axis allies, and, after only four days fighting, Paulus's 6 German Army, the strongest army on the whole of the eastern front, was left surrounded and isolated. Paulus could have withdrawn the bulk of his troops at the cost of losing nearly all his equipment, if he had been a man of energy and decision ready to defy the dictator's standstill order. But Paulus was more fearful of the Führer than intent on using his own initiative, and he obeyed the dictator to the very end as Hitler directed the detail of the defence of the siege, firstly from his faraway home in Bavaria and then from his Rastenburg headquarters; Paulus earned in return contempt and abuse, and the threat, uttered in the privacy of the dictator's own circle, that 'he would be court-martialled after the war'. Over 200,000 German troops were lost at Stalingrad together with another 100,000 men who became casualties outside the pocket. By the end of February 1943 the army and SS losses in Russia from the beginning of the war, in dead and missing alone, had exceeded the million mark. And the

Soviet winter offensive showed no signs of abating as it forced the German Army out of the Caucasus and back into the Ukraine.

Hitler had had very fixed misconceptions as to the political, economic and military strength of the Soviet Union, and, in the main, he continued to hold them until the time of his death. And there appears to be no evidence that the German intelligence organizations before 1941 attempted to disabuse him or indeed had the necessary information on which to base any contrary views. Similarly, Hitler had a poor opinion of the military potential of the United States, and he rejected, often in the most violent terms, warnings that he received from some of his advisers regarding North American industrial and economic wealth, telling his generals, in March 1941, that such USA production forecasts were 'pure humbug' and that the United States could be no great danger to Germany even if it did come into the war.

Although Germany's fate would appear to have been finally sealed as early as December 1941 when Hitler declared war on the United States of America, the effect of the Anglo-American alliance was not to become apparent until the turn of 1943. At sea their war effort had admittedly been very powerful, and British air attacks had tied down substantial *Luftwaffe* forces in the defence of Western Europe, for the night bombing of German cities, some of it extremely heavy, had become a regular feature of the air war. But only forty-one German divisions had remained in the west in defence of Scandinavia, occupied France and the Low Countries, and many of these divisions were of low fighting value.

Up to November 1942, notwithstanding Hitler's premonitions and nervousness about the western seaboard of Europe, the ability of the British and the Americans to fight a war by land had not been taken very seriously in Rastenburg, and for this reason the Axis defeat at El Alamein and the Anglo-American landing in French North Africa had come as unpleasant tidings to the OKW and as a surprise to the German public, where the exploits and significance of Rommel and his African panzer army of less than four divisions had been much exaggerated by Goebbels's propaganda ministry and by the German press. Hitler's military reaction was, however, immediate, for he ordered, in quick succession, the entry of German troops into unoccupied France and the disarming of the rump of the French Army there, and the landing of fresh German and Italian forces in Tunisia.

The German staff officers accompanying Göring on a visit to Rome at the end of 1942 had assured their Italian allies, with customary braggadacio, that the new panzer army of three panzer divisions allotted to the Tunis force would 'be in Morocco inside three months'.* This was almost prophetic for, roughly within five months' time, 5 Panzer Army, with the remnant of Rommel's Panzer Army Africa and all other Axis troops in Tunisia, were in prisoner of war camps stretching from Tunisia to Morocco. The Axis loss amounted to over 200,000 men, of whom more than a half were German. The tide of the whole war, both in the east and in the west, had already turned.

---

* This high level optimism was at variance with the pessimistic opinions of the men on the spot, Rommel and Nehring.

CHAPTER TWO

The Fortress

Instead of remaining in Berlin at the centre of government, the Führer, following in the footsteps of the last imperial Kaiser, had taken to the field as the *de facto* Commander-in-Chief, with his own personal command staff, at the opening of each of the lightning wars. But when Hitler moved to the hutted camp near Rastenburg in midsummer of 1941 for what was to have been the short campaign to overthrow the Soviet Union, he was to remain in the wet and gloomy Görlitz forest almost without a break until November 1944 when the invading Russians were already setting the German border villages aflame. For over three and a half years of the war the government of the Reich and of the occupied territories of Europe was directed from wooden army sheds and concrete bunkers not far from the Lithuanian frontier, through party representatives and government liaison officers and the field echelons of the armed forces.

Hitler's system of government was entirely personal in that it revolved about himself, and he claimed to have solved the contradiction of opposites between the competing demands of the political and the military leadership that had plagued the old Empire, in that he had united all authority in his own person. In truth the problem still existed in a more acute form since the dualism remained, but within his own head, where his brain was unable to cope with the stress of the conflicting daily claims made upon it. Isolation and seclusion from the reality of the day to day activity in the capital made matters worse. In his great East Prussian military camp, he was, he told Goebbels, sick of the sight of generals, and 'after the war he would never want to see a general again'. By then Hitler was a full-time field commander as, day by day, he directed the detail of operations on all the various fronts; many major questions of war direction could not be put to him since his daily time-table at his closely guarded headquarters did not permit it, and weighty decisions on the most important matters of state were postponed, often indefinitely. It had been noted, too, by Goebbels, by Bormann and by the O K W war diarists, that the stress of war was having its effect in that the Führer was tiring and his powers of decision were becoming impaired so that it was often impossible to get a firm answer out of him. And so, outstanding questions were dealt with, or neglected, by the competing agencies of the party, the military and the government.

But this period also saw a change in the status and responsibilities of the old party men, Hitler's veteran associates and proven comrades-in-arms who had been in the movement since the start. Himmler's powers as Minister of the Interior, as Chief of Police and as Commander-in-Chief of the general and armed (*Waffen*) S S were undiminished, but, since the Führer had shut himself off in monastic seclusion, Himmler now shared less of his company and confidences. This applied, too, to Ley, the party and labour leader, and to Goebbels, the Minister for Propaganda and the party *Gauleiter* of Berlin, whose duties kept them in the capital. Göring, the Commander-in-Chief of the *Luftwaffe*, Minister for Air Transport, and the Plenipotentiary for the Four Year Plan, had suffered a serious eclipse in his standing with the Führer on account of Germany's failures in the air war. But as these old party associates declined in their importance and their closeness to the Führer, there had arisen in 1943 a new consortium, called by Goebbels 'the committee of three' or 'the three wise men of the east'; Bormann, the head of the Party Chancellery, Lammers, the head of the Reich Chancellery, and Keitel, the Chief of the O K W. Of these Bormann was the most important. These three men had the dictator's ear and began to override not only the administration but also the older party organization with its roots in the capital; in this way Führer control came to be exercised over an increasingly wide field of government through Bormann direct to the many party *Gauleiter*. And although Keitel's significance could be discounted, since he was used by Bormann, as by Hitler, as a figurehead to give the appearance of solidarity with the armed forces, Bormann and Lammers were viewed with distrust and dislike by Goebbels, Himmler and Göring. These three *alte Kämpfer* disliked and mistrusted each other, but, for the time being, at Goebbels's urging, they prepared to forget their own differences in a joint effort to unseat the others.

Similarly within the body of the Reich the powers of the *Gauleiter* had been extended and consolidated. The Nazi administration had always made a virtue of its claim that it was revolutionary, without roots, antecedents or ties with the past, without reliance on written constitution, legal precedent or tradition. Party organs had been superimposed upon the governmental framework, so that the most important decisions of state should depend entirely upon the Führer *as party leader*; much of the other main business of the state was conducted, not by the civil service, the local government and the jurists, but by party officials. This situation had always existed from as early as 1934; but from 1940 onwards the authority of party representatives had grown rapidly; the redistribution of power was then belatedly regularized in the autumn of 1942 when forty-two defence districts were established, each to coincide with the party *Gau* borders, the party *Gauleiter* being named as the defence commissar with authority over all government and administrative bodies in the area, and ranking as the equal in military matters to the commanders of the local military districts. So it came about that the status of those ministers who did not at the same time hold high party office, declined, so that, receiving neither audiences nor instructions from the dictator, their business became confined to minor routine. Matters considered to be of concern to the people, particularly those in the public eye, were handled by the party. By degrees even the military within the Reich became entirely subordinate to party control.

The German military were forbidden, by Hitler's orders, to criticize the organization of the high command, and Hitler himself boasted that the German command structure was the envy of the world. In reality, like the Reich administration, the high command was how it had chanced to develop or what Hitler had decided it should be at the time. When, for example, the dictator had assumed the post of Commander-in-Chief of the Army in December 1941, it had been intended that this should be a temporary measure. The makeshift arrangement was convenient, however, to the dictator and soon became permanent; but since he was interested only in fighting battles and had neither the inclination nor the time to carry out all the other tasks of the Army Commander-in-Chief, much of what was left of the OKH was to be broken down and handed over to the control of authorities outside the army.

The bulk of the OKW, the Armed Forces High Command, had remained in the Berlin Bendlerstrasse, while a large part of the general staff of the army and the OKH remained in its peacetime location at Zossen, about twenty-five miles south of the capital. The main part of the *Luftwaffe* High Command, the OKL, and of the German Navy, the OKM, were in or near Berlin.*

Within the Rastenburg headquarters, known as the Wolf's Lair (*Wolfsschanze*), Hitler lived in a closely barricaded and guarded compound, his military representatives there being Keitel and Jodl, Schmundt, his chief adjutant and head of the Army Personnel Office, and the liaison officers and adjutants from the three armed services and the SS. The OKW operations staff (*Wehrmachtführungsstab*) under Warlimont, Jodl's deputy, was, however, removed from Hitler and Jodl, in a completely separate compound. Zeitzler, the Chief of the Army General Staff, together with a small OKH field echelon, lived a few miles away in the Mauerwald, near Angerburg, and rarely saw the Führer except at the times of the daily briefings.

Zeitzler had formerly been a colonel in the OKW and a subordinate of Jodl's; then, after a short period of service in Russia, he had gone to von Rundstedt's Army Group D in France where he had gained some credit as a live wire for his part in the repulse of the British-Canadian raid on Dieppe. He was known personally to the Führer, and his middle class origins (he was the son of a pastor) apparently commended him to Göring, Goebbels and to the party. But, most important of all, he was a great friend of Schmundt, Hitler's chief military aide and military secretary. Zeitzler gave off an air of confidence and breezy optimism, unlike his predecessor Halder who, according to the dictator, was a pessimist and a prophet of doom, always infecting the army groups with his wailing. So Zeitzler, in the autumn of 1942, had replaced Halder, and was promoted directly to general, jumping the intermediate rank of lieutenant-general, as Jodl had done before him.

The effect of Zeitzler's appointment was to debase the post of Chief of General Staff since, as the German Army was by then Hitler's personal instrument, Zeitzler could only be regarded as the Führer's man. The new Chief of the Army General Staff, a major-general only since 1942, had, in the eyes of the army group commanders, none of the advantages of seniority, experience or authority. On taking up his post he made it entirely clear to his staff that loyalty to and confidence in the Führer was the order of the day.** The sun shone brightly on Zeitzler. The Führer's court took note of the favour bestowed on the new chief and was friendly towards him; even Jodl expected to profit by the new spirit of co-operation between the OKW and the remnant of the OKH. Keitel and Jodl were to hope that Zeitzler, as their former colleague in the OKW, would acquiesce to the OKW assuming an overall directing control over the eastern front. In this they were doomed to disappointment for Zeitzler disassociated himself from the pair and, profiting by the temporary

* The military accommodation at Zossen was largely underground and was excellently camouflaged by woods and country houses. By the end of 1944 Zossen was to house both the OKW (Maybach I) and the OKH (Maybach II) as well as the great military signal centre for the Reich (Halle 500 or *Zeppelin*). The OKL functioned from Wildpark-Werder and the OKM from Bernau.

**To his subordinates Zeitzler was blunt, even brutal, and choleric.

weakness of Jodl's personal position *vis-à-vis* the dictator (caused by Jodl's presumption in disagreeing with Hitler's strategy in the Caucasus), adroitly did away with the overlapping of some of the dual command responsibilities in the east and won back some of the ground lost by Halder to Jodl in the preceding nine months.

As far as Zeitzler was able, he excluded Keitel and Jodl from all discussion and business concerning the Russian front and, later on, pointedly absented himself from Jodl's Führer briefings. In the first year of his office he enjoyed Hitler's confidence but not necessarily that of his own general staff subordinates or of the army groups in the east, for he tended to be a mouthpiece and telephonic link between them and the Führer. Zeitzler failed as a chief of general staff and he may not have had that strength of character lent to him by some post-war writers. Yet, for all that, he was able and, according to Speer, a man of backbone who would defend his views with vigour.

In February 1943 Zeitzler's army general staff had suffered another decline when Hitler decided, presumably on the prompting of Guderian, to reorganize the panzer arm in the hope of injecting into it new *élan*. With scant consideration as to the possible effect on the remainder of the German Army, all mobile troops were removed from the control of the army general staff, of the OKH, of the Replacement Army and of the military districts, and were put directly under Guderian in his newly created appointment of Inspector-General of Panzer Troops. Guderian was responsible neither to the OKH nor to the OKW but only to Hitler, and some idea of the extent of his new responsibilities may be gathered by the fact that his panzer arm was henceforth to include all tank and all armoured reconnaissance units, armoured infantry, motorized infantry, all anti-tank units and armoured trains; only the artillery arm succeeded in resisting Guderian's efforts to take over all assault gun units; what remained of the former mobile troops that were not taken over by Guderian, the horsed cavalry and cyclist units, were redesignated, paradoxically, as infantry.* Guderian in this way became a separate and independent Commander-in-Chief of Panzer Troops within the Reich, with the complete responsibility for all panzer troops in the armed forces.**

This reorganization was to leave the high command and the armed forces in even greater disarray.

Towards the close of 1942 the Russians, recovering quickly from the summer defeats, had gone over to the second of the great winter offensives of the war, and, by the spring of 1943, had retaken much of the territory lost in the previous year. But the return of the fine spring weather that had dried out the soil and restored some of the mobility of the German Army could not be made use of, for Hitler was no longer free, as he had been in 1942, to strike a devastating blow at his Soviet

* Armoured reconnaissance units could be equipped with tanks or armoured cars; armoured infantry were those panzer grenadiers who were carried in armoured personnel carriers, the remainder being the motorized or lorried infantry. Assault guns *(Sturmgeschütze)* were turretless tanks mounting direct fire (usually high-velocity) guns to give fire support to infantry; they could also knock out tanks. The assault gun was not meant to be an indirect fire S.P. gun; although manned by the artillery it was, in all essentials, a tank.

**Jodl, Zeitzler and Guderian were all on unfriendly, even hostile terms.

foe, since the German Army and the *Luftwaffe*, reduced in numbers and in equipment, were tired and disorganized. The Führer was forced, too, to take account of the increasingly threatening situation in the west, for he could not allow himself to be caught, in the event of an invasion, with the bulk of his ground forces locked in battle nearly two thousand miles to the east.

In 1941 and 1942 the Channel and Atlantic beaches had been comparatively lightly held, and then mainly by second-class or refitting formations. Yet the Anglo-Canadian raid at Dieppe, in August 1942, had been crushed remarkably quickly. By early 1943, however, the situation in Western Europe was by no means as encouraging for the German defenders. Contrary to Hitler's expectation, the Japanese had not called down on their own heads the whole of the United States war effort in the area of the Pacific, and Washington, having sufficient resources for two wars, had decided to give priority to that against Germany. The enormous U-boat sinkings of allied shipping that had reached a peak in 1942, far exceeding the rebuilding rate, had suddenly fallen off and were decreasing rapidly, with heavy casualties to the U-boat attackers caused by increased air cover and by the rapid progress of British naval technology, particularly in the development of a radar so sensitive that it could, so the Germans believed, pick up an exposed periscope. The large tonnage of allied shipping used for the North African landings had come as a great surprise to the German dictator, and thereafter the great troop and supply convoys arrived, virtually without loss, in the Mediterranean and in the British Isles, enabling a great build-up of American forces there. The Italian colonial empire in Africa had been completely overrun by the British and, with the Axis loss of the North African coast, the *Luftwaffe* command of the air over the main Mediterranean sea-way had vanished, so that it could only be a matter of time before the Suez sea route to the Middle and Far East would be reopened once more for allied shipping.

From 1941 onwards the British had won air superiority within the operating radius of their single-engined fighters, but bombing beyond this range had had to be carried out in the protection of darkness. The bombing offensive against Germany had been growing steadily and, in 1942 and 1943, severe raids were becoming a nightly event, a thousand heavy aircraft often attacking a single target, city after city suffering the greatest destruction. Already, by March of 1943, Goebbels had said that he 'feared to think what Germany would look like at the end of only another three months', and that 'by next spring a great part of the Reich would be in ruins'. Then, during the summer of 1943, the air raids grew rapidly in intensity as the United States Air Force began its heavy daylight bombing, at first unescorted and then with the protection of recently developed long-range pursuit planes that had a performance which the German home defence fighters could not equal. So it was that, in the summer of 1943, the *Luftwaffe* lost, finally and irrevocably, air mastery over the whole of the Reich and the occupied territories.

The key to the loss of Germany's air superiority lay in the restricted capacity of its aircraft industry, in fuel shortages and in indifferent higher direction and command. But since each of Germany's three enemies had an aircraft production that exceeded that of the Reich—in the case of the United States by many times—and all of them had adequate sources of aviation fuels and abundant manpower, the *Luftwaffe* could not survive.

The loss of air superiority by itself was deadly enough in that it exposed the homeland, its peoples, its industries and its communications to air attack, but its effects grew in geometrical progression in that it struck not only at Germany's war potential and production but it also took away one of the very foundations on which victory in the land and sea battle must be based. Nor could the German Army fight even a defensive battle with hope of enduring success if it was to operate in conditions of air inferiority.

The glorious victories won by the German Army between 1939 and 1942 had been due to the strength and the imaginative use of air power and armoured and mobile troops. But by 1943 the air power had been lost and the panzer arm was no longer capable, by itself, of carrying out even operative tasks deep in the enemy rear; at the best, German tanks were gradually being restricted to tactical roles, supporting attacks, putting in counter-attacks and covering withdrawals. The reason lay jointly in the loss of air support and in the falling off of German tank strength in comparison with the rapidly expanding armoured forces of Germany's enemies. As with the case of aircraft, the German motor and armoured industry was hardly a match in resources and productivity for any one of its three principal enemies, and it was fully extended in trying to replace casualties caused by battle or by the wear and tear of mileage and weather on the eastern front.

On the high seas the Axis situation was no more favourable. The Italian Fleet was port-bound in Taranto and Spezia because of a shortage of fuel oil deliveries from Germany and because of its unwillingness to challenge the British Mediterranean Fleet. Elsewhere German surface raiders had been hunted out of existence and the German Grand Fleet, two battleships, four heavy and four light cruisers and thirty destroyers, had proved unable even to interfere with the British escorted Arctic convoys to Murmansk. Except for its U-boats the German Navy was no longer of strategic or military significance, since, without air cover, surface fleets were vulnerable and largely ineffective. By 1943 Hitler had concluded that all big fighting ships were so entirely obsolete as to be extinct (*Saurier*) and he subjected Raeder to hour-long abuse for what he considered to be the German Navy's failure.* At the end of January Raeder was retired and replaced by the submarine-specialist Dönitz, but the battleships, instead of being scrapped as originally intended, took refuge in the Norwegian fiords while the cruisers were used as naval training units in the Baltic. From then onwards priority was given to the building of U-boats and light coastal craft.

The Baltic remained a German lake since the Soviet fleet there had been held in check by minefields and anti-submarine nets laid across the Gulf of Finland. The Red Baltic Fleet, consisting of two old battleships, two cruisers, forty destroyers, over 100 motor torpedo-boats and ninety-three submarines, remained bottled up near Kronstadt, except for a score or so of submarines that managed to penetrate the barrage. Of the 1,700 Axis vessels that sailed the Baltic in 1942 only twenty-six were sunk by enemy action, the Germans claiming to have destroyed ten Soviet submarines during that year. The Royal Air Force caused more disruption to German shipping and the U-boat training in the Gulf of Danzig at this time than did the Soviet Baltic Fleet. During 1943, however, the situation in the Northern Baltic began to change with the threefold increase of the Soviet Baltic air arm to about 900 aircraft. German patrol vessels and minelayers, many of which were converted fishing vessels, lacked both armament and speed and could no longer

---

* This was done in the presence of Keitel, after the *Hipper* and *Lützow*. with a squadron of large destroyers, had been driven off with loss by a much inferior Royal Navy escort in the Barents Sea on 31 December 1942.

patrol the mined and netted areas in daylight because of the heavy air attacks, and Soviet craft began to sweep and penetrate the mine barrage.

The Black Sea was controlled by German Navy light flotillas, including a few small submarines (brought down the Danube from Germany), with *Luftwaffe* air and some Rumanian naval support. The Soviet Black Sea Fleet, made up of an old battleship, five cruisers, fifteen destroyers and about fifty submarines, sheltered in Caucasian ports, declining to put to sea without air cover.

A few German submarines had entered the Mediterranean through the Straits of Gibraltar—there were never more than about a dozen on operations there at any time—but, in the main, German naval activity was restricted to light surface units in the coastal waters off South France and Italy and among the Greek islands, where supply and troop movement took place either by night or by using small unescorted coasters. Since the Greek peninsula and islands were outside the radius of the allied single-engined fighters in the Mediterranean, the *Luftwaffe* continued to have air superiority over this area until 1944.

The French Atlantic ports of Brest, La Rochelle and Bordeaux were essential to the German Navy as bases for long-range U-boat operations, La Rochelle and Bordeaux having the added advantage that they were beyond allied close-fighter range. Elsewhere along the French Atlantic and Channel, the sailing of German coastal shipping was only safe at night and when covered by protective minefields and light escorts.

By June 1943 the battle line on the eastern front ran from near Petsamo in the Arctic Circle due southwards through Finland to Lakes Onega and Ladoga, past encircled Leningrad and due south again across Old Russia to Velikie Luki, then eastwards in the great Rzhev salient that still threatened Moscow, then southwards again, taking in two further big salients of Orel and Kharkov, both jutting eastwards one to the north and the other to the south of Kursk; the fighting line then ended at the Sea of Azov, on the northern bank near Taganrog and on the southern at the Taman bridgehead covering the crossing of the Kerch Straits to the Crimea. This German front from Leningrad to the Black Sea covered 1,700 miles, in addition to a frontage of nearly 200 miles in the far north held by 20 German Army in Finnish Lapland.

In the west, facing the Anglo-Americans, the German-held territory stretched from Petsamo in Finland round the North Cape to Narvik and down the Norwegian coast to Skagerrak, Jutland and the German Bight, then along the Channel and Atlantic coast to the Pyrenees, a distance in all of nearly 3,000 miles. In the Mediterranean the coastline to be defended ran for more than 4,000 miles from the Pyrenees to the Turkish border.

During 1943, as the strength of Germany's military position had declined, Goebbels had sought to give its situation a positive meaning by coining the idea of Fortress Europe, since this suggested a certain sense of security to the now beleaguered inhabitants of the Reich. The fortress was to be given walls, the Atlantic Wall along the western coast and, after August 1943, the East or Panther Wall in Russia running from near Leningrad due southwards to the line of the Dnieper.

The real strength of a fortress or of any fortified area depends, of course, on the strength of the fortifications and field works, and on the numbers and fighting value of the forces manning the perimeter defences and forming the mobile reserves that it is so essential to have ready at hand to destroy any enemy penetration. For as soon as the walls of the stronghold are breached in strength in any one place, the remaining defences are useless.

The idea of a fortress usually presupposes a garrison closely united by race, or by interest and loyalties, under a single effective command. But by far the largest part of the population of Fortress Europe was made up of the inhabitants of occupied territories, French, Belgians, Dutch, Danes, Norwegians, Poles and the many peoples of Czechoslovakia, Yugoslavia, Greece and Albania, nations that had been at war with the Axis and were now suffering from the brutalities of the occupying powers. In the east the Lithuanians, Latvians, Estonians, Belorussians, Ukrainians and Russians, although they might at first have been ready to throw off a Soviet reign of terror, were little better pleased to have another tyranny in its place. Some of these inhabitants of the Fortress, particularly in the Balkans, had never laid down their arms, but, taking to the hills, had waged a bitter and merciless war on the Axis troops. Others in Western Europe, in Poland and in Russia, had been slower to form resistance organizations until they had become confident that Germany had not in fact won the war. Intelligence and armed partisan organizations then grew apace, some nationalist and others communist in their origin and control. All were united in their hatred of the Germans.

Nor was the situation among Germany's Axis partners much better, for they were allied only in name. The most valiant and able fighting men were the Finns, whose formations in the closely forested and mountainous northern regions were superior to those of the Germans, and, indeed, were without equal anywhere. But the Finns, no less than the Japanese, kept themselves aloof from Hitler's conduct of the war, and, having reached the line of the Svir, the Finns were content to sit there and let the fighting continue with the shedding of German blood rather than their own. Nor did they even regard themselves as Germany's allies, but merely brothers-in-arms who happened to be fighting a common enemy, the Soviet Union; Finland relied heavily, however, on Germany both for food and for arms. Finland was not at war with Britain or the United States.

The situation with the other members and associates of the Axis was different yet again, for by 1943, Rumania, Hungary, Bulgaria and Slovakia had degenerated to the position of unwilling German satellites. The Rumanian and Hungarian dictators were from time to time summoned to the Führer's presence and subjected to violent and acrimonious harangues, while their forces and peoples were openly despised by the German troops occupying their countries. After two years of war in which their resources had been used in the furtherance of Germany's interests, the leaders and peoples were rapidly becoming as anti-German as before they had been anti-Russian. The Hungarians and Rumanians were at each other's throats. Bulgaria, allied to the Germans, although little esteemed by them, formed one of the occupying powers in the Balkans; the Bulgarians were at war with Britain and the United States but not with the Soviet Union; and they were the blood enemies of the Turks, the Greeks and the Italians. There was disunity everywhere.

In due course the property and peoples of the Axis allies were to be treated by the Germans little differently from those of the occupied territories of the defeated nations; governments and peoples allied to the Germans were to be kept in the war, that they would willingly have left, by the use of German armed force and the

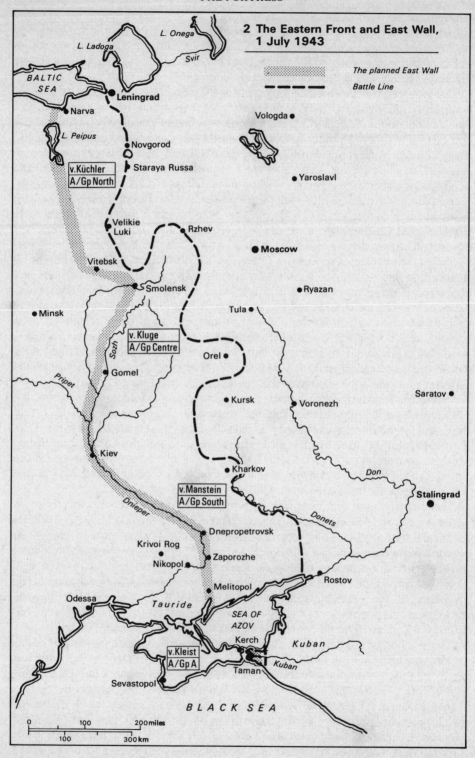

2 The Eastern Front and East Wall, 1 July 1943

The planned East Wall

Battle Line

L. Onega

L. Ladoga

Svir

BALTIC SEA

Leningrad

Narva

Vologda

L. Peipus

Novgorod

Staraya Russa

v.Küchler
A/Gp North

Yaroslavl

Velikie Luki

Rzhev

Vitebsk

Moscow

Smolensk

Ryazan

Minsk

Tula

Sozh

v.Kluge
A/Gp Centre

Orel

Gomel

Pripet

Kursk

Voronezh

Saratov

Kiev

Kharkov

Don

Dnieper

v.Manstein
A/Gp South

Stalingrad

Donets

Dnepropetrovsk

Krivoi Rog

Zaporozhe

Nikopol

Melitopol

Rostov

Odessa

Tauride

SEA OF AZOV

Kuban

Kerch

v.Kleist
A/Gp A

Kuban

Sevastopol

Taman

BLACK SEA

0   100   200 miles

100   300 km

German concentration camp. For German arrogance was such that it was impossible for its leaders or for its peoples to realize that any nation's destiny must be regulated by its own preservation, not by Germany's interest. For Germany was stripping these countries of their resources and manpower in an effort, from 1943 onwards, to keep the enemy as far as possible from the soil of the Reich. In such a situation it would have been criminal for any Axis satellite statesman, whatever his political persuasion, not to have put the interest of his own country first. But any attempt to leave the war was regarded as treachery and brought immediate German reprisals, with the imprisonment or shooting of leaders and the mass execution of hostages or troops, not necessarily by the SS, for the *Luftwaffe* and German Army also bore some of the blame for carrying out the criminal orders issued from Rastenburg.*

Mussolini's Italy had at first been in a privileged category, since in 1940 Italy had been Germany's only ally. Hitler had once, in the early twenties, been an admirer of Mussolini, and there existed between the two men a peculiar bond of friendship interlaced with much mutual distrust. Hitler had felt that any ally was better than none, and Mussolini had been eager that Italy should share the spoils for which it had not been obliged to fight. But the unfavourable turn that the war had taken from 1941 onwards had put a strain on the dictators' friendship. The German foreign office, the party and the military representatives, although priding themselves on their correctness, became exasperated by Italian methods and by Italian failures. In the Balkans the Italian occupation authorities introduced policies not only independent of, but also purposely directed against, those of the Germans. The population of the Italian homeland, already tired of a war that they had never wanted, became deeply concerned at the nearness of the Anglo-American threat and resentful of the presence of the German forces there.

Throughout the whole of Europe, among both the victors and the vanquished, the Germans were both feared and detested. In the Greater Reich itself, although the population was, for the most part, still determinedly and staunchly behind its leader, it was, in 1943, for the first time severely and sorely troubled about the course of the war and its outcome. The situation was very different from that of a year before. Goebbels had been much shaken by the sudden change in Germany's fortunes. It gave him the creeps, he said, merely to look at the map and see how much ground had been lost in the east, and the mere thought of the Anglo-American invasion 'hanging over all of them' left him depressed. The Führer could not understand, Goebbels said, why the Soviet Union, with its enormous losses in men and equipment, had not already collapsed, but it was impossible to know what Stalin had left in the way of reserves. If only, Goebbels continued, the Soviet Union could be finished off quickly, the *Wehrmacht* could then face the coming invasion with new confidence.

What was even more disturbing to the little Minister for Propaganda were the reports reaching his office of the drop in morale of the German people, and for this he blamed the defeat in North Africa, the air war over Germany, the failure of the U-boats and the reduction in the German food ration. The nation was deeply worried, he thought, because it could not see how victory could be won or how Germany could get out of the war. The allied Casablanca declaration of January 1943 had been used by Goebbels to impress on the Reich that no acceptable terms

---

* The *Luftwaffe* bombing of the towns of its Axis allies was another of Hitler's reprisals.

could be expected from west or east; this had given the people new resolution but it had also depressed morale since it had confirmed that the war would have to go on to the bitter end against overwhelming odds.

The internal Reich postal service was always liable to interception, and correspondence of interest found its way to Goebbels's desk. German citizens were now daring to complain about the war, the way it was directed, about the party, 'even criticizing the Führer himself'. The Führer's apparent indifference to the plight of the people had been remarked on, in that he had not made a single visit to the heavily bombed areas; nor was he doing much to remove public anxiety, since he no longer made radio or press addresses to brief the nation on the progress of the war. It was known, too, that many of those unfortunates that had lost husbands and sons, reported missing in the east, were now listening regularly to Soviet German language propaganda broadcasts, in spite of the draconian penalties that they would suffer if caught, in order to hear the nightly lists of German prisoners in Red Army hands. Goebbels and the party had been further embarrassed by the great quantity of prisoner of war mail received from the Soviet Union, most of it having an anti-war or an anti-Nazi propaganda bias written in by the soldier at the direction of the communists as the price of despatch. This mail had been held back by the party, but Goebbels had come to the conclusion that it could be held no longer and that each letter would have to be delivered personally by a party representative in order to nullify the Soviet propaganda by an official Nazi explanation, and, presumably, to report back to the party the reaction of the recipient.

Goebbels himself had no military training and little military understanding and he had been obliged to accept what he had been told by the Führer and the OKW, making use of, and falsifying, this in his propaganda offensives at home and abroad. In some respects, knowing no better, he had become the dupe of his own propaganda, but as the truth of the situation gradually became understandable he showed himself, in the privacy of his diary, to be concerned, at times even aghast, at Germany's perilous situation. The war direction was failing, he thought, in that it took too little account of the effects of the loss of air superiority, not only on home defence but also on the waging of war as a whole, and it was apparently exerting little effort in trying to rectify the situation. Goebbels had for so long echoed his master in decrying United States war production, that it came as an unpleasant surprise to find that the clouds of American fighters appearing so frequently over the Reich were superior to the German, and that the enemy bombers could pin-point targets 'with amazing accuracy from a height of 25,000 feet'. Taking his cue from the OKW and the army general staff, he had sneered for years at the inferiority of enemy ground troops, British, American and Russian. By 1943, however, he was revealing to his diary 'that it was not true that British troops lacked experience or skill' and was marvelling how 'any [German] soldier of any rank returning from the eastern front continues to emphasize the absolute superiority of our own men over the Red Army—yet all we do is to retreat and retreat!'.

Goebbels had come to realize that German foreign politics and diplomacy had withered and died. He knew that peace, with either east or west, was necessary for Germany's survival, and he urged this course on the dictator. The Minister for Propaganda tried, too, to get Himmler and Göring to support him. The wary Himmler did not intend to commit himself. Göring, continually bullied by Hitler, was thoroughly demoralized and had become what Koller, the latter-day Chief of Air Staff, called, 'His Master's Voice'. Yet Göring well knew the peril threatening the Reich and he regretted that Germany had ever gone to war at all. Terrified of the Führer, however, the only initiative he would permit himself was to abuse von Ribbentrop, the Foreign Minister, as if the whole war was of Ribbentrop's making.

The Axis defeats in Stalingrad and North Africa and the rapidly increasing military strength of the Soviet and Anglo-American powers gave to the world the clearest indication that, unless Germany's enemies fell out amongst themselves, the Axis could not win. Japan had shot its bolt and was beginning to suffer telling defeats in the Pacific, so that Tokyo voiced its fears to Berlin and Rome urging that they should both make peace with Moscow—but *not* with London or Washington. Above all, the Japanese had wanted to keep the Mediterranean closed to British shipping and they ventured to give to Berlin their opinion that 'since an Anglo-American landing in France was most unlikely' the Germans would be well-advised to regard the Mediterranean and Italy as *the* main defensive front in Europe. Italy, too, not unnaturally, wanted to concentrate on the defence of the Mediterranean. Finland was considering how it could best extricate itself from the war. Antonescu, the Rumanian dictator, wanted peace with the Anglo-Americans, but a continuation of the war against the Soviet Union. Germany's allies, jointly or severally, succeeded in persuading von Ribbentrop, at least temporarily, that peace must be made with east or west. But Hitler's reaction to any suggestion of diplomacy was either an outright and angry rejection or one of vague deferment—a dishonest half-promise to consider a peace initiative when the auspices might be more propitious and Germany might obtain better terms.

The Italians and Rumanians pooled their intelligence as to what was happening at the Führer's headquarters, and the Japanese, doubtful of Hitler's version, frequently asked Germany's European allies for frank briefings as to the war situation in Europe. In January the Italian liaison officer in Rastenburg reported to his capital that 'everything was concentrated in the Führer's hands, and the slightest initiative depended on the dictator, even the most trivial allocation of units, for the general staff no longer had any say in the matter'. And Antonescu, the Rumanian head of state, and his foreign minister, returning that month from Rastenburg, told the Italians that Hitler 'was fully taken up with the Russian question and tortured by serious obsessions' and that 'in his fixation on Russia he fails to take account of America and England'. But when Antonescu had suggested to Hitler a positive strategy in the east, perhaps the taking of Moscow and Leningrad and the consolidating of the line of the Volga, the Führer changed his tune with the retort that 'what counted now was to hold out in Russia and to neutralize the offensive of the Anglo-Saxons'. Antonescu continued that, 'faced with this nightmare conception of going absolutely nowhere in the east that would eventually drain away all our resources', he (Antonescu) had asked von Ribbentrop if it were not timely to resuscitate and unite Europe by a moral and political initiative. Von Ribbentrop, in reply, had said that such action was not possible 'until Russia had been beaten: Europe *must* hold out—and that is all'. The internal situation in Germany, thought Antonescu, was very serious and he had noted a certain uneasiness in the German high command, a crisis of confidence in public opinion and morale, a crisis in the system; a crisis above all in German manpower and in strategic reserves. The German Army was tired; and 'the troops who had been through four or five campaigns were now as if under the influence of drugs'.

Notwithstanding Hitler's boasting that he was so well-read in Clausewitz it is certain that he did not understand that war is a political act, the mere continuation of policy by other means, and that political failures could not necessarily be made good by feat of arms. For Hitler had come to regard war as a military rather than as a political matter. The Führer could not maintain the dualism between politics and military leadership and he had become confused in his aims. And, as the editors of the OKW diaries have said, too often Hitler the general put Hitler the politician into an impossible position, because he over-estimated his military capabilities and believed that all problems could be solved by force, while Hitler the politician and Hitler the economist frequently left Hitler the general in the lurch by giving him tasks impossible to perform.

There seems to be little doubt that Hitler prized his reputation as a military leader rather than that as a statesman and that he wished to rank in the annals with Napoleon, Caesar and Alexander. Keitel, Jodl and Schmundt told him that he already did so. This had eventually led him to neglect politics and affairs of state while he acted the war-lord, clad in the field grey tunic and dark trousers of his own design, the uniform without rank insignia that he was to wear throughout the war. But Hitler had learned his generalship listening to generals as they gesticulated in front of maps, and this is what he himself had become, a map general, except that he had little or no idea of battle conditions or what was practicable in war. This in turn led him to place his trust on chinagraph markings denoting walls, defensive lines, fortresses and bastions, whereas on the ground there was in reality virtually nothing, neither troops, nor defences nor topographical features capable of being defended. But adventurer as he was, he had determined to fight it out to the bitter end, from a fortress without walls and without a roof, without defences and without reserves, with tired and divided garrisons and, for the most part, an enemy population within its boundaries.

From a fortress in the old days one could always make sallies, even though these might be only diversionary and not fatal to the enemy. But without seapower and with the loss of air superiority, German sallies in the west or in the Mediterranean were out of the question. In the east, against the Red Army, where there were no seas to cross and where local air superiority could still be gained and maintained, such sorties might still have been possible. But the Führer's insistence on a rigid defence and the holding of more territory than his troops could encompass rapidly exhausted the small reserves that might have been available for a mobile offence or a mobile defence. For the same reason the Germans had not been able, since the start of the war against the Soviet Union, to collect or husband theatre reserves of any consequence, let alone a central OKW mobile reserve within the Reich held at a state of readiness to reinforce the theatres, together with sufficient *Luftwaffe* resources to give air cover so that such formations might move and fight.

Much of Hitler's war strategy was illogical and was unrelated to what was practicable and to the realities of the situation. He had long ago ceased to interest himself in world politics and had never had any other long term aim except the mastery of Europe and world domination by armed force. In Germany's decline he was resolved to keep Europe in subjection and, obsessed with upholding his own personal military prestige, to hold on to every foot of occupied soil. The Führer could always find reasons convincing to himself for justifying the dissipation of German formations in far-flung territories. The allies must be kept out of Italy and away from the borders of the Reich. Italy itself must for this reason be covered by large garrisons in Corsica, Sardinia and Sicily. The security of the Balkans was only sure if strong Axis forces held Crete and Rhodes and the many Greek islands; these island garrisons would, according to his reasoning, fulfil secondary roles in that they would bar the Dardanelles to the British, should they try to win a direct sea transport link through to the Russians, and the near presence of German troops would deter Turkey from coming into the war against the Axis. In the far north large forces sat idle in Lapland while others guarded the long Norwegian coast, although the likelihood of a major allied landing there was remote. But Petsamo nickel and Swedish iron ores were essential to the war economy, said the Führer, and unless strong forces remained in the north, Sweden, 'growing more insolent with each Axis defeat', might come into the war. The coast itself was covered by outposts, and island garrisons were deployed as far afield as Lofoten in an effort to get even more security. There was always some geographical feature of strategic importance, however limited this might be, just over the horizon; these were often occupied to prevent their seizure by the enemy. It was a conception dangerous in its infinite scope.

In Russia and the Ukraine terrain was held, often against military logic, for what was considered to be an economic advantage—foods, ores, timbers, even Russian manpower that might be mobilized by the enemy; communication centres were designated and defended as bastions or strong points, again merely to deny their use to the enemy; great rivers were marked out as defensive lines, even 'walls', unmindful of the fact that for five months of the year the rivers were frozen over, and that there were not sufficient troops available to fortify or to defend the over-extended river frontages. For the genius of the Führer had drastically revised many of the theories that he had learned from earlier German general staffs, and he had formulated some very bizarre doctrines. He no longer had the means to launch the powerful blitzkrieg offensives, and had, perforce, to put his trust in defence. But he had come to the conclusion that since 'the attackers needed to overcome a well prepared strong point must outnumber the defenders by three to one', then all the advantages must necessarily remain with the defenders, who can thereby defeat up to three times their own numbers.

The weaknesses in this argument are obvious. The 'three to one' calculation is neither immutable nor always true. Nor does a closely defended sector or a surrounded bastion or strong point necessarily attract or hold any given number of enemy troops. And a besieged fighting man is effective only as long as he can be supplied and properly supported by air and ground weapons. But if this defensive strategy is carried to such lengths that it denies to one's own defenders both tactical and strategic mobility, tying formations, even whole armies, to the defence of terrain, at the same time removing from their commanders the freedom to redeploy, move and even to attack, then one has already lost all initiative to the enemy. For he who attempts to hold everything holds nothing. The Soviet High Command was not slow to take advantage of this novel situation in that it disengaged its forces at will, leaving the battle line lightly held, without danger of counter-attack or follow up, so amassing enormous Red Army and Red Air Force reserves with which to destroy, systematically, vast sectors of the German held eastern front.

In the west, although in a different element, the situation was to prove much the same, for German troops had been dispersed from Petsamo to the Pyrenees and from the Channel Islands to Crete in a way that was contrary to all basic strategic principles, without securing the coastal perimeter one iota. For the Anglo-American enemy, enjoying air and sea supremacy, could land at will anywhere, playing, as Schramm has said, ducks and drakes with the defenders.

By mid 1943 the war was already lost both politically and militarily. The Bolsheviks and the Anglo-American capitalists, united only in a common determination to destroy Nazi Germany, showed no signs of relaxing their efforts. The Casablanca declaration made it clear that Germany itself could expect no terms and certainly would not be regarded by the victors in the same light as its Axis satellites. For Germany, far from being permitted to return to its 1938 frontiers, would be occupied and probably truncated or partitioned, its leaders being made answerable for the past. The enormity of their grisly crimes, as yet, only the Nazi hierarchy knew.

CHAPTER THREE

Kursk and the East Wall

The German Army had, since the beginning of the war, already taken over four million Red Army prisoners, and this high figure, coupled with the estimate of the casualties in Russian dead and wounded, had encouraged Hitler to think that Stalin's reserves must be running out. But, gambler though he might have been, the Führer was no longer willing to attempt to force a final decision in the east, because of what he believed to be the imminence of an invasion in Western Europe and in the Mediterranean. For, by midsummer 1943, the German Army was very much out of balance, having 168 divisions (3.1 million men) in the east, together with six SS and twelve *Luftwaffe* field divisions and 3,800 tanks, but only seventy-five divisions (1.4 million men) together with five SS and ten *Luftwaffe* field divisions and 1,300 tanks elsewhere. In France there was a total of only forty-four divisions and 860 tanks (of which a half were French), while in Italy the German forces stood at seven divisions and 570 tanks. The forces in France, in particular, were in no way ready to withstand invasion, and for this reason the dictator concluded that a strategic offensive into the depths of Russia was out of the question for the summer of 1943.

Hitler, however, was unwilling to surrender all initiative to the enemy and remain on the defensive awaiting the next blow. Since he was virtually powerless at sea and in the air, he was unable to interfere with any Anglo-American preparations for invasion, even if he had been aware of where these were being made; so he was forced to turn his attention to the east once more. He had for some time past been reading the history of the German 1916 offensives at Verdun launched in the third year of the First World War with the object of pinning and destroying allied reserves. So, in the third year of the Second World War, he arrived at a plan similar to that of Verdun in that it would have as its aim the destruction of the remaining enemy strength on the main fighting front.

The basis of the Führer's new plan was to launch a major offensive with very limited territorial objectives, to be made immediately the ground had dried out after the thaw and before the Anglo-Saxons could begin an invasion of the continent. The object was to destroy or capture men and equipment and so remove, at least for the time being, the offensive power of the Red Army. The Soviet enemy would then be forced to remain quiescent while the *Wehrmacht* turned about to hurl back the invaders from the west. This was the broad reasoning that the dictator forced upon his military staff. Keitel, of course, agreed with him. Jodl's main interest was to get his hands on the OKH divisions as quickly as possible and redeploy them in the west; and since he wanted divisions fit for battle and not burned-out shells, he was against *any* German offensive into Russia, limited or otherwise. Zeitzler, together with Field-Marshals von Manstein and von Kluge, two of the four army group commanders on the eastern front, agreed with Hitler in that they were all opposed to any more adventures involving large scale and deeper penetration into Russia. But, since they well knew that divisions would in any case be removed from them before autumn for the west, leaving them dangerously understrength and exposed should there be another winter Russian offensive, they were only too willing to make use of the German formations for a limited summer offensive before these were taken away, perhaps for good. Zeitzler, in particular, desperately wanted a solution to the impasse on the eastern front. His battle sectors were over-extended and the divisions there had been drained of their fighting strength. Above all Zeitzler wanted to shorten the line in order to thicken up the defences, but since this usually involved withdrawals from salients, Hitler would not hear of it, both for reasons of prestige and because he maintained that the war economy could not stand the loss of further territory and resources.

In this way the tug of war between east and west, Zeitzler and Jodl, and between the army general staff of the OKH and the *Wehrmachtführungsstab* of the OKW, was accentuated, with the new element, what was in fact almost a third general staff, Guderian's General-Inspectorate of Panzer Troops, introducing a further dimension in the dissension. For, according to Guderian's post-war account, he had an overriding interest in building up armoured reserves in both troops and equipment to be ready for the Second Front, and for this reason he was entirely against the new venture.

This was the general background behind the new offensive. There were, in addition, other compelling and more particular motives that Hitler was not so ready to stress to his military subordinates. For the past year the *Wehrmacht* had suffered an unbroken run of major defeats and Hitler dearly wanted a victory, something quick and spectacular, however transient, 'that would shine out to the world like a beacon', and restore, in some part, his own military prestige. And the dictator had been encouraged by the limited tactical success of von Manstein's counter-attacks in the area of Kharkov in the previous March, when the great winter Soviet offensive had finally petered out. But, above all, his attention was drawn back to May 1942 when the dangerously exposed Red Army salient at Izyum, just south of Kharkov, surrounded on three sides by the German forces, had been foolishly used by Timoshenko as a jumping-off place for a major offensive. Timoshenko's attacks had been held, and von Bock's immediate counter-offensive, supervised by Hitler and Halder, had cut off the great Izyum bulge at the shoulders, with Paulus attacking southwards while von Kleist moved northwards to meet him. The larger part of two Russian fronts (small army groups) had been concentrated in the bulge ready for the Red Army offensive, and these were destroyed in the course of a few days fighting. The Germans had suffered 20,000 casualties, against a Red Army loss of 214,000 prisoners, 1,200 tanks and 2,000 guns.

This was the type of victory that the Führer hoped to repeat in April 1943, and the battle maps of the eastern front appeared to offer the ideal setting for such an operation. Just to the north of the 1942 Izyum battlefield, between Kharkov and Orel, the Red Army line bulged westwards forming three sides of a square, in the centre of which was the city of Kursk, this bulge being contained by German forces to the north, west and south. It was known that the Soviet High Command was repeating its actions of a year before in that it was moving two reinforced fronts into this closely packed area, presumably closing up in preparation for an offensive. It only remained for von Kluge's Army Group Centre and von Manstein's Army Group South to attack the salient, one from the north shoulder and the other from the south, and, their spearheads meeting just east of Kursk, cut off and destroy the whole of Rokossovsky's Central and Vatutin's Voronezh Fronts. According to the German estimates of the time there were seventy-five Soviet rifle divisions and forty-two tank brigades (about 2,400 tanks) within the Kursk salient, supported by 2,600 aircraft. In all probability this estimate was too low since Soviet post-war accounts give the total strength of the two fronts as 1.3 million men, 3,600 tanks and 3,000 aircraft, with a further 1,500 tanks held in reserve by Konev's Steppe Front standing outside and immediately to the east of the salient.

Planning for the German offensive had begun in March and it had originally been intended to attack in April, but the date was frequently postponed because of delay in assembling the troops and because Model, the commander of 9 Army forming the main assault force from the north, on whose opinion Hitler attached great importance, repeatedly asked for additional troops.

On 4 May Hitler held a planning meeting with the principal commanders and staffs to discuss the new offensive, to be known as *Citadel*, but he was by no means certain what he wanted to do. Zeitzler, on the other hand, appeared quite confident and von Kluge and von Manstein were still in favour of the offensive. Model was understood to have his doubts, based mainly on the known Soviet strength within the salient and the great depth of the Red Army defences that were growing week by week. It was obvious that the Russians expected a German attack. The enemy field works were so daunting to the north and to the south of the bulge that some brief consideration was given by the German commanders to the alternative, to break into the salient from the west face, but this was dropped since it offered little prospect of a double envelopment that would trap Rokossovsky and Vatutin behind the rapidly closing pincers. The only other course of action would have been to have played a waiting game throughout the summer and let the Red Army attack first from out of the salient, as Timoshenko had in fact done the year before at Izyum, since this would give the German some advantage in that the decisive battles that followed would be fought in the open. This course had much to commend it. But those who argued against it reasoned that there could be no guarantee that Stalin would go over to a major offensive there before the next winter, and meanwhile the fine dry summer weather, so essential to German mobility, would have been lost. The whole concept of the *Citadel* offensive had been to attack early, in the late spring or beginning of the summer, so that forces could then be withdrawn for the west. To wait could only play into the hands of the Anglo-Americans. Such was the German dilemma, and the mere thought of it, as Hitler said, 'made his stomach turn over'.

All these factors were talked over during that meeting on 4 May. Hitler was uncertain, doubtful whether the offensive should begin until the Russians should attack and in two minds as to whether the offensive should be launched at all, for he knew full well the value of the stake he was committing to this battle. Von Manstein was to have twenty-two divisions, of which six were panzer and five were panzer grenadier, and in all nearly 1,200 tanks; Model was to have twenty-one divisions, of which six were panzer and one panzer grenadier, totalling over 900 tanks. Over 1,800 aircraft were in support and a further seven German infantry divisions held the west flank of the bulge. About fifty divisions and over 2,000 tanks, with a fighting strength far exceeding that of the whole of the *Wehrmacht* forces in France at that time, were to be thrown into a single battle, the outcome of which would probably be decided in a few days.

The Munich conference broke up in disorder for there was little common ground among the Führer's several army staffs. The Führer, forced to come to some resolution, had come down in favour of attack. Guderian had been angered by the decision and by the removal of his remaining assets, including the untested Mark V Panthers and the Porsche Mark VI Tigers and Ferdinands, and he had fallen foul of his old enemy von Kluge, who thereupon challenged him to a duel, inviting Adolf Hitler to be his second.*

On 1 July the Führer addressed a meeting of senior commanders, all leaders down to corps commander being present, for he had finally decided to go ahead with the offensive and had resolved to put a bold and determined face on his decision. He opened with a preamble on the war situation, in which he roundly blamed Italy as being the cause of his misfortunes. Rumania and Hungary were unreliable and Finland was at the end of its resources. At all costs Germany must hold on to the conquered territory—it could not exist without it and the German soldier must be made to understand that where he stood there he remained. Under no circumstances would he give up the Balkans, but he would, if necessary, replace the Italian troops there by Germans. Crete, too, would be held rather than give it up to the enemy to become another airfield runway. In Russia he did not doubt that many crises were in store, but he believed that the Red Army would be dormant throughout the summer preparing for another winter offensive. He had no intention of withdrawing from the Orel salient since 'it was to Germany's advantage to tie down Soviet troops', nor did he propose to await an enemy offensive and hit the Russian on the rebound, that is to say by a counter-offensive, for he was certain that Germany must seize the initiative and attack. He was prepared to admit that *Citadel* was a gamble, but he himself believed that it would come off, and this conviction he based on events of the past when, against all military advice, *he* had decided to march into Austria, Czechoslovakia, Poland and the USSR.

Reason enough, one might have thought, to have abandoned *Citadel* immediately.

In Moscow some very similar scenes were being enacted. Stalin, like Hitler, was the *de facto* Commander-in-Chief of all the Armed Forces and, in addition, was the Commander-in-Chief of the Red Army and of all ground and air forces in the field. As in the case of the *Wehrmacht*, operational command was exercised from the dictator's office (in Stalin's empire from the Moscow Kremlin) direct to the many fronts in the battle areas. The organization of the ground element of the Red Army was very similar to that of the German Army, but the high command system approximated more to that of the German Empire in the First World War.

---

* The Mark VI Tiger (weighing about 60 short tons) had been developed by both Porsche and Henschel, the Porsche (Tiger P) being found unsatisfactory because of difficulty in manoeuvre and because of the lack of a secondary machine-gun armament. Many of the Tiger Ps were converted to turretless tank-destroyers with a L71 88 mm gun (Ferdinands). The Mark V Panther (weight about 50 short tons) had excellent sloped armour and carried the L70 75 mm gun.

The Red Army stood paramount and included the Red Air Force, and the Red Fleet occupied a secondary and inferior position. The high command of the Red Army, an extempore organization developed out of the peacetime Ministry of Defence, carried out all war planning, as directed by the head of state and the Red Army Commander-in-Chief, that is to say Stalin, and by the political and military committees of which Stalin was both the chairman and the director. The Red Army General Staff was purely a planning and executive body; although in some respects its position was comparable to that of the Great General Staff of the German Empire, it was, however, entirely dependent upon Stalin.

By midsummer 1943 Stalin had evolved the command system that, except for a few minor changes, was to continue until the end of the war. He himself was the Commander-in-Chief, with Zhukov, a former tsarist cavalry non-commissioned officer, as his deputy. Vasilevsky, a captain of the old tsarist army, was the Chief of General Staff. In reality Zhukov was not Stalin's deputy and Vasilevsky was only a part time chief of general staff; both were Stalin's advisers, executives and trouble-shooters, travelling to the various fronts as his eyes and his ears, gingering the front commanders and, on occasions and when instructed to do so, taking command of fronts or groups of fronts in time of crisis. The real duties of the chief of general staff were carried out largely by Antonov, Vasilevsky's deputy, another former tsarist officer, who briefed the dictator nightly on the battle situation on all the fronts. Antonov briefed, and he carried out orders, but he rarely discussed situations or made suggestions.

The probable German intention to attack at Kursk had been noted in Moscow in the first week in April, when Zhukov had sent a written report to Stalin mistakenly suggesting that the enemy was about to open another summer strategic offensive 'deep to the east towards Ryazan, so enveloping Moscow from the rear'. This, too, was Stalin's reading of the enemy preparations. Zhukov said he was against making a pre-emptive attack on the enemy but would prefer to await the German offensive. This opinion was shared by Vasilevsky and the general staff. Stalin instructed Rokossovsky and Vatutin, the front commanders at Kursk, to let him have their appreciations and recommendations. Rokossovsky, like Zhukov and Vasilevsky, favoured remaining on the defensive, but Vatutin's Voronezh Front hedged its appreciation in provisos, hinting that it might prove better, in certain circumstances, to attack out of the Kursk salient rather than wait for the enemy to begin. On 12 April, although it was known that the German offensive was not yet imminent, Stalin was clearly worried in case heavy German attacks should result in another Izyum, and he was fearful for the safety of Moscow. His natural inclination, like Hitler's, was to strike first before the enemy blow should fall, but he lacked confidence that his own troops could mount a victorious offensive in summer, for, before this time, the successful Red Army operations had all been in midwinter when the German troops, lacking cold weather equipment, clothing and supplies, had been at a disadvantage.

As the spring turned into summer Zhukov and Vasilevsky kept to their opinion that no offensive should be mounted until after the enemy had first blunted and then dissipated his strength against the formidable Kursk defences. But then, in May and June, Vatutin, nervous and highly strung, had begun to press, firstly Vasilevsky and then Stalin, that the Red Army should begin the offensive, urging the dictator not to lose the benefit of the summer weather. Vatutin's frequent pleas began to have their effect, so that Vasilevsky said it took all his own efforts and those of Zhukov, to dissuade the dictator. What was happening in Munich and Rastenburg was in fact being mirrored in the Kremlin and in the general staff building in Frunze Street, with endless discussion and argument on whether or not to attack first, and Vasilevsky noted, with concern, how nervous and irritable Stalin was becoming. He would not accept the one advice or the other, but frequently veered between the two opinions. On 10 and 20 May, and again on 2 June, the German offensive appeared to be imminent and the Russian fronts stood to, only to be stood down again some days later. Vacillation and the strain caused by the prolonged waiting affected Stalin's temper. Rages and abuse became more frequent. And so the long wait dragged on until the first week in July.

Meanwhile planning continued for the first Soviet summer offensive of the war, this to be mounted as soon as the German attacks on Kursk had been held and defeated, for Hitler was in no way right when he had forecast that the Red Army would lie dormant until the next winter. Stalin was determined to reoccupy Kiev and to force von Kluge's Army Group Centre westwards since, notwithstanding the recent German evacuation of the Rzhev salient (to find the necessary troops for the *Citadel* operation), the enemy still stood only 200 miles distant from Moscow.

On the late afternoon of 4 July, in hot, thundery and rainy weather, the Germans at long last began their offensive on the Kursk salient. Stalin did not go to bed that night. Towards the end of the following day Rokossovsky, facing Model in the north, was already under great enemy pressure, and he telephoned Stalin to ask for reinforcements. But his gratitude on being given another army was short-lived when it was redirected a few hours later to Vatutin (facing von Manstein). For Vatutin, according to Stalin, was 'in the gravest situation'.

In Army Groups Centre and South no pains had been spared in the preparation of the offensive. Reconnaissance and planning were carried out extensively, minute details being taken into account; air photographs were available for the whole of the Kursk salient. The troops were carefully briefed and rested and units were reinforced and, where necessary, re-equipped.

Yet there were many weaknesses on the German side that would have been more apparent to a Russian than to an Anglo-American observer, since he, the Russian, often suffered from the same deficiencies for exactly the same reasons. Hitler—like Stalin—was obsessed by numbers and was little concerned with real fighting strength; in consequence the enormous number of divisions that were deployed on both sides of the eastern front was misleading because a large proportion of these were mere shells, although still bearing a divisional number with a divisional organization and still being commanded by generals. In bayonets, however, some could hardly have matched a full strength battalion. Both dictators apparently found some personal reassurance in these inflated orders of battle and closely filled battle maps, and they used them to frighten their enemies and, in Hitler's case, to deceive his allies. But whereas Stalin used many of these shells as cadres for later re-embodiment as full scale divisions when reinforcements became available, Hitler was rarely able or willing to do so. For the Führer was determined not to break up burned-out or understrength divisions in order to provide reinforcements for the others, nor yet to bring them up to strength; and so these remnants remained at the battle front. Only the *Waffen SS* had a plentiful supply of men and equipment that was to raise the fighting value of its formations far above those of the German Army.

In order to keep up the number of army divisions in the field, Hitler had already made a number of reserve divisions (that were in reality home service basic training organizations of Fromm's Replacement Army and in no way organized or fitted as field divisions) available to the army groups outside the Reich. Most army (but not SS) field divisions, whether motorized or infantry, were in the process of being reduced from nine infantry battalions to six. Other skeleton divisions in the east were fused into corps groups (*Korpsabteilungen*) in order to economize on supporting artillery and services, but each of them still retained its divisional identity; these so-called corps groups had barely the fighting strength of divisions. So nonsensical was the reinforcement policy that twenty new divisions had been recently raised on the eastern front taking the numbers of those lost in Stalingrad, in addition to another thirty divisions with completely new numbers and titles; these fifty divisions had received adequate reinforcements but little equipment, and they were side by side with other battle tried formations that had been allowed to drop to below thirty per cent of their establishment strength. All divisions, whatever their strength, had suffered severely from losses of trained and experienced leaders, and this robbed the formations of much of their efficiency. Yet the fighting spirit, loyalty and cohesion of these troops was still surprisingly high; in any case, the Red Army troops facing them suffered from many of the same defects and deficiencies.

Hitler intended that the Kursk operation should be a tank battle because he wanted a quick decision based on a double armoured envelopment. He had already allotted to this single battle nearly every tank that he could raise, more than four times as many German tanks as he had at that time in the whole of France and the Netherlands; but the numbers had been found not only by exhausting Guderian's meagre reserves and emptying the proving grounds and factories, but also by introducing assault guns into the panzer regiments instead of tanks and by ruthlessly removing armoured fighting vehicles from the rest of the eastern front. So it came about that, on 30 June, a few days before the Kursk offensive, there were in the 200 miles between Orel and Kharkov nearly 2,600 tanks, but only 890 tanks over the remainder of the Russian front.

If Hitler was determined to fight an offensive battle on the eastern front he could have done it in no other fashion than in the way that he did, by concentrating all available forces in the area that he considered to be vital, which happened in this case to be the sector where the Red Army had also built up its formations ready for the summer offensive. Only too rarely in the latter half of the war was the Führer willing, or able, to comb out subsidiary sectors in order to amass a mobile reserve for the purpose of regaining a major tactical, let alone a strategical, initiative. Whether or not Hitler had amassed sufficient armour to defeat the 5,000 Soviet tanks said to be in the Voronezh, Central and Steppe Fronts, and whether he had sufficient infantry divisions to penetrate the great depth of the Soviet defensive works and open them up for the panzer formations, is of course another matter.

But Hitler, like Guderian, his former mentor, was obsessed by tanks, their numbers and mobility, and he was staking all on what he hoped was to be the lightning armoured blow, although there could be no question of achieving any

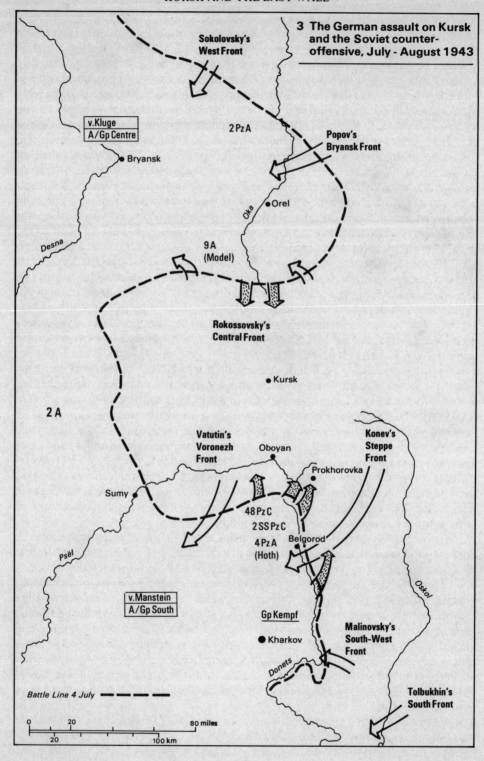

3 The German assault on Kursk and the Soviet counter-offensive, July - August 1943

Sokolovsky's West Front

v.Kluge
A/Gp Centre

● Bryansk

2 Pz A

Popov's Bryansk Front

Desna

Oka ● Orel

9 A (Model)

Rokossovsky's Central Front

2 A

● Kursk

Vatutin's Voronezh Front

Oboyan

Konev's Steppe Front

Prokhorovka ●

Sumy ●

48 Pz C
2 SS Pz C
4 Pz A (Hoth)

Belgorod ●

Psël

v.Manstein
A/Gp South

Gp Kempf

● Kharkov

Oskol

Malinovsky's South-West Front

Donets

Tolbukhin's South Front

Battle Line 4 July ━ ━ ━

0   20   80 miles
20   100 km

surprise. In this particular sector, however, with its close and well defended areas, infantry, artillery and engineers were to be at a premium in a situation where the presence of tanks could actually be a hindrance. And no land battle could be brought to final victory without a favourable air situation.

The *Luftwaffe*, like the panzer arm, had achieved a concentration of war planes in the battle area but it was still outnumbered by the Red Air Force. Qualitatively the *Luftwaffe* aircraft were probably still superior to the Soviet enemy, but the superiority was very much less than it had been at the beginning of the war, since the Red Air Force had been largely re-equipped with aircraft of modern design. Then again, the experience and training of *Luftwaffe* pilots in Russia was considerably lower than in the west and in the Reich, where the defending airmen had to combat the far superior air forces of the Anglo-Americans, for it was *Luftwaffe* policy to draft the newly trained and the less proficient to the eastern front. The shortage of aircraft fuels was already curtailing training and restricting operations. In consequence the *Luftwaffe* could guarantee a measure of air superiority for only a few days over the battlefield but could not bind itself to interdiction programmes to isolate the fighting area or even to dislocate the movement of Soviet reserves. The *Luftwaffe* action, like that of the ground troops, was to be based on the sudden massive blow; thereafter it could not keep up the intensity of its attacks.

Hitler's adventurist gamble was a single throw of the dice; if it failed there could be no second chance since there were no reserves and no alternative plan. There was nothing for von Kluge and von Manstein to do but attack and keep moving forward; if they should come to a standstill they were beaten and, unless they could extricate themselves, the attacking forces would be faced with annihilation.

These were some of the doubts that assailed Adolf Hitler as Commander-in-Chief. If the German Army attacked it could expect the bloodiest of losses that it could ill afford, even though the offensive brought victory and the destruction of the Voronezh and Central Fronts. If the operation was unsuccessful the losses would be even greater with the danger that Army Groups South and Centre would suffer so crippling a blow that they would, thereafter, be in no position to defend the Ukraine and Central Russia. If the German Army did not attack at all in Russia, but did what Jodl suggested and removed German divisions from east to west, then Stalin, as strong as ever, would himself launch a major offensive against Army Groups Centre and South, weakened by the withdrawals. The soundest tactical solution would have been to have awaited a Soviet offensive from out of the Kursk salient, for, with the benefit of hindsight one can now assume that this would have been made in August or September at the latest. As it transpired, the Second Front was still ten months away. But Hitler was not to know that, and he was already faced with the possibility of the collapse of Italy and the probability of the Anglo-American landings there.

And so the German offensive against the Kursk salient opened late on the afternoon of 4 July. Of the three earlier imponderables, the weather, the location and strength of the Soviet reserves, and the date and place of the landings in Western Europe, the first appeared to have been decided. For it began to rain, almost incessantly for days on end, turning the firm ground into a quagmire that bogged down vehicles and tanks.

Hoth, one of von Manstein's most experienced commanders and a veteran tank leader in Russia since 1941, had begun his 4 Panzer Army offensive at about 3 p.m. on 4 July. After heavy bombing raids and diversionary probes by infantry formations, von Knobelsdorff's 48 Panzer Corps successfully pushed home its attack against 6 Guards Army of Vatutin's Voronezh Front. The Germans were at first of the opinion that the defenders had been surprised, an opinion reinforced by the absence of any weight of artillery defensive fire. After dark, Hausser's 2 S S Panzer Corps made some limited attacks to secure observation posts for the next day's fighting, but then at 10.30 p.m. the Soviet artillery at last opened up with a very heavy fire over the whole area.

During that night the rain never stopped, washing away roads and tracks, but at 5 a.m. the attack was taken up again by both 48 and the S S Panzer Corps, 48 Panzer breaking through the first Soviet line of defence and reaching its objective two hours later against what it described as a relatively light opposition. The *Luftwaffe* 8 Air Corps, after early morning air battles with whole regiments of Red Air Force bombers trying to get through to attack the German airfields in the Kharkov area, had already established a measure of air superiority over the battle area, although this did not prevent repeated and heavy Soviet air attacks on tank concentration areas. Then, during the morning of 5 July, the skies opened to let fall a deluge of water that turned the many streams into torrents impassable to tanks. It took twelve hours before the sappers could bridge them and 48 Panzer Corps reported that the whole area was infested with mines.

The Soviet delay in reacting to the attacks was caused by the referring of the situation by Zhukov and Vasilevsky, the men on the spot, to Stalin in the Kremlin, persuading him on the telephone that this was indeed the long awaited offensive and asking for permission to fire off the prepared artillery fire programme. Hoth soon found that the Soviet artillery, once it had started in earnest, warmed to its task, keeping up an ever increasing intensity of fire hardly affected by the massive bombing attacks made by the *Luftwaffe* on the Soviet gun areas. In the centre, to the right of 48 Panzer Corps, Hausser's S S divisions had breached only the first of the Soviet defence lines by nightfall of 5 July, and Breith's 3 Panzer Corps (of Group Kempf) had secured a small bridgehead over the Donets to the south of Belgorod. At the end of the second day's fighting the Germans had made only three small penetrations, nowhere more than seven miles deep, and Hoth came to the conclusion that, contrary to expectation and previous experience, the Soviet infantry was tolerably trained and of good morale. The nature of the ground, the mines, the gullies and the waterlogged soil made the tank going difficult, and German infantry was sorely needed—but was not to hand—to clear the enemy out of the scattered villages and standing corn. As it was, the Soviet rifle formations could not be overrun, and when hard pressed they simply withdrew under cover to alternative positions.

On 6 July the 4 Panzer Army attack towards distant Kursk continued, and 8 Air Corps flew 1,700 sorties, a half of them being *Stuka* dive-bombing attacks, but German air power was insufficient to support both 48 Panzer and 2 S S Panzer Corps and, at the same time, cope with the steadily mounting air opposition; on that day Katukov's 1 Tank Army moved from the Voronezh Front reserve close in behind 6 Guards Army.* Early on 7 July, however, Hoth's two panzer corps,

* The *Stuka* was the single-engined Ju 87 dive-bomber.

together with 3 Panzer Corps on their right flank, began to make steady progress and for a fleeting hour or so it looked as if they might achieve freedom of manoeuvre and break through the closely defended area. Both Vatutin and Stalin had been thoroughly alarmed since 6 July and had started to thin out the flanking sectors of the south face of the salient, combing out artillery and anti-tank guns in order to reinforce the threatened area. Late that day Hoth's advance was met by heavy tank attacks on both flanks, and a steady stream of Red Army formations was drawn forward into the battle.

By 9 July Hoth was still fifty-five miles from Kursk and ninety miles from Model's 9 Army and the momentum of the German attack had gone. Casualties had been heavy and the troops were already tiring. The Porsche Tiger tanks, the Panther tanks and the Ferdinand assault guns on which Hitler had placed great hopes had not proved a success; and the tactical employment of the heavy tanks may have been at fault for, instead of exploiting the very effective 88 mm guns with which the heavy tanks were fitted by using them for long-range sniping tasks, they were put in the forefront of battle as was usually the practice. In close combat in the copses and orchards it was soon found that a Russian T 34 at point blank range could hole a Tiger as easily as a Tiger could destroy a T 34.*

Meanwhile, 100 miles to the north, Model's 9 Army had had only limited success against Rokossovsky's Central Front. At first Soviet resistance was weak and the Red Air Force, in particular, had appeared to lack determination. By nightfall on 5 July, Model had made a penetration six miles deep on a frontage of twenty miles. This was the extent of his success and he was not to advance much further. On the next day resistance stiffened rapidly and German infantry clearing the settlements and numerous copses and woods, suffered heavy casualties, over 10,000 men falling in two days. On 7 July, 9 Army was short of both infantry and of tank gun ammunition and Model was asking Zeitzler for the immediate despatch of 100,000 rounds. German tank losses in the minefields were heavy, and the Red Army continued to sow mines, thickening up the minefields at the rear as Model's men gapped them from the front. Within forty-eight hours the impetus of the 9 Army offensive had been broken and the attack came to a standstill. By 10 July it was already accepted, even in Rastenburg, that there could be no quick victory, and the war diarist began to record suggestions made at the daily briefing conference about 'attrition to use up the enemy reserves'.

By 10 July an Anglo-American force started disembarking in Sicily and two days later the presence of 'nine allied formations' was reported there. It became obvious that the Italians did not intend to fight any longer. Hitler, fearing that the loss of Italy and the Italian-held Balkans might open up his southern flank, required the O K W to overhaul the emergency military plans already prepared for such a contingency. On 13 July von Kluge and von Manstein were called to East Prussia, according to von Manstein 'to be informed of the Führer's decision to break off the *Citadel* offensive and move a number of divisions, including those of Hausser's 2 SS Panzer Corps, to Western Europe'. Von Manstein, according to his own account, told Hitler that the Red Army tank reserves were fast running out and urged in vain that the battle should be continued. Failure to do so, he added, would unleash the Soviet tank forces against Army Group South's long salient down to the Donets basin and the Black Sea, for if Hausser's S S men were taken

---

* The T34 was the standard Soviet medium tank weighing just under 30 (short) tons and mounting a 76 mm (later a 85 mm) gun.

from him much of his offensive power would be lost.

On or about 13 July Hitler did undoubtedly warn von Manstein of the *possibility* that formations *might* be withdrawn shortly to face the new danger in the west, in accordance with battle plans already drawn up by the OKW from the time of the fall of Tunis, for the 10 July landings marked the beginning of a new stage of the war in that Germany was at long last to be forced actually to fight by land from two sides, rather than stand guard over a second front. The time was soon to come when a number of German formations were permanently lost to the war effort as they were shunted across Europe in an effort to plug gaps in the west, the east, the south-east and the south. Hitler may, of course, have used the Anglo-American landings merely as an excuse to extricate himself from an offensive that was not going well and in the success of which he himself had doubts, yet it is more probable that he called off his attacks for the reasons he gave. What is to be questioned, however, is von Manstein's version that Hitler's final decision to break off the battle was given on or about 13 July, this being represented by von Manstein as the reason for Army Group South's failure.

The Führer did fear an allied landing in Western Europe, but he had reason to believe that this was still a few months away. The landing of what he believed to be nine Anglo-American divisions in far-away Sicily, did not as yet pose any great threat to Fortress Europe, and it is unlikely that the landings by themselves would have caused any substantial redeployment of the *Wehrmacht*. But what Hitler was afraid of was an internal collapse in Italy that would have lost both Italy and the Balkans to Fortress Europe. For the time being, however, and contrary to what von Manstein has since said, it was intended that the Kursk offensive should be continued without the withdrawal of troops to the west.

The Kursk battle situation was, however, slowly turning in the Red Army favour. In the south von Knobelsdorff's 48 Panzer Corps had become bogged down against the dug-in tanks of Katukov's 1 Tank Army, and, though it reckoned Soviet tank losses to be enormous, its own were admitted to be staggering. Further to the right, Hausser's 2 SS Panzer Corps had been drawn into an armoured battle against over 800 tanks of Rotmistrov's 5 Guards Tank Army near Prokhorovka, while great air battles were being fought out overhead. Soviet striking power, instead of diminishing, seemed to be increasing. Then, that same day, about 150 miles to the north, Stalin began his own offensive, known as *Kutuzov*, against the east face of the Orel salient held by Rudolf Schmidt's weak 2 Panzer Army, this new offensive being aimed at taking Model's 9 Army in the rear. Schmidt was removed from his command at that critical time by the Gestapo, and from 13 July to 5 August Model commanded 2 Panzer Army in addition to his own.* The new *Kutuzov* offensive, launched by Popov's Bryansk and Sokolovsky's West Fronts from the northern flank, made good progress and, on 17 July, Model was forced to withdraw 9 Army back from the Orel salient in order to escape being cut off. Two days later the OKW war diarist noted that 'operation *Citadel* is no longer possible on account of the violence of the enemy counter-offensive'. Thus, the 19 July would appear to have been the date on which the *Citadel* offensive was abandoned, and the reason for the German failure rested mainly on the Soviet strength in the area of Kursk rather than on the intended withdrawal of 2 SS Panzer Corps and other formations to the west.

* Schmidt's brother had been arrested on a charge of treason, and among his correspondence had been found letters from the general critical of the régime.

On 22 July Hoth's 4 Panzer Army and Group Kempf, both part of von Manstein's forces, 'continued their planned withdrawal'. Overall, however, the battle situation was deteriorating sharply. *Luftflotten* 4 and 6 had made extravagant claims during the early days of the fighting saying that they were flying from 3,000 to 4,000 sorties daily and destroying up to 200 enemy aircraft each day, with the lightest of *Luftwaffe* losses.* After the third week of the month, however, air superiority over the battlefield had been lost in the face of 'much increased Red Air Force activity and bad weather'. Popov was forcing a gap between 9 Army and 2 Panzer Army and there was a wave of partisan attacks against the German operated railway system in the rear areas, the German war diarist reporting up to sixty separate attacks being made each day.

Not until 25 July, when battle front conditions were looking serious throughout the Ukraine and when *Citadel* had failed completely, did Zeitzler receive from Hitler the order to begin the removal of Hausser's 2 S S Panzer Corps to the west. And the reason can be attributed to the dismissal and arrest of Mussolini on that same day. For Hitler was sure that Italy was about to leave the war.

The *Citadel* offensive had little hope of success because the plan for the offensive was badly conceived. Frequent postponements had led to a loss of surprise. But, if the offensive had been launched earlier, say in April, the German formations would not have been ready and the outcome would in all probability have been no different. After the German experience of attacking the city of Stalingrad in the late summer of 1942, the plan to attack a well entrenched and strong enemy was of doubtful wisdom, whatever the strength of the German forces. *Citadel* was undertaken as a gamble in the hope of snatching an early victory before the Anglo-Americans made a major landing in Europe, but Hitler and his high command had little idea that Stalin was by then almost ready to begin his own massive summer offensive. Hitler and Göring had never been close to the realities of the fighting on the eastern front and even Zeitzler had no recent experience of war there. It was noticeable that the more distant the opinion from the fighting line, the more sanguine it became. Zeitzler appeared confident, von Kluge was inclined to scepticism, and Model had little confidence in the outcome.

Before 1943 the Germans in Russia usually succeeded tactically but failed strategically. At Kursk they failed strategically because they were unsuccessful tactically. The whole concept of *Citadel* reflected the bankruptcy of Hitler's political and military leadership. At Kursk the European Axis lost all strategic initiative in Russia and was never to regain it. Instead the German Army reeled back, being driven for the rest of the war from defence line to defence line, being outflanked, enveloped and surrounded, falling back to the old 1938 Reich eastern frontier and beyond. Between July and October 1943 the total German loss from all causes was not much short of a million men; less than half of these could be replaced.

Stalin's offensive strategy at this time was not always clear even to his principal military advisers, for he was a man both of obsession and impulse. He had originally directed that his front commanders should themselves decide when the time was opportune to go over to the counter-offensive after *Citadel* had run its course; but

* '15 aircraft lost on 7 July against 205 lost by the enemy'.

then, when the defensive battle was at its height, it was Stalin who again took complete control and tried to decide every move. By 15 July, when the Voronezh and Steppe Fronts had held the final enemy thrusts, Stalin began to goad everyone forward into the counter-offensive, so that Zhukov and Vasilevsky had the greatest of difficulty in persuading what they called the 'heated and grudging' Supreme Commander that occasional pauses were going to be necessary for preparation and resupply.

The initial operations, *Kutuzov* in the Orel salient and *Rumiantsev* in the area of Kharkov, were only two of the many offensives that were to be taken up along the whole length of the eastern front. To the south of the Sea of Azov, Petrov was to keep up pressure on von Kleist's Army Group A in the Taman bridgehead and the Crimea, while Tolbukhin's South Front attacked von Manstein's right flank along the Black Sea littoral. Malinovsky's South-West Front had the task of freeing the area of the Donets basin in the centre, and Vatutin and Konev were to attack out of Kharkov on von Manstein's left wing. Rokossovsky's Central, Popov's Bryansk and Sokolovsky's West Fronts were joined in an onslaught against von Kluge's Army Group Centre; a little to the north Eremenko's Kalinin Front was to be made ready for yet another offensive before the end of August against Army Group Centre near Smolensk.

Stalin had in fact reverted to his earlier strategy of attacking frontally, a succession of hammer blows from Velikie Luki in the north to the Kuban in the south, and when, in early August, Zhukov, according to his own account, had suggested that the withdrawing Germans should be surrounded instead of being driven off westwards, the dictator had retorted that the enemy 'was still too strong for that'. Nor would he change his opinion when Zhukov returned to the theme later in the month. Stalin wanted the enemy off Soviet soil and above all wanted to reoccupy Kiev as quickly as he might. On 25 August, at a defence committee meeting that day, he was demanding immediate action to prevent the enemy stabilizing his positions on the line of the Dnieper, and a stepping-up of the tempo of the offensive so that von Manstein should not have time to strip and scorch the area through which he was being forced to withdraw.

During the autumn it so happened that the centre of gravity of the Soviet effort and their main successes came to lie in a line through Kiev towards the Carpathians, in thrusts that were eventually to separate Army Groups A and South and threaten them with envelopment. But the indications are that this was not the result of a long-sighted and carefully co-ordinated Soviet military strategy with this end in view, for it appears to have been the development of Stalin's short term demands, often based on political and economic considerations and the opportunist exploitation of German military weaknesses. The Kiev-Poltava-Carpathian axis eventually proved to be the corner-stone of the 1943 and 1944 Soviet operations in Central Europe.

On 25 July Hitler had sent for von Kluge to instruct him to prepare to pull out of the Orel salient immediately, as the formations to be withdrawn from there were needed for the west, and he told the protesting army group commander that he (the Führer) was no longer the master of his own decisions. Four days later a German radio intercept unit listened to a trans-Atlantic radio telephone conversation between Churchill and Roosevelt in which the probable defection of Italy from the Axis was discussed between the two statesmen. This confirmed Hitler's fears, and, on 1 August, he ordered the immediate withdrawal of von Kluge's troops in the area of Orel.

Von Manstein had been forced to hand over some of his armour to von Kluge to help stem the Soviet attacks, and then he had had to divert panzer formations away from Kharkov to his own southern flank to hold back a new offensive there by Malinovsky's and Tolbukhin's fronts. But no sooner had he found these mobile forces by thinning out his troops in the Kharkov sector than Vatutin and Konev attacked once more from the south face of the Kursk salient and reached open country. During August German troops of Army Group South were being forced back nearly everywhere.

On 27 August Hitler came to see von Manstein at Vinnitsa. Von Manstein asked for more freedom to make his own decisions and asked Hitler either for reinforcement formations or for permission to evacuate the Donets basin. Hitler ordered that the industrial area of the Donets should continue to be held and he fobbed off objections by promising von Manstein that he would give him additional troops to be withdrawn from von Kluge's and von Küchler's army groups. The Donets basin was soon lost, anyway. According to von Manstein, the Führer was almost entirely preoccupied with the threatening situation in Western Europe and the Mediterranean. Von Manstein, beset by his own difficulties, was later to criticize Hitler for being incapable of discerning priorities and for using arguments that events subsequently proved to be irrelevant. But it must be remembered that they were not irrelevant at the time. Italy had collapsed and was about to leave a great vacuum in the Balkans, and Jodl was to note that the Führer was perturbed about the danger of a landing in South-East Europe that might win over the Balkan States and even bring Turkey into the war, 'such an event giving promise of a quick allied victory'. During the month of September the possibility of an allied invasion of France or the Netherlands came to the fore once more.

The Führer's problems, real though they undoubtedly were, proved cold comfort for von Manstein. Only the day before this Vinnitsa meeting, Rokossovsky had attacked Army Group Centre; von Kluge, who soon found himself in difficulties, hastened to Hitler in East Prussia to resist any transfer of troops back from himself to von Manstein, and von Manstein therefore got nothing. This was to become the pattern throughout the German Army, for not only did the bickering Jodl and Zeitzler compete in trying to draw off formations from each other's theatres, but the army group commanders in the east themselves vied against each other, and against Zeitzler, when the OKH passed on Hitler's orders to give up divisions to assist their neighbours. Their usual reaction was a visit or a telephone call direct to the tired Hitler, who, by now, when faced with the necessity of making a decision between competing demands, having no reserves of his own to offer, often gave in to the last caller.

Since the failure of *Citadel*, Zeitzler had been recommending to Hitler the fortification of a new line running from the Narva and Lake Peipus to Belorussia down the course of the Sozh to Gomel, then along the Dnieper to the area of Zaporozhe, and finally due south to Melitopol and the Sea of Azov. It was intended that this line, known as the East Wall or Panther Line, should hold the Red Army in check. The Führer had refused earlier requests to begin defensive works, partly because he was in principle opposed to rear defences that, so he reasoned, might encourage his field commanders to withdraw, and partly because all available fortification materials were required for the construction of the Atlantic Wall in France. Some work had been carried out by the army groups on their own initiative after it had become obvious that the Kursk offensive had failed, using civilian labour, but since this labour lacked concrete, steel, barbed wire and mines, the defences developed merely as earthworks. Not before 12 August were the army groups given official sanction to develop the line as best they might, but this order gave them no authority to withdraw their troops back on to the wall.

The value of this defence line was to prove largely illusory since the defences, left to the labour organization and to the rearward troops, were often so poorly sited as to be useless. The Dnieper itself was hardly an obstacle since its entire length could not be covered by observation and fire; after it froze it was not an obstacle at all. The Dnieper bend in the south formed an extended salient that might prove costly and dangerous to defend, but no sooner had von Manstein been forced out of the Donets basin than the Führer decided that Krivoi Rog and Nikopol, inside the bend, were essential to the German war economy, and that the holding of the Dnieper bend was necessary to cover the Crimea; for if the Crimea were to be lost this would become an air runway controlling the Black Sea, so endangering Rumanian oil and having a decisive effect on the war attitudes of Turkey, Rumania and Bulgaria. Once again the political and economic governed the strategical, but the strategical was based on the tactically impossible.

The Führer put as brave a face on the position as he could, and he told Goebbels that the situation in the east 'could be managed' by withdrawing on the Dnieper; if only, he continued, he could have had fifteen to twenty first-class divisions there, he would undoubtedly have repulsed the Russians. Unfortunately, however, 'he had been forced to commit these to Italy'. Goebbels could only wonder and confide to his diary that even the neutrals were amazed at the change in Germany's fortunes, for 'they cannot imagine that our fighting spirit has sunk so low—indeed many regard the withdrawal as a political manoeuvre to prepare for a Soviet peace'.

The German officers and men, moving back on foot in scattered regimental groups across the hot and arid Ukrainian and Tauride plains, fighting by day and making strenuous forced marches by night along main roads and railway lines, were frequently out of touch with formation headquarters, orienting themselves, often without maps and compasses, as best they might. Every man knew that his safety depended on the group and he took good care not to become separated 'from his own mob (Haufen)'. Propaganda pamphlets offering safe conduct were showered on them from the air, but all feared captivity more than death. The unkindest blow was yet in store for them when they saw the little that had been prepared in what was already vaunted as the East Wall.

Here we must, for the moment, leave the German Army on the eastern front in those months of July and August, much of it falling back towards the East Wall disorganized by casualties and the loss of equipment, and the officers and men much discouraged by the defeat at Kursk. In the far north Dietl's 20 Army stood virtually idle in Lapland as security for Finnish nickel and Swedish iron ores. From Leningrad southwards, von Küchler's Army Group North had, as yet, not had to give much ground, although its front was frequently under attack. Its neighbour, von Kluge's Army Group Centre, was being forced back steadily in the area of Smolensk and was fighting off Rokossovsky's attempt to outflank it from the south. But the greatest losses had been inflicted on von Manstein's Army Group South, that was in danger both of being split from Army Group Centre and of being penetrated on the right and cut off from its own newly reconstituted 6 German Army on the Black Sea coast and von Kleist's Army Group A in the Crimea. Von Manstein himself, against Hitler's intentions, tended to let his own fulcrum gravitate to the north, preferring to keep a strong link with von Kluge, his northern neighbour, at the expense of that with von Kleist in the Crimea. But the truth of the matter was that it was impossible to find sufficient troops even to make a pretence at covering the vast extent of the linear East Wall.

CHAPTER FOUR

The Mediterranean

German strategy to the south of Fortress Europe had been based on closing the Mediterranean water-way to British shipping and on commanding the sea exits at Gibraltar and Port Said, and it was for this purpose that the *Wehrmacht* had been sent to control the Mediterranean skies and waters and to reinforce the Italian armies on the North African shore. Admittedly, other reasons, apart from that of prestige, soon presented themselves to support a German presence there. The Führer was interested in having German forces on Italian soil as some security for his ally's actions; this had been recognized by Mussolini, who had originally been reluctant to accept them. Then again, during that glorious short summer of 1942, Hitler, drunk with success, had imagined that the forces in North Africa formed a great strategic pincer that was to join List's forces coming down from the area of the Caspian Sea. After the sobering defeats of early 1943, the *Wehrmacht* in the Mediterranean came to be regarded as the buttress of the Italian armed forces and the defenders of Fortress Europe in the south, firstly from the outpost line on the North African coast and then from the Greek coasts and islands and from Corsica, Sardinia and Sicily. By May 1943, when Tunis fell, the O K W intention was to deny the Balkans to the enemy, because of its oil and industrial ores, and, as Alfieri, the Italian Ambassador in Berlin, had realized, to keep the Anglo-Americans and their bombers as far as possible from the borders of the Reich.

The Italian dictator Mussolini was the minister for all three of the Italian armed services, exercising field command through Marshal Ambrosio, the Chief of the Armed Forces Staff and head of the high command (*Comando Supremo*), to whom the chiefs of staff of the army, navy and air force were theoretically subordinate. In fact, however, the channel of command was not so clearly delineated for, rather in the German fashion where the O K W controlled the so-called O K W theatres, the *Comando Supremo* commanded the Italian Army formations in the Balkans (except in Croatia and Slovenia) directly, and not through Roatta, the Chief of the Army General Staff.

The Italian Army in the Balkans came under General Rosi's Army Group East and was made up of Dalmazzo's 9 Army in Albania, Vecchiarelli's 11 Army in Greece, and independent corps in Herzegovina, Montenegro and the Aegean, totalling in all the equivalent of twenty-three infantry divisions. Rosi was responsible directly to the *Comando Supremo*. The troops in Italy, on the other hand, and those in the occupied territories outside of the Balkans, came under the Army General Staff. The ground forces in Italy, grouped under Crown Prince Umberto's Army Group South, consisted of Feroleto's 5 Army in Piedmont, Liguria and

Tuscany, Arisio's 7 Army in Calabria, Campania and Apulia, and Guzzoni's 6 Army in Sicily and Sardinia. Gariboldi's 8 Army was in the area of Venice and Venezia Giulia, reforming after its disastrous defeats in Russia; Vercellino's 4 Army was in occupied France (Provence) and Robotti's 2 Army was in Croatia and Slovenia. The Italian Army in Italy and the adjoining occupied territories amounted to thirty-two infantry, six motorized and nineteen coastal divisions, although many of these were divisions only in name since they were in the process of being formed or reformed.

All the German forces in the Central Mediterranean were technically subordinate to the Italian *Comando Supremo*. In practice, however, matters stood very much otherwise, for Field-Marshal Kesselring, the German Commander-in-Chief South, while keeping up the appearance of subordination to the Duce and to the staff direction of Ambrosio, was in fact directly under Hitler's orders, and on day to day matters dealt with the O K W in Rastenburg and with von Rintelen, who was both the Military Attaché in Rome and the permanent German representative at the Italian armed forces headquarters.*

Previous to June 1943 Kesselring had also been the commander of *Luftflotte 2* in command of all *Luftwaffe* forces throughout the Mediterranean, in addition to being Commander-in-Chief South; but that summer the situation was partially regularized when von Richthofen assumed command of 2 Air Fleet and when the responsibility for air operations in the Eastern Mediterranean was made over to Fiebig, the *Luftwaffe* commander in the Balkans. Von Richthofen dealt directly with Göring's O K L but appeared to be subordinate to Kesselring for operations—a somewhat unusual situation in an O K W or an O K H theatre, and this owed its origin to the fact that Kesselring, as a *Luftwaffe* general officer, had previously centralized both appointments in his own person. So it came about that Kesselring was to command army formations, even corps and divisions, directly, but air formations only through von Richthofen, any use of air power being subject to O K L approval or veto. Control was further complicated in that in Sicily and in Italy a proportion of the ground fighting troops, mainly parachute formations, were found from Student's *Fliegerkorps XI*, technically under von Richthofen, but in practice, like the army, directly under Kesselring. In such a tangled skein of command the relationship between Kesselring and von Richthofen gave rise to difficulties and misunderstandings.

When the equivalent of six German divisions had been lost in Tunisia there were very few German fighting troops left in Italy. That May Hitler had offered the Italians another five divisions, but Mussolini was little interested in accepting them. In June, faced with the possibility of an allied invasion of Sicily, Sardinia and Corsica, new German divisions began to form, being based largely on training cadres and rear elements of those divisions that had been destroyed in Africa. On 7 July a new Hermann Göring Panzer and a new 15 Panzer Grenadier were being formed in Sicily, a new 90 Panzer Grenadier Division in Sardinia and a S S brigade in Corsica. A further panzer and one more panzer grenadier division were on the Italian mainland. *Luftflotte 2* was said to include about 900 aircraft of all types of which only a half were serviceable.

The Axis forces in Sicily came under Guzzoni's 6 Italian Army numbering over 200,000 Italians and 40,000 Germans, the Italian organization consisting of the

---

* Kesselring, a former officer of Bavarian artillery, had been transferred against his will to the newly forming *Luftwaffe* in 1933; he was forty-eight years of age when he learned to fly.

equivalent of four field and four low quality and poorly equipped beach divisions. 7 Italian Army was responsible for the defence of the Italian peninsula in the south, 5 Italian Army covered Rome and to the north, and 4 Italian Army centred on Nice in part of occupied France. There were two Italian field and two coast divisions in Corsica and about six divisions in Sardinia. The Italian air force in the south was reported to have 800 aircraft of which only 300 were fit for battle.

In the Balkans the occupation forces were made up of German, Italian and Bulgarian troops. The command of the *Luftwaffe* in the theatre came under Fiebig, but German ground troops were under Löhr, a *Luftwaffe* general commanding Army Group E; he was also the Commander-in-Chief South-East. Löhr controlled his ground troops through subordinate army headquarters, the Commander German Troops Croatia (four divisions), the German Serbian Command (one German and three Bulgarian divisions), the Commander Salonica-Aegean (one division), Commander South Greece (two divisions), and a number of other small static commands; his only mobile field reserve was 68 Corps of one panzer and one light division; there were, moreover, two German divisions on Crete and another division on Rhodes. In addition there were about twenty-three Italian divisions in the Balkans and the Greek islands, under General Rosi's Army Group East, not including eight divisions of 2 Italian Army in Croatia and Slovenia. Since the Balkans were beyond the range of allied fighters, the Axis still controlled the skies above the coast and the many Greek islands, and this German air activity very much restricted the daylight operations of the British fleet off the northern coasts of the Eastern Mediterranean. The Italian Navy, based mainly on Spezia, Taranto and Genoa, played only a minor part in the battle for the control of the Mediterranean during this period. The small German naval contingent of torpedo boats on the Italian coast, and the dozen submarines based on Toulon, were always active.

The *OKH Fremde Heere West* intelligence appreciation of 2 July noted the unfriendly, even hostile, attitude of the Italian population towards German troops and the drop in the fighting value of the Italian Army. 'The German relationship with the armed forces [that is to say with the Italian officers] was generally correct but the Italian occupational policies in the Balkans [since they were often deliberately aimed against the German interest] were "incomprehensible".' Another tendency that had become apparent to German military liaison officers and planners was a newly encountered Italian insistence on a measure of independence from what had been complete German military control.

The enemy air offensive on towns and airfields in Sicily, Sardinia and on the Italian mainland was steadily mounting and, on 4 July, it was reported that about 100 enemy vessels were approaching the Mediterranean through the Straits of Gibraltar. At the Führer briefing conference on 9 July, it was thought that the Anglo-Americans might next invade Sicily, Sardinia or even mainland Calabria; yet the underlying assumption shared by both the Führer and Jodl was that Greece was more likely than Italy to be the final allied objective, and that landings on the Italian islands or on the boot of the Italian peninsula would probably be made only as an intermediate step to an invasion of the Balkans—the Achilles heel of the Axis. For an invasion of Greece, or so it was reasoned at the OKW, would present the German high command with the problem of moving reinforcement formations southwards over 800 miles of very poor road, whereas an invasion of Italy could be met with an immediate Axis reaction and speedy troop movement over a good rail and a first-rate road network. An occupation of the Balkans offered good political and military advantages to the allies, together with, what was regarded in Rastenburg as, 'crippling economic disadvantages to Germany'; the local populations were hostile to the Axis, and Hungary and Rumania were believed to be strategic targets of paramount importance to the Anglo-Americans because of their oil and mineral deposits and because, so Hitler said, the British had an interest in securing the Balkans against Soviet penetration and control. This obsession that the Balkans were the primary strategic target in the south, originating mainly from Hitler and Jodl, was to distort all German thinking for the next nine months.

German intelligence organizations, and this applied particularly to the *Fremde Heere West*, usually tended to exaggerate the strength of the Anglo-American forces threatening to invade Fortress Europe. On 4 July, Kesselring, using intelligence provided not only from his own sources but from the OKW and the *Fremde Heere West*, came to the conclusion that the allies had about forty divisions available in the Mediterranean ready for an invasion, and that about eighteen of these could be lifted 'in the first wave'.* The *Fremde Heere West* strategic appreciations at this time were generally in line with what the Führer thought.

It was known in Rastenburg that Italy was falling away from the Axis, and Jodl began to bemoan the German difficulties, the problems of co-operating with Axis allies and the inter-service frictions within the *Wehrmacht*. He began to look enviously at the Anglo-Americans. The British had now re-established naval control over the Atlantic and Arctic, while the Americans were fast clearing the Pacific. Both were delivering what appeared to be closely co-ordinated hammer blows from the air, one by day and one by night, against Fortress Europe from north and south. Jodl even suspected that their strategy was linked to that of their Soviet ally. In North Africa both Americans and British had shown that they could operate and fight without any apparent loss of efficiency under a single allied commander and a unified command; this led Jodl to believe that the Anglo-Saxon political and military war direction was completely united and was motivated by a single aim and a common method. These qualities that Jodl credited to the enemy high command, if they had been known, would have caused some surprise in London and Washington.

———

The United States war direction had been split on the basic question as to whether the war against Japan should not have been given an absolute priority over the war in Europe, and American public opinion and a substantial element in the American political and military leadership would probably have had it so. The British, on the other hand, were obliged first to fight the enemy on their own doorstep. There were other fundamental political and strategic differences between the two western allies. The British had the gravest mistrust and detestation of communism and of the aggressive aims of Stalin's Soviet Union but these were little shared by the United States administration of the day; on the other hand American policy makers were suspicious of Britain, and of Churchill in particular, and were determined that United States forces should not be used to help shore up Britain's colonial empire or its power interests in Europe.

* In all the allied resources there totalled in fact 34 divisions.

There were further divergences of opinion as to the military strategy to be followed in the war in Europe. America, as a continental power, believed that Germany could only be brought down by destroying its land forces, and that the quickest and most efficient way of doing this would be by invading the mainland of Western Europe from the British Isles, and then occupying Germany. The United States military leadership was, quite rightly, entirely unconvinced by any Royal Air Force argument that Germany could be put out of the war by bombing alone; nor could naval blockade be more successful since Germany could draw on its occupied territories for food and raw materials. The United States for this reason was doing its utmost to get its newly formed ground forces into action against German troops as soon as possible.

The British were of opinion that the Anglo-American forces were not ready to carry through a successful Second Front landing and they eventually convinced their ally that such an invasion was not practicable during 1942. The United States war leadership had then agreed, with some misgiving—since it was unwilling to divert its attention from the coast of France—to the joint landings in French North Africa at the end of that year; but at that time there certainly had been no intention, let alone agreement, that Italy should then be invaded; the Balkans had not even entered into the joint planning as a possible war theatre, except in so far as the British supported the governments-in-exile and gave encouragement and some very limited supplies to the guerrilla partisans of those countries.

It had then become necessary to postpone the Second Front from 1943 to 1944, much to the chagrin of the United States, but American political and military opinion still remained reluctant to undertake any further campaigns in the Mediterranean except, possibly, against the south coast of France. As against this, the British wanted to occupy Sicily and so open the Sicilian Strait and the sea-way to Mediterranean and Far East shipping; they had a further interest, too, in seizing Sardinia and Corsica as a springboard into Central Italy or into South France. Washington was naturally unwilling to keep its own forces idle after the fall of Tunis, and so it had eventually been agreed at Casablanca and at the Washington Conference in the following May that Sicily should be occupied and that there should be 'further exploitation' to eliminate Italy and to contain German forces. Further than Sicily 'and its exploitation' the Americans were not, for the moment, prepared to go, since they regarded the Mediterranean theatre as a subsidiary and one that must rob the Second Front landing of much of its strength.

On the British side there were some, Churchill and the Chief of the Imperial General Staff among them, who, while not necessarily advocating a weakening or a delaying of the 1944 Second Front, proposed attacking the Reich by way of Italy during 1943, since they reasoned that the immediate and the pressing need was to fight Germans and draw off as many divisions as possible both from the Channel coast and from Russia. As an additional point of argument they stressed that, whereas the Germans could easily switch large numbers of divisions from France to Russia and back again since the east-west rail communications in the summer months were good and had a large capacity, it was much more difficult, so they contended, for the *Wehrmacht* to shunt its ground strength from north to south because of the restriction to traffic in the Alpine passes.

It may be said of course that the allies had no clear strategic aim in the Mediterranean after the occupation of Sicily and that the Americans were the unwilling partners, in that they did not want to be in the Mediterranean in the first place. But they were subsequently drawn more deeply into the adventure by the inviting prospect of a possible Italian collapse, since this held out the expectation of a rapid occupation of the whole of the Italian peninsula. This resulted in the agreement formulated at the Quebec 'Quadrant' conference in late August of 1943, when the allies determined to eliminate the already tottering Italy from the war, to seize Sardinia and Corsica, to establish air bases in the area of Rome 'and further to the north', and to exert pressure on the Germans *in North Italy* so creating more favourable conditions for a landing in North-West and South France.

This strategic concept agreed at Quebec was in fact never to be materially changed from the American or the British side, although Churchill was, from time to time, to attempt to press on the Americans his own variations on this theme. He still had the great interest in the Dardanelles imputed to him by Hitler, although he wanted to open the Bosphorus to Russia-bound shipping by bringing Turkey into the war on the allied side and not by an invasion that could only have made Turkey an enemy; and he was much in favour of seizing the enemy occupied Greek islands that controlled the Mediterranean approaches to the Dardanelles, except that he had not the air resources available to do it. Churchill was, naturally, intensely concerned in the fate of the Balkan countries, but his general staffs knew that Crete must be taken before the Balkans could be invaded from the south and that fighter cover over the coast of the Greek mainland was going to be essential to any such invasion, large or small. Churchill was left then with his own strategic brainchildren, most of them political but some of them military, some of them sound, but most, if not all, of them impracticable for the time being.

The Anglo-American councils of war and their war direction, far from providing the unified and far-sighted high commands that Jodl imagined them to be, were in fact divided politically and militarily on the great strategic questions of the day and were fraught with political, national and personal suspicions and jealousies. Human nature and political and national prejudice being what they are, the situation could not have been otherwise, and it is remarkable, in retrospect, what the western alliance did in fact achieve. Inter-allied co-operation between Moscow and the west was generally very poor, almost non-existent, and for this the Soviet Union was primarily responsible.

The allied strength in the Mediterranean, not including the four United States and three British divisions that were earmarked for the removal to the United Kingdom in preparation for the Second Front, stood at nineteen Commonwealth and British divisions, four United States and four French divisions, twenty-seven divisions in all.

The national war aims and the intricate relationships of the enemy statesmen and of their military staffs were largely unknown to Hitler and Jodl; Hitler, in particular, credited Churchill with a much greater influence in the allied councils of war than he did in fact possess. The Balkans was the theatre in which Germany was most vulnerable, politically, economically and militarily, and the opening of the Dardanelles, regarded in Rastenburg as Churchill's obsession since his failure there in the First World War, would have done away with the need for the costly allied Arctic convoys to Murmansk. In the German view it would have been greatly to the allied advantage to have overrun South-East Europe, and the OKW tended to overlook the allies' paramount need for single-engined fighter cover over the assault beaches; and so the Balkans became one of Hitler's major pre-occupations that caused him to keep 60,000 German troops in Crete alone, long after that island had been strategically bypassed. But neither Hitler nor Jodl can be blamed for failing to deduce the intentions of the western allies when those allies themselves were both uncertain and divided as to their next action. When the allies did in fact invade South Italy, Jodl said that he could not credit that it was part of the enemy's strategy to fight his way step by step, mile by mile, over difficult mountainous country, all the way up the whole of the length of the Italian peninsula; nor indeed was this in reality the Anglo-American intention at the time, for the allies imagined that when Italy surrendered, the German forces would withdraw northwards as rapidly as they were able. Both the Germans and the Anglo-Americans misread each other's intentions. Jodl, like Hitler, remained convinced that the allies would use Sicily or Sardinia as a stepping-stone into South Italy, and that the boot of Italy would itself be used as a jumping-off base for an invasion of the Balkans across the Adriatic. So both of them came to believe that *the holding of Italy* by German forces *was essential to the defence of the Balkans*. This was one of the principal reasons that made Hitler resolve to fight for every foot of Italian soil.

In reading the western allies' news accounts of the time and the post-war memoirs of their commanding generals in the field, one might perhaps attach undue importance to the military events in those corners of the Mediterranean theatre where fighting took place. Whereas the overrunning of Sicily came to be regarded by some Anglo-Americans as a resounding victory, in Rastenburg it was seen as a series of minor battles against relatively few German troops in an out of the way island. The enemy ground strength in the Mediterranean was mainly British, and British troops were regarded as dogged and slow under an uninspired and somewhat hesitant leadership, so much so that the Führer was still confident that he could, if he so wished, contain, if not repulse, enemy landings. Hitler kept the south flank of Europe in a grand perspective from Spain to Turkey, and he feared an Anglo-American invasion from the Mediterranean not because he held the allied commanders or troops there in particularly high esteem but because he thought he could foresee the political effect that such landings might have on his allies and on the non-German populations within the fortress. A successful landing, indeed the mere presence of Anglo-American troops within the fortress, however far removed and however insignificant their numbers, could have set Italy and the Balkans ablaze, and induced the Hungarians and Rumanians to withdraw from the war, or even to change sides, as some security against the threat of a Soviet occupation. The enemy landing in Italy was in fact followed by some of the political and social consequences that he feared.

Even before the fall of Tunis the OKW staffs had been directed to produce contingency plans to safeguard against Italy's leaving the war, for the Italians were to be kept in the Axis by force. Mussolini, notwithstanding his apparently cordial relationship with Hitler, held Germans in no great favour; nor did he have their confidence. Ambrosio, the Chief of the Armed Forces Staff, and Roatta, the Chief of the Army General Staff, were much mistrusted in Rastenburg. Yet the three Italians spoke with different voices; Ambrosio was reluctant to let more German ground troops into the country; Mussolini was at first absolutely against it, though he did want a substantial increase in air support, either *Luftwaffe* formations or the delivery of German warplanes; after the Sicily invasion he was forced to ask for ground troops; Roatta had from the beginning requested German motorized troops, and for this he came to be suspected by Jodl of a sinister plot in trying to draw German formations to the south of Italy 'where they might be trapped by the allies'. The Italians themselves feared, what was in fact being secretly prepared in Munich, a German operation to take over the kingdom by force.

The German plans that began as early as that May provided for a total occupation of Italy (codename *Alarich*) and the Balkans (*Konstantin*), the military action against the Italian armed forces having the codename *Achse*. Von Rundstedt, the Commander-in-Chief West, was to be ready to intern 4 Italian Army on the French riviera and to secure the French-Italian Alpine passes for German use. Löhr, the Commander-in-Chief South-East, had been ordered to plan the disarming, firstly of 11 Italian Army in Greece and then the other Italian formations in the Balkans. An army staff, based on Munich and eventually to be known as Army Group B, was already in being under Rommel, who, in the event of *Alarich* and *Achse*, was to become Commander-in-Chief Italy, taking under command Kesselring and his forces in the south. Meanwhile Rommel's staff was to plan the seizure of the Austro-Italian Alpine crossings and the movement of more German divisions into North Italy.

On the 10 July Montgomery's 8 Army and Patton's 7 Army landed side by side on the southern coast of Sicily and it became obvious that the Italians intended to fight no longer, and that the two German divisions in Sicily, still theoretically under Guzzoni's command, would have to resist as best they might with very little *Luftwaffe* support. Elsewhere 76 German Corps with one panzer grenadier division was on its way to the area just north of Rome, while 14 Panzer Corps had panzer divisions near Salerno and near Bari and a panzer grenadier division north of Cosenza. Mussolini, thoroughly alarmed at the situation in Sicily, now wanted another German motorized corps for Italy and increased *Luftwaffe* support, for this lack of air power, he told the Germans, 'had been the root of all the Axis troubles'; at all costs he wanted the German formations already in the centre of Italy to move south into the battle area for 'if the English cannot be dislodged then Sicily is lost'. That same day, on 13 July, he sent a teleprint message to the Führer pointing out 'the moral and military effect it would have, not only on all Italians but on all Germans as well, if the enemy were to be successful in this, his first, attempt to gain a foothold in Europe'. Kesselring, too, was in favour of moving more German troops into Sicily.

Jodl, however, saw the situation differently, and on 15 July he summarized his views in an appreciation for the Führer. Jodl was firmly opposed to moving any more troops into Sicily since 'Sicily could no longer be held and the Italian traitors were asking for more German formations in order that they might be destroyed by the allies'. It was impossible, he said, to say where the enemy's next landing would be, Corsica, Sardinia or Greece, but he did not expect a Second Front invasion from the British Isles at that time. Germany needed, Jodl thought, to hold South Italy in order to cover Greece, but 'it might not be possible to hold Italy south of the Appenines unless the Italian military command could be sorted out'. Germans must be put into key positions, the *Comando Supremo* must be done away with and all dissident Italian personalities arrested. For Jodl, the Bavarian, could, if need be, out-Prussian the Prussian. On 17 July the Führer had accepted most of

Jodl's ideas, for he, too, could see no point in sending further troops to the south and losing his last reserves, and he told Kesselring to defer for the moment the movement of any more troops of 29 Panzer Grenadier Division to Sicily. Meanwhile the Duce was recommending to Rastenburg and even trying to order, through the *Comando Supremo*, that 29 Panzer Grenadier should move immediately from South Italy to Sicily and that 3 Panzer Grenadier Division should quit Rome for Calabria. The German formations politely ignored the Italian instructions and remained where they were awaiting orders from Rastenburg. The only action taken by Hitler to reinforce the two hard pressed divisions in Sicily had been the movement of some parachute regiments from South France and of *Luftwaffe* air formations from France and the Balkans.

On 19 July the Duce, accompanied by Ambrosio and Alfieri, joined the Führer at Feltre in North Italy for a two hour meeting. Ambrosio, after a private conversation with Keitel, had become convinced that the Germans had not the strength to keep the allies out of Italy; Ambrosio had then impressed upon Mussolini Italy's hopeless military position and had begged him to put the true facts to Hitler, 'that Italy must be out of the war in fifteen days'. Mussolini was unwilling and fearful, replying that 'Hitler would not give Italy liberty of action', and so he said nothing at the conference. Instead the meeting took the form of a two hour Hitler-harangue in untranslated German, roughly on the lines of an agenda drawn up by Jodl and Warlimont, and to this the Führer added his own touches. If all the regions containing raw materials of military importance from North Norway to the Balkans and from the Ukraine to France could be safeguarded, then the war could be continued indefinitely; it was simply a question, said Hitler, of mobilizing manpower and will-power—the well-worn theme that he was to continue until the last days of his life. Hitler blamed the Italians for being the cause of their own misfortunes due to their inefficiency and lack of resolution, and he made it clear that Italy could expect to get little from German war production. The Führer rounded off his monologue with the promise that in August London would be 'razed to the ground in the course of a few weeks by the reprisals air fleet'; in addition, new wonder weapons would be brought into service and the submarine war resumed with new and improved U-boats.* According to what Mussolini said after the meeting, Hitler had promised, over their private luncheon, 'to send all the reinforcements Italy would need'. The impression that Keitel left with Ambrosio, on the other hand, was entirely to the contrary, and Mussolini's staff remained dissatisfied and unconvinced. The only concession that Hitler had made to Mussolini and to Italian susceptibilities was the agreement that Rommel should not be re-employed in Italy; as a result the field-marshal was sent to take up the German command in the Balkans.

On 25 July Mussolini, having been outvoted in the Great Council of the Fascist Party, was arrested, but the new Badoglio government hastily assured the German representatives in Rome of its intention to continue the war with renewed vigour. An entry in the OKW war diary on that day noted the Führer's firm decision to hold Italy and the Balkans, and immediate orders were sent out to von Rundstedt, Kesselring and Löhr to prepare the preliminary moves for *Alarich* and *Konstantin*, all troop movements to take place under the pretext of guarding against Anglo-American sea or air landings, so that German formations might occupy areas of

---

* The Italians were unmoved, for they had, they said, 'heard it all before'. 'If he really has these weapons', they commented to each other, 'why does he not use them instead of talking about them.'

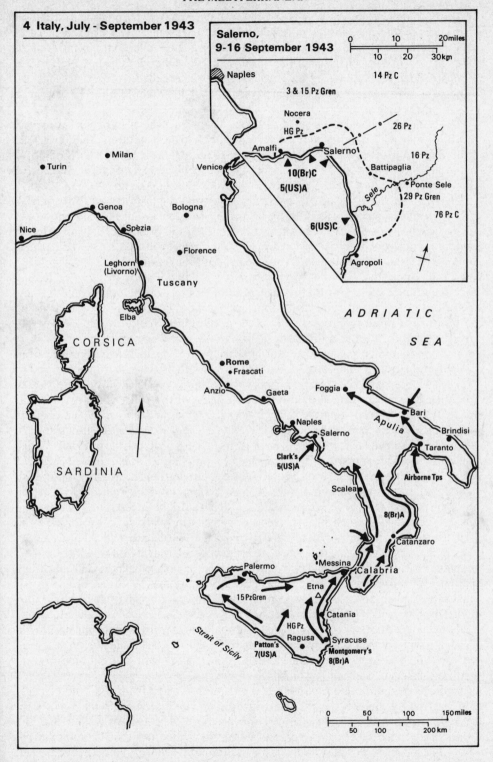

4 Italy, July - September 1943

Salerno, 9-16 September 1943

0 10 20miles
10 20 30km

14 Pz C

Naples

3 & 15 Pz Gren

Nocera

HG Pz

26 Pz

Amalfi

Salerno

16 Pz

Venice

Battipaglia

10(Br)C

5(US)A

Sele

Ponte Sele

29 Pz Gren

6(US)C

76 Pz C

Agropoli

Milan

Turin

Genoa

Nice

Spèzia

Bologna

Florence

Leghorn
(Livorno)

Tuscany

Elba

CORSICA

ADRIATIC

SEA

Rome

Frascati

Anzio

Gaeta

Foggia

Naples

Bari

Salerno

Apulia

Brindisi

SARDINIA

Clark's
5(US)A

Taranto

Airborne Tps

Scalea

8(Br)A

Catanzaro

Palermo

Messina

15 PzGren

Etna

Calabria

Catania

HG Pz

Patton's
7(US)A

Ragusa

Strait of Sicily

Syracuse

Montgomery's
8(Br)A

0 50 100 150miles
50 100 200 km

strategic or tactical importance without, for the moment, exciting Italian suspicion or armed resistance. Rommel was ordered to return immediately from Salonica to continue his former planning tasks at the still disguised headquarters in Munich; Löhr took back his old post from Rommel as the Commander-in-Chief South-East. In addition, Hausser's 2 SS Panzer Corps was recalled from Russia and von Kluge and von Manstein were again warned that they would be called upon to give up more troops.

The next ten days was a period of hectic German activity in South Germany, South France, the Balkans and Italy, so that the battle situation in Sicily, as seen from Rastenburg, was of comparatively minor importance. On 21 July the Führer had reluctantly allowed the movement of part of 29 Panzer Grenadier Division to Sicily, but as late as 4 August the dictator still could not make up his mind whether to give up the island or not. Kesselring, who was in ignorance as to Rommel's activities and proposed role in Italy, continued to believe that Badoglio intended to stay in the war. Hitler meanwhile had received the detail of the transatlantic telephone conversation between Churchill and Roosevelt that made it clear that Italy was asking for allied terms, together with other reports that Roatta had told the Commander of 2 Italian Army when in Venice that 'Badoglio intended to play for time in his dealings with Germany and then get out of the war'. The Italians meanwhile were reinforcing the Alpine passes and, by objections and delaying tactics, were attempting to prevent the movement into North Italy of what was to become the nine German divisions of Rommel's Army Group B.

The real tactical control of the German troops in Sicily had been removed from Senger und Etterlin, the German liaison officer with Guzzoni, and transferred to Hube's 14 Panzer Corps that arrived in the island on 18 July, for the OKW intended that Kesselring should be free to deal with the internal situation that might develop on the mainland. A week later Kesselring was informed by a personal liaison officer sent from Hitler, of the OKW plan (*Schwarz*) whereby the *Luftwaffe* general Student should, in the event of *Achse* being ordered, seize Rome, arrest the Badoglio government and release the Duce, using for this purpose 3 Panzer Grenadier Division and 2 Parachute Division. Kesselring, normally an optimist, was appalled at this plan and on 5 August he reported to Rastenburg that he thought the OKW fears were groundless since he still believed in the goodwill of the Italians; and Kesselring disagreed emphatically with the plan to seize the capital since 'if 5 Italian Army [with five divisions near Rome] should put up even the slightest resistance, a successful operation would hardly be possible, and six German divisions in Italy could be put in jeopardy'. In a marginal note on Kesselring's appreciation Jodl wrote 'the Führer doubts that the *Schwarz* operation is possible—and so do I'. Hitler was undeterred, however, even by his own doubts, and at the beginning of August he allocated to Kesselring a new 10 Army headquarters under von Vietinghoff to take under command all German field formations in Central and South Italy. It was part of von Vietinghoff's task, said Hitler, to secure the German communications and line of retreat. The German field organization had now taken on a more regular pattern.

In the Balkans the Commander of the Italian Army Group East was largely disregarded by the OKW, and it arranged with the *Comando Supremo* a joint reorganization and redeployment of troops there. The OKW settled that the boundary be changed between 11 and 9 Italian Armies and that 11 Italian Army should be brought directly under Löhr's command; 68 German Corps was then put under 11 Italian Army with the addition of a German chief of staff to the Italian army commander; this corps then took over the key area of the Peloponnese, so that the main coastline and islands came under German control. Further up the Adriatic coast a number of German formations infiltrated the Italian command in that they were made subordinate to the Italian Army in the Albanian and Montenegro area, and German fortress battalions and liaison personnel were allotted to Italian formations and coastal batteries.

In the event of *Achse* being ordered Löhr had at his disposal on the mainland six German mountain and light divisions, a single panzer division, two reserve and two SS divisions, in addition to four Bulgarian and two Croat divisions. On 26 August von Weichs's Army Group F took over the Balkan command as Commander-in-Chief South-East, and Löhr and his Army Group E, subordinate to von Weichs, took over the coastal command in Greece and the Aegean Islands.*

The British official historian has concluded that Montgomery's picture of his own Sicilian successes was 'fanciful'; this may or may not be the case, but there is little doubt that Montgomery, determined and systematic though he undoubtedly was, was a very cautious field commander. If the thrusting Patton had been allowed more freedom by Alexander, the British army group commander, 15 Panzer Grenadier Division might have been cut off in West Sicily. But, whatever the underlying reasons for their actions, neither Montgomery nor Patton caused Kesselring or Hitler any great uneasiness, although the allied armies had the advantage of numbers, the freedom of the seas and heavy air and naval gun support. If the Italian resistance is largely disregarded, then less than four scratch German divisions held between eight and twelve allied divisions for a period of more than four weeks. In the German war diaries the enemy was described, almost daily, as 'timid' and 'cautious'.

At some time between 6 and 9 August, the Germans made up their minds to evacuate Sicily, the 10 August being set as the day on which the retirement was to begin. Yet on 11 August the decision was still being argued in Rastenburg. Kesselring said afterwards that he gave the order on his own responsibility, although this seems somewhat unlikely. What is apparent, even from the entries in the OKW diary, is that Hitler, Jodl and the OKW were much preoccupied elsewhere. The withdrawal from Sicily took place with little enemy interference so that, by 17 August, the OKW diarist noted, with some satisfaction, that 60,000 German troops with vehicles and equipment had reached the mainland. It is not improbable, however, that this figure included about 13,000 wounded, and it is known that in reality numbers of tanks and guns and some equipment were abandoned. The German casualties in Sicily are not known, but they were estimated to be about 20,000 men, roughly the same as those suffered by the allied armies.

The Badoglio government had already taken secret steps to surrender Italy to the Anglo-Americans, and this encouraged the Americans to agree to the projected invasion of the mainland at Salerno south of Naples, the limit of the range of allied single-engined fighters; the surrender was to be announced as the landing was made and the Italian armed forces were required to co-operate with the allies and

---

* In addition HQ 2 Panzer Army was brought from Russia, so that this, and HQ Army Group E (later HQ Army E), formed in reality two army headquarters.

'to resist any German attacks against them'. Much could not be expected from the Italians, however, as they held the Germans in great fear. A plan to land a United States airborne division near Rome to stiffen the Italian resistance had to be abandoned when it became clear that the Americans might be left in the lurch to fight on their own. Montgomery's 8 Army was to cross the three mile narrows of the Messina Straits a week earlier than the Salerno landing and advance north-east up from the toe of Italy.

On 14 August, when Kesselring had come to understand the role that was likely to be played by Rommel, he asked to resign. Although this was refused by Hitler, it probably caused the Führer to revise his earlier ideas in that he decided for the present that, in the event of *Achse* being ordered, he would keep the Italian theatre split between Rommel's and Kesselring's army groups in the north and the south, both coming directly under his own command. The Italo-German military conference of 15 August, held in Bologna, was attended by Rommel and not by Kesselring, however, and it was at this meeting that Jodl repeated the view of the German high command that the next enemy landings would come either in Sardinia and Corsica as stepping-stones to South France, or in Central Italy to create a base for crossing into the Balkans. Von Vietinghoff's 10 Army was redeployed to meet a likely enemy landing in Central Italy, Hube's 14 Panzer Corps, with two panzer divisions and one panzer grenadier division taking up positions near Gaeta and Salerno, while Herr's 76 Panzer Corps was withdrawn to a line Scalea-Taranto-Brindisi leaving only a single battalion south of Catanzaro across the Calabrian narrows to delay the movement of Montgomery's 8 Army in the difficult mountainous country there. Student's *Fliegerkorps XI* with two divisions remained near Rome. On 3 September British and Canadian troops crossed the Straits of Messina into Calabria; the 8 Army movement inland was described by the German war diarist as slow and hesitant.

During the first week in September the tension between Italian and German troops became acute and an S S agent within the Italian armed forces high command reported, on 4 September, intercepting telephone conversations concerning the proposed surrender to the allies. On 7 September the O K W prepared an ultimatum to the Italian government demanding freedom of German military movement without any further Italian attempt to restrict it, and Jodl drafted an appreciation of the German action to be taken should the Italians reject the German demand. According to Jodl's reckoning there were more than seventeen German divisions either in Italy or about to enter it, and these could not be reinforced further from Russia or from the O K W theatres since further formations were simply not available. The O K W had, in all, only fifty-four German divisions to engage 116 divisions of the enemy and combat up to 200,000 'bandits'; each division defending Europe was trying to cover over 100 miles of coastline and the situation was likely to become critical both in the Balkans and in France. To disarm the Italians and still hold Italy was going to take too much German strength, and for this reason Jodl was in favour of holding on to the Balkans, perhaps with the exception of Rhodes and Crete, but of withdrawing from South Italy and Sardinia 'to the Appenines'. Up to four divisions might then be moved from Kesselring to von Weichs to protect the Balkans in case the enemy should cross the Adriatic from Apulia. This recommendation by Jodl was a departure from the view that he had held earlier and it failed to move Hitler.

In the early evening of 8 September the Italian surrender was announced by radio from Algiers and London, a little prematurely, as it so turned out, since the Salerno landings did not begin until the following day. At 8 p.m. that same night Hitler ordered *Achse* and the task began of rounding up and disarming not only the numerous Italian troops in the homeland but the equivalent of about thirty Italian divisions in the Balkans and in South France. This was carried through successfully within a matter of days with very little resistance. In the Balkans numbers of Italians were disarmed by, or voluntarily handed over their weapons to, the partisans, and some Italians took to the hills becoming guerrillas themselves. Only in North Italy and on some of the Greek islands was there any real fighting between the former Axis allies. Churchill's forlorn attempt at putting lightly armed troops without air cover on to the Dodecanese islands of Cos and Leros, to encourage Italian resistance and so open the entry to the Dardanelles, ended without any gain and the loss of five British battalions, mostly in prisoners, and a number of Royal Navy warships sunk. Meanwhile, on 11 September, the Führer had ordered that in those cases where Italian troops had offered armed resistance or had allowed their arms to fall into the hands of partisans, the Italian officers were to be shot on the spot, and the men sent to Russia. On 18 September, when German troops attacked the Italian held Adriatic island of Cephalonia, the O K W ordered that no Italian prisoners should be taken.* Non-resisting Italian troops, after being disarmed, were to be treated as enemy prisoners-of-war and transported to Germany.

Clark's 5 United States Army, made up of a British and a United States corps, began landing in the area of Salerno on 9 September. Von Vietinghoff's divisional commanders had just been briefed that their role would be to delay and withdraw, when, to their surprise, both panzer corps, totalling two panzer and three panzer grenadier divisions, were ordered to concentrate on the west coast ready to destroy what appeared to be powerful allied forces in the Gulf of Gaeta, before Montgomery's 8 Army should arrive in the area. At first the advantage went to von Vietinghoff, for the German build-up was quicker than the allied, and the Anglo-American tactical handling was faulty. By 13 September over 1,000 British prisoners had been taken, so that von Vietinghoff and Balck, the temporary commander of 14 Panzer Corps, much encouraged, had come to the conclusion that the British troops were not fighting at all well. The Americans, too, were being pushed back, and 10 Army began to talk of pursuit, so causing Jodl and the O K W propaganda and press section to release news items hinting that 'another Dunkirk was in the offing'. By the next day, however, the advancing panzer troops were coming under the heavy gunfire of the naval ships lying off shore and Balck reported that 'the remaining British were not numerous but their resistance was exceptionally tough'. Nor could the Americans be dislodged further. And although the German intercept service had reported that the enemy was planning to evacuate his beach-head, the two panzer corps noted that 'in their view this was certainly not the enemy's intention'. By 16 September the Salerno battle was over and the Germans disengaged and began a slow withdrawal northwards before setting up a defensive line; they had suffered only 4,000 casualties, about half the number lost by the Anglo-Americans, and their field command had displayed remarkable tactical

* *Kriegstagebuch des Oberkommandos der Wehrmacht,* Vol. III 2, 18.9.43, p. 1119 and 23.9.43, p. 1133; Gert Fricke, *Das Unternehmen des XXII Gebirgsarmeekorps, (Militargeschichtliche Mitteilung Nr. 1/67),* p. 49; also *Le Operazioni della Unità Italiane nel Settembre-Ottobre 1943 (Ministero della Difesa Stato Maggiore dell'Esercito — Ufficio Storico)* Rome. 1975, p. 490 *et seq.*

skill. On the higher command level the gambler's throw was successful only in that it had reinforced the caution in the minds of the already over-deliberate allied field commanders.

The second week in September saw the surrender of the Italian Fleet to the British and this left only a dozen U-boats and some German light S-boat flotillas in the Mediterranean waters. Mussolini was released, on 12 September, from Italian captivity by *SS Hauptsturmführer* Skorzeny's armed *coup* before being set up by the Germans as the puppet head of the German occupied state of the North Italian Republic that even Franco declined to recognize, for the new republic was treated by Berlin as enemy territory with its population and resources entirely at German disposal. Eventually the republic was to be forced to cede to the Reich the northern territories of Venezia Giulia and the Alto Adige. Hitler justified severing any remaining links of friendship with the former Italian dictator when he became aware that Mussolini had actually *wished* to leave the war at some time prior to the capitulation. That was reason enough.

The defection of Italy and the allied invasion of the Italian mainland had led inevitably to a grave weakening of the German position in the Balkans. The guerrilla leader earliest in the field there had been Mihailovic, who, supported by the British and with close ties to the royal government-in-exile, had drawn his followers mainly from the Serb Cetniks. Mihailovic was bitterly anti-communist and had a natural interest in preserving both the royal and the Serbian political ascendancy after the war. In the German view he had been aided, more or less openly, by the Italian occupation authorities against the communists and against the Germans; in fact, Mihailovic's connection with the Italians had been based on what he could get out of them. Tito's partisans, on the other hand, had a much wider appeal to the many peoples and factions within Yugoslavia, since they claimed to be supra-national with both communist and non-communist support, and promised land reform and relief from unemployment and poverty. Tito had received some very limited material support from the Soviet Union and, from May 1943 onwards when Anglo-American missions were accredited to him, rapidly increasing military aid from the western allies.

Tito was regarded by the Germans as a more dangerous enemy than Mihailovic, and this was soon to be recognized in London and Washington. Tito was the bitterest enemy of the Germans, and of the Cetniks, whom he eventually destroyed. As a good communist, he was deeply suspicious of the west, though he took its aid. And although he had close political and emotional ties with Moscow, he was, in company with all foreign communists, heartily mistrusted there. Before September 1943, neither Mihailovic nor Tito was a serious problem to the German Commander-in-Chief South-East, but the capitulation and invasion of Italy changed the whole situation almost overnight in that it brought to Tito a flood of Italian arms and equipment and nearby British administrative support: his forces, instead of being urban guerrillas or mountain bands, were quickly established as divisions and corps, and they began to govern, control and administer the extensive territories they soon occupied.

The complete change in Tito's fortunes was apparent to von Weichs when he wrote to Jodl on 21 September, emphasizing that he was fighting a regular war not partisan bands, 'for Tito's forces were now well equipped, well organized troops fit for operational | strategic | as well as tactical tasks, and were led with energy and drive'. The enemy strength had been increased by about 20,000 Italians that had

1 Hitler, Colonel-General Zeitzler, Admiral Dönitz and *Reichsmarschall* Göring

2 Field-Marshal Keitel, Chief of the Armed Forces High Command (OKW)

3 Colonel-General Jodl, Chief of the OKW Operations Staff

4

5

4 Colonel-General Guderian,
Inspector-General of Armoured
Forces (1943–1945) and acting Chief
of the Army General Staff (1944–1945)
5 Colonel-General Blaskowitz, Commander Army Group G in Southern
France (1944)
6 Field-Marshal Model, Commander
of Army Groups in the east (1943–
1944) and in the west (1944–1945)

6

8

7 Field-Marshal Kesselring,
Commander-in-Chief Italy (1943–
1944), and West (1945)
8 Field-Marshal von Rundstedt,
Commander-in-Chief West (1943–
1945)
9 Field-Marshal Rommel, Commander Army Group B Italy (1943) and
France (1944)

10

11

12

13

14

10 Field-Marshal von Kluge, Commander Army Group Centre (1943) and Commander-in-Chief West (1944)
11 Field-Marshal Schörner, Commander of Army Groups in the east (1944–1945)
12 Red Army troops move up to the East Wall
13 German troops bogged down on the eastern front
14 S (or E) fast torpedo boats, the most active element of the German surface fleet

15 Italian troops moving up near Catania, Sicily
16 German coast watch on Jersey, the Channel Islands

gone over to them, and the partisans had been re-equipped with the arms of six Italian divisions. By the end of the year Tito's regular troops were estimated as eleven corps, each up to 15,000 men strong, in addition to the two 'overseas' brigades equipped and organized by the Anglo-Americans. The partisans had their own supply, equipment and repair services, together with a military government administration; as many as twenty different newspapers were published in the Tito-held areas. In the German view, Tito took Russian advice but British supplies, and they said that he differed from Mihailovic in that, whereas his troops were always fighting, Mihailovic was content to remain on the defensive while the Germans and communists destroyed each other.* This war was being fought in a particularly brutal fashion in that the Titoists were as ready as the Germans to take reprisals, often against the innocent; and since the Germans at first refused to accredit the partisans with the status of combatants they murdered Yugoslav prisoners out of hand; this, Tito's forces repaid in good measure.

The weight of the German forces in the Balkans lay in Yugoslavia, particularly in Croatia, for the Greek resistance was not as extensive or as well organized as Tito's; nor was there any bandit activity in the Greek islands except in Crete. Yet the German armed strength was never sufficient to quell Greek insurgency, let alone carry through a contingency operation planned in the spring of 1943, aimed at occupying European Turkey and both sides of the Dardanelles-Bosphorus Straits; this plan was abandoned in that same autumn for lack of troops. By November the Führer had come to believe that a new allied landing in the Peloponnese was unlikely, but his opinion, and that of the OKW, changed month by month. An allied crossing of the Adriatic was always considered possible and Kesselring was required to have ready a plan for an offensive on the Italian mainland southwards into Apulia, in case the allies should move the weight of their forces from South and Central Italy across the Adriatic into the Balkans. Kesselring, however, protested to the OKW that the project was impossible unless the OKW could allot him substantial ground and air reinforcements.

Back on the Italian mainland the six divisions of von Vietinghoff's 10 German Army were no longer withdrawing, except under the heaviest of pressure, for Hitler was threatening the direst of penalties against any officer who failed to maintain his position or fell short of his duties. Senger und Etterlin's 14 Panzer Corps, in the west opposite 5 United States Army, and Herr's 76 Panzer Corps on the eastern Adriatic flank opposite 8 British Army, had to be forced back over difficult mountainous country from one line to the next. Sardinia and Corsica had been evacuated by German troops and 10 Army was Kesselring's only command, with *Fliegerkorps XI* his only reserve. In the north, and entirely separate from Kesselring, Rommel sat at Canossa with Army Group B, having under command no army headquarters, but four corps and nine divisions; he had no troops in battle and he was responsible only for the security in the North Italian Republic and for the safety of the Alpine passes and the land communications to the Balkans. The army organization in Italy was top heavy and, on 6 November, Hitler finally decided to regularize the situation. A single commander was needed and he came down in favour of Kesselring who was at long last given the united Italian command and designated as Commander-in-Chief South-West and Army Group C. Rommel's formations in North Italy were brought under a new 14 Army under

* According to German intelligence 21,000 rifles, 2,000 machine-pistols, and 16 guns were delivered in February 1944 alone from the British held Adriatic island supply base of Lissa.

von Mackensen (from 1 Panzer Army in Russia) and were subordinated to Kesselring; Rommel and his Army Group B headquarters were withdrawn into the OKW reserve. Hube, the one-armed veteran from the First World War who had escaped captivity in Stalingrad, replaced von Mackensen in Russia where death was to await him.

Meanwhile Churchill had been condemning as scandalous the allied lack of progress in Italy and the failure of the commanders there to make good use of the open flanks in the Adriatic and Tyrrhenian Seas. It was largely as a result of his pressure that a sea-borne landing of Lucas's 6 (US) Corps, consisting of an American and a British division, was made on 22 January 1944 at Anzio well behind von Vietinghoff's 10 Army line that stretched roughly from Gaeta to Ortona. The aim of the landing was, however, by no means clear, certainly not to those who took part. At the politico-strategic level there was talk of a lightning strike across the waist of Italy to the Alban Hills and beyond, cutting the main trunk roads to the south and taking in the capture of Rome. But little was defined in the directives or orders as regards the mission, objectives or timings. Between the levels of army and corps the mission had been watered down to 'an advance *towards* the Alban Hills', and Clark, the Commander of 5 Army, laid particular stress that the Anzio beach-head should hold and not be destroyed in any German counter-offensive. If the allied leadership hoped that Hitler or Kesselring, or the German formations under their command, would be panicked into a rapid disengagement and withdrawal to the north of Rome, they completely misunderstood both the Führer's strategy and the tightness of his military control.*

The allied corps achieved complete surprise on empty beaches, and it is possible that it could have occupied Rome and the Alban Hills and cut the two main routes to the south in the space of the first few days. Whether the corps could have continued to have controlled these key areas after the arrival of Kesselring's reserves, is, of course, entirely another matter. To have been effective in this difficult role the allied force would have been obliged to resort to fast moving warfare with tank forces and armoured infantry, although these tactics could only have been successful, and then for a very limited period, provided that the corps could have been kept supplied. In fact, Lucas's 6 Corps, made up principally of two infantry divisions, with some armour, was not equipped for such a task.

In Rastenburg the Anzio landings had not been linked with the attempts of the enemy 15 Army Group to fight its way northwards, but were regarded, instead, as the first of many landings expected in the Mediterranean, the other threatened areas being South France, the North Italian coastline down to the Tiber estuary, and the Balkans from the Adriatic to the Dodecanese. The Anzio landing, so the Führer declared on 27 January, had a significance far beyond the battles for Rome and for Central Italy, 'for the invasion of Europe planned for 1944 had already started'.

Hitler's plan to destroy the invading force involved the rapid movement of part of von Mackensen's 14 Army from North Italy to the Anzio area, together with a

---

* The allies appear to have had little conception of the true workings of the enemy high command. Wavell, in 1942, wrote that 'Hitler was a figure-head', while Alexander was reputed to have told Lucas at the beginning of 1944 that a successful Anzio operation 'might make the Second Front unnecessary'.

division from the Balkans and another from France, two divisions from 10 Army and some reinforcement from the Reich. The dictator ordered that every soldier in 14 Army should be absolutely clear of what was involved. It was not enough, he said, to make correct tactical judgements and to give clear orders; every leader and every soldier must be inspired by a fanatical will for victory, and he must be filled with a crusading hatred against this enemy that was waging a pitiless war of annihilation against the German people. The battle, he continued, must be fought with the utmost ruthlessness, not only against the enemy but also against 'our own leaders and troops who are found wanting', so that the enemy would know that the German fought as well as ever and would realize that the Second Front, when it came, 'would drown in the seas of blood of the Anglo-Saxon troops'. Two days later, on 29 January, Hitler again stressed the need for a victory after the 1943 string of defeats—defeats that he was apt to write off 'as a run of bad luck (*Pechsträhne*)'—*in order to frighten off the enemy from further landings.*

The Anzio landing involved only a handful of allied and about eight German divisions and its importance must of course be kept in perspective. The landing is of particular interest, however, in that it illustrates how even this minor battle, like those in all other theatres, was fought right down to its tactical detail by Hitler personally, by telephone and by map appreciation, in his distant Rastenburg headquarters. Kesselring and von Mackensen, and corps and divisional commanders, had their tasks closely defined and controlled by the dictator. On 27 January Hitler sent to Kesselring, through Jodl, tactical guide-lines for the offensive: 'since, on their recent showing [presumably Salerno], the British seemed to have less defensive staying power than the Americans', the British sector of the beach-head would be the one selected for the main attack, and the main thrust would be made, as selected by Hitler from the map, from north to south immediately to the west of the Rome-Anzio road. Westphal, Kesselring's chief of staff, felt obliged to point out to Jodl that the broken ground there made any advance most difficult and he suggested that the open fields to the east of the road be used for the axis; and, 'after due consideration, the Führer approved the change'. For some unknown reason Kesselring, when giving out his orders at 1 p.m. on 30 January, used the words '14 Army will attack concentrically from coast to coast'. These words reached Hitler's ears and, just after midnight, Jodl was on the telephone repeating the Führer's countermand 'there was no question of a concentric attack—the English would be attacked first, exactly as instructed, by a main thrust and thrown into the sea, and only then would the Americans be dealt with'.* During the battle the Führer was to tell Kesselring exactly how the attacks were to be carried out and how he was to use his Tiger tanks, artillery and infantry. And the dictator required to be minutely briefed on the detail of von Mackensen's battle situation maps and plans for the attack.

Hitler's plans for the offensive had to be postponed when, on 30 January, Lucas's 6 Corps on the beach-head attacked northwards up the Anzio road and the area immediately to its east. At first it gained several miles. Then, after being counter-attacked on its flanks, its losses became heavy, and it fell back beyond its starting point. Von Mackensen's losses had not been light, and fourteen days' delay for regrouping and reinforcement was necessary before Hitler's own offensive

*Whether Hitler was right in his choice appears to have been indirectly questioned by Jodl's personal representative at Kesselring's headquarters; this liaison officer later reported on the first rate impression made by prisoners of war from the British division.

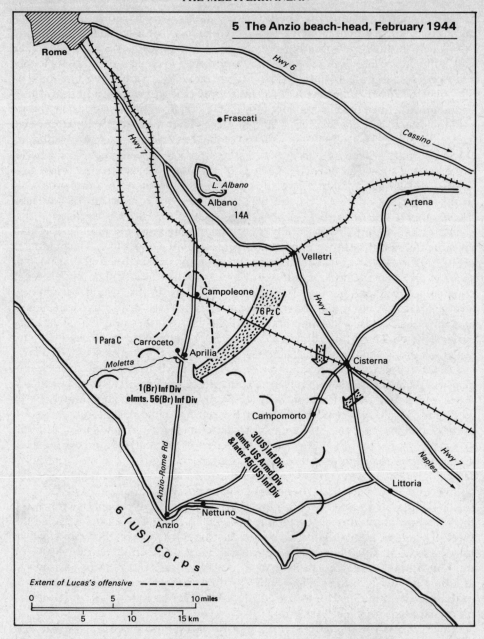

5 The Anzio beach-head, February 1944

Rome
Hwy 6
Frascati
Cassino
L. Albano
Albano
14A
Artena
Velletri
Campoleone
76 Pz C
Hwy 7
1 Para C
Carroceto
Aprilia
Moletta
Cisterna
1 (Br) Inf Div
elmts. 56 (Br) Inf Div
Campomorto
3 (US) Inf Div
elmts. US Armd Div
& later 45 (US) Inf Div
Naples
Hwy 7
Littoria
Nettuno
Anzio
6 (US) Corps

Extent of Lucas's offensive - - - - - - - -
0   5   10 miles
5   10   15 km

could be mounted. On 6 February Hitler personally briefed von Mackensen and gave him detailed orders as to how the offensive was to be conducted, and he reserved to himself the timing of the attack. The dictator had come to see a German breakthrough being made 'in the fashion of the Western Front in the First World War with massed artillery and waves of infantry'; as soon as the enemy front had been pierced the tanks would reach the coast (a distance of less than seven miles) in a single bound.

The offensive began on 16 February, the main effort being made exactly where Hitler had directed it, on and to the east of the main Anzio road, although this sector had recently been taken over by United States regiments from the British division that had previously held it; there was, however, a British brigade in depth on a commanding tactical feature of paramount importance a thousand or so yards to the rear. The battle raged for four days under lowering skies and over open water-logged country with miles of wire, minefields, weapon pits and trenches, and with shell-holes and scrapes everywhere, so that the German diarist was to record that the conditions, for the first time anywhere, actually did approach those of the First World War. Between 16 and 23 February German artillery fired 22,000 shells on this mile or two of front, a high figure by German standards at that time. Much of the American forward defended localities had been overrun or bypassed, but the German advance was finally brought to a standstill on the British reserve line, mainly, said the diarist, by the effects of field artillery and naval gunfire. On 19 February a flanking thrust by tanks of the newly arrived United States armoured division, together with a frontal counter-attack by the British brigade, caused von Mackensen's troops to fall back several thousand yards with a heavy loss in prisoners.

In the early hours of 20 February Kesselring reported to the OKW that the foe was fighting 'with toughness and bitterness' for every foot of ground, and that the enemy infantry had sited and constructed its defensive positions with great skill. German casualties were mounting and Kesselring was of the opinion that the enemy troops, fully realizing the gravity of their own situation, would continue to fight on as bitterly as ever. Kesselring believed that he might be able to renew the attack a little further to the east, but the Führer forbade this as being too near the present *Schwerpunkt*. The dictator himself marked out a new sector for attack near Isola Bella 'where the enemy was weak'. This attack, delivered on 29 February against the American coastal flank in the east, and lasting only one day, also failed.

Any German hope of destroying the beach-head had now disappeared, although Hitler continued to threaten it verbally, with unfulfilled promises of reinforcements and uncompleted battle plans. And he ordered twelve officers, in the main junior leaders who had been in the fighting, to be brought to Rastenburg to be cross-examined by him, personally and individually, as to the reasons for the failure. Rarely can any *Supremo* have shown openly, and without regard for the self-respect and susceptibilities of his commanders and staffs, what little confidence he had in the senior officers about him or in the higher command in the field.*

---

*After the battle Kesselring admitted that the only numerical and material superiority that the allies enjoyed at Anzio was in the air and in naval gunnery; otherwise they were much outnumbered by the attacking Germans. Kesselring said that he regarded the success of the mixed allied 6 Corps as a remarkable achievement.

CHAPTER FIVE

The East Wall Breached

Before 1943 the Soviet armament industry was turning out more guns, tanks and aircraft than were being produced by Germany, and the quality of the guns and tanks was equal, and sometimes superior, to that of their German equivalent. From 1943 onwards, however, the German armament production began rapidly to overtake that of the USSR.

At the beginning of 1942 Todt, the Minister for Armaments, had been succeeded by the energetic Speer, one of the very few men who had direct access to Hitler, and Speer soon began to use his position and abilities to reorganize and rationalize German industry. Göring and the office of the Four Year Plan were edged aside, and Thomas's Economic and Armament Department was removed from the OKW and Keitel's and Göring's control, and was taken over by Speer's organization. Göring's deputy, Milch, and Speer's deputy, Saur, formed a single executive body to concentrate on fighter production.

Speer began to use up such stocks of strategic raw materials that had accrued, and, motivated by the spur of total war, although many of the measures were in fact much less than total, German war production began to show an immediate and most remarkable improvement. In 1942 German industry had turned out only 14,000 military aircraft, but in 1943 the output rose suddenly to 25,000. During 1944 the aircraft production was to outstrip that of the Soviet Union, reaching 34,000 combat and 3,000 training aircraft, although it must be taken into account that fighters were being produced at the expense of bombers. The graph of tank production showed a similar rise, from a 1942 figure of only 4,300 medium tanks and assault guns, to a 1944 high, approaching the armoured production of the Soviet Union, made up of 11,000 medium tanks and assault guns, 5,200 heavy tanks and 1,600 tank destroyers, together with 10,000 armoured vehicles of other types.* Even more significant was the improvement in the design of German fighting vehicles that had done much to redress the earlier inferiority, since the new Tiger and King Tiger were superior to the Soviet K V tanks while the improved Mark V and the upgunned Mark I V were to prove a match for the T 34.** In 1942 German gun production stood at only 12,000 artillery and 2,400 tank guns; by

* The assault gun, as already explained, was a turretless tank. True tank destroyers were assault guns mounting a high velocity armament, although the name was sometimes given to self-propelled anti-tank guns on obsolescent tank chassis.

**The K V weighed over 50 tons and mounted either a 85 mm gun or a 152 mm gun-howitzer. The upgunned Mk IV weighed about 25 tons and carried a high velocity L 48 75 mm gun.

THE EAST WALL BREACHED

1944 these figures had risen to 40,000 artillery and 15,000 tank guns a year.*

Hitler and his advisers had, through ignorance and wilfulness, failed to face the seriousness of Germany's position until too late. Three years that might have been used to improve the equipment position of the German forces had been largely wasted. Yet, in spite of this, Germany's armament position *vis à vis* the Soviet Union had greatly improved in 1943 and showed every indication of continuing to do so. Key raw materials, however, were being used up at a rate that gave rise to anxiety, since forty-seven per cent of Germany's iron ores were imported, mainly from Sweden and France, together with a hundred per cent of its needs of manganese and bauxite, mainly from Russia and the Balkans, forty-five per cent of its copper requirement from Sweden, seventy-five per cent of its wolfram from Portugal and all its chrome from Turkey. The immediate and pressing difficulty lay in the shortage of oil since this was now restricting operations and curtailing training, for although seven million tons of oil were being produced within the Reich, Rumanian imports by way of the Danube had been cut to three million tons because of transportation difficulties. In all, the superiority of the combined resources of the USA, the British Commonwealth and Empire and the USSR over Germany has been estimated at about nine to two.

The western allies had mounted a somewhat complicated deception plan during the late summer of 1943 in order to make the Germans think that the invasion of France was imminent.** This involved air and sea and electronic intelligence operations off the coasts of Western Europe to confuse the enemy, test his reactions, bring his fighters into the air and, if possible, to pin his forces. The results were certainly not as effective as the allies had wished, mainly because the resources allotted to the operation were insufficient to give a credible appearance of the existence of large-scale forces concentrated and poised ready for invasion. During the summer and autumn of 1943 the likelihood of a Second Front was believed in Rastenburg to be possible but not probable, and von Rundstedt's command in France and the Netherlands continued to be used as a reinforcing theatre for Russia, the Balkans and Italy.

In September 1943 Blumentritt, von Rundstedt's chief of staff, had written to Jodl remonstrating against the continual removal of good and complete formations that were exchanged for burned-out shells from Russia or were not replaced at all. For Blumentritt reasoned that the invasion in the west must come eventually and that time was running out. Jodl was of two minds. When he heard the press announcement that Eisenhower had been returned to the United Kingdom to assume the supreme command over the forces preparing for the invasion of Western Europe, he had, somewhat surprisingly, told Hitler that he was inclined to think that the Anglo-American Second Front 'was just one big hoax' that would never come off.*** Hitler would probably have liked to have thought that this was true but it was a view that he could not share. Like Blumentritt he was forced to

---

* The Soviet 1944 production was said to be 29,000 AFVs and 32,000 aircraft of *all* types and 56,000 field and anti-tank guns: British 1944 production 5,000 tanks and 26,000 aircraft: United States 1944 production 17,500 tanks (29,500 in 1943) and 96,300 aircraft.

**This deception plan was known as *Starkey*.

*** It is of interest to note that United States staff officers working on the invasion plans at this time recorded (October 1943) the entirely unfounded suspicion that the British regarded the invasion as 'a gigantic deception plan' and the armies as 'an occupying force' that would land only after the expected German collapse,

admit that an invasion of the Channel or Atlantic coast could not be long delayed, but he pinned his hopes on the German ability to throw the Anglo-Americans back into the sea; he would then be able to concentrate all his forces against the Soviet Union.* Influenced by the contents of Blumentritt's letter to Jodl, Hitler had signed the *Wehrmachtführungsstab* draft Directive 51, his last numbered directive, giving absolute priority to the German forces in Western Europe for the supply of reinforcements and equipment, this meaning that the eastern front would, for the next few months, receive nothing at all.

If an Anglo-American invasion in the west was likely from February 1944 onwards, a series of Soviet winter and spring offensives was certain even before February. During the whole of 1943 Hitler and many of his senior commanders and staffs had believed that the Red Army was near exhaustion, and time after time they had continued to be surprised by the rapidity and the strength with which the Soviet fronts had returned to the offensive. And for every German soldier killed in Italy in the fall of 1943, fourteen fell in Russia.

The causes of the German failure in Russia during 1943 were the same as those that gave rise to the defeats of 1942, an inadequacy of resources, particularly of aircraft, tanks and motor vehicles and of motor fuels, and the insistence by the Führer on a rigid defensive strategy. Together these lost the Germans both the strategic and the tactical initiative. Hitler has rightly been blamed by his leading commanders for his demand that every foot of territory be held secure. Von Kluge, the Commander of Army Group Centre, sounded the note of truth when he told the Führer, on 14 October, that the Soviet success was due not so much to overwhelming strength, but to Soviet mobility and flexibility that enabled the Russian to amass a preponderance of troops and equipment at the decisive points on the whole battle front.

It was impossible that Germany could be victorious against the three great power coalition, and the defection of Italy and the deposing of Mussolini had had a depressing moral effect not only on Hitler but on the German public at large. Goebbels continued to press the need for immediate peace with either east or west. But for Hitler it was all or nothing, victory or annihilation, and resignation or suicide was out of the question. The German Army might of course have deposed the dictator and then sought peace. Hitler had, however, safeguarded himself against a *coup d'état* by centralizing the police and security organizations under Himmler and by keeping the numerous SS formations independent of the army, and he blamed Mussolini for not having set up the equivalent of an Italian SS as a counter against the King, Badoglio and the Italian Army. The *Luftwaffe*'s and the German Navy's loyalty to Hitler was never in doubt and Goebbels reasoned that the senior German Army generals, nearly all of whom owed their rank and position to the Führer, were unlikely as a class to head a military uprising.

Although Hitler may have had no reason to doubt the loyalty of the German Army, he had not been entirely satisfied with the resolution and political conviction of his commanders or of the officer corps, for he had come to the conclusion that armies that had their basis on a firm spiritual and ideological foundation were superior to those of the *bourgeois* states. He believed that the existence of political commissars within the Red Army had made it formidable, and, during the last eighteen months, he had introduced his own form of commissar organization into

---

* The words he used were: 'If only the landings can be thrown back into the sea then no further problem will exist, for we can remove our forces from France as quickly as we like'.

the armed forces. The German Army, in particular, had been wholly penetrated by these commissars, usually army officers who had been given rigorous and specialized Nazi political training and who were largely independent of the commanders to whom they were accredited. These 'National Socialist Guidance Officers' were Hitler's party controllers and spies within the armed forces.

Although it was of course unthinkable that Hitler would have agreed, it might be argued that it would have been in Germany's interest if the dictator had returned the leadership of the armed forces to its professional officers, a course that had been urged upon him by von Kluge and von Manstein. An immediate withdrawal would have been necessary from the Baltic States, Belorussia, the Ukraine and the Crimea, and from Italy, France, Scandinavia and the Balkans in order to have shortened the frontages and accumulated reserves, although such a withdrawal would have cut off the sources of raw materials so prized by Hitler. Such a measure *might* possibly, even at this late hour, have brought the war in the east to a stalemate, provided that Germany was not engaged in fighting a war on two fronts. The Anglo-American intervention in Western Europe was likely, however, to be the final decisive factor in the outcome of Germany's fate, as Hitler himself said that it would.

Von Küchler, the Commander of Army Group North in the sector from Leningrad to the Volkhov, had already given up a number of divisions to von Manstein in the south so that there remained to him only forty-two understrength infantry divisions and one panzer grenadier division to hold over 500 miles of closely forested and marshy front; he had no reserves and virtually no tanks. On 30 December von Küchler presented his sorry situation to the Führer at the midday Rastenburg conference and he protested against having to reinforce other army groups in the east. Now that he was so weakened it was his turn, he so reasoned, to have to withstand a Soviet offensive, and he believed this to be imminent. Von Küchler's troops still stood forward of the East Wall and he now asked for permission to fall back on these defences near the 1940 frontier between the Baltic States and the Soviet Union; this was refused by Hitler on the grounds that such a withdrawal would leave the Finns exposed and would make it certain that they would leave the war. It became obvious that von Küchler's subordinate, Lindemann, the Commander of 18 Army, took the more optimistic view that he could hold his present position against a Soviet offensive; the Führer always accepted the opinion that coincided with his own, and von Küchler lost the day.

On 14 January von Küchler's fears were realized when Lindemann's army was attacked on both its flanks by Govorov's Leningrad and Meretskov's Volkhov Fronts. German troops were cut off in Peterhof and Novgorod, and Lindemann, in spite of orders to the contrary, was forced to give ground. Von Küchler, well aware of the Soviet intention to encircle 18 Army, and seeing his two corps threatened with immediate destruction, appealed to Hitler to sanction Lindemann's further withdrawal and allow the besieged troops in Novgorod to break out. The Führer refused, but made the half-promise that he thought he might be able to move a single panzer division from Army Group Centre to assist Lindemann.

Inured to hardship though the German defenders were, the Soviet offensive had burst on them with a fury that none had expected, amid scenes that none had ever experienced before. Von Küchler began to order withdrawals on his own responsibility. The Novgorod garrison had to abandon their seriously wounded and try to get out under cover of darkness. Elsewhere to the north-east, troops fell back under heavy enemy artillery fire while the Red Air Force bombed and machine-gunned all movement. German formations became mixed and confused, and fighting units took in as reinforcements leave and baggage men and stragglers. The *Luftwaffe* field divisions were the first to disintegrate and the supply echelons failed. Scaremonger rumours ran up and down the front and there were numbers of cases of panic and flight.

On 28 January von Küchler virtually signed his own dismissal order when he persuaded Hitler that 18 Army must fall back to the line of the River Luga, though he could offer the dictator no assurance that this could be held. Hitler, choosing to ignore that if Lindemann had not withdrawn his army it would have been surrounded, used the events to argue that the fault lay with von Küchler for having advised the withdrawal in the first place. That same day he remarked bitterly to Zeitzler at the midday conference that the experience of the last three years, if it had shown anything, had proved that when one retired from a position in order to shorten the front or to build a firmer defence line, the new position could never be held. On 29 January von Küchler was retired and replaced by Model, who had acquired a reputation as a lion of the defence.

Model started to move troops over from his right hand 16 Army to reinforce 18 Army on his left, and so consolidate the line of the Luga. But as soon as 16 Army had been weakened it came under attack from a new and heavy Soviet offensive further to the south mounted by Popov's 2 Baltic Front, so that the whole of Army Group North appeared to be in danger of envelopment. On 15 February Hitler was forced to agree that Model should withdraw Army Group North out of Russia to the East Wall. Finland then asked Moscow for an armistice.

As in the north, so it was in the south. By the beginning of October von Manstein had averted disaster in that he had managed to get the bulk of his forces back to the East Wall and behind the Dnieper from Loev in Belorussia to Dnepropetrovsk in the Central Ukraine; von Manstein continued, however, at Hitler's insistence, to hold bridge-heads forward of the river both at Dnepropetrovsk and in the great triangular area east of the Dnieper from Zaporozhe to Melitopol and the Molochnoye Lake near the Sea of Azov, this being the only land approach to von Kleist's Army Group A and 17 Army in the Crimea. The linking Hollidt's 6 German Army that held this triangle was, at the Führer's whim, sometimes under von Manstein and sometimes under von Kleist.

When the field formations began to arrive back in the East Wall they were appalled to see what little had been done, and that very badly. Even more alarming to see was the panic of the German rearward troops in the base areas, with occupation and rearward officials using valuable motor transport to evacuate women, supplies and materials for their own comfort. This was noted, too, by the SS field formations arriving in the area, and their reports soon reached Hitler's ears where they were to serve as yet another bitter reproach against the whole German Army.

During October and early November the Soviet pressure in the Ukraine, particularly about Kiev, became overwhelming, Vatutin's 1 Ukrainian Front renewing its attacks, apparently undeterred by earlier failures and losses. The Red Army casualties, in the German view, were very heavy, since much of its infantry were

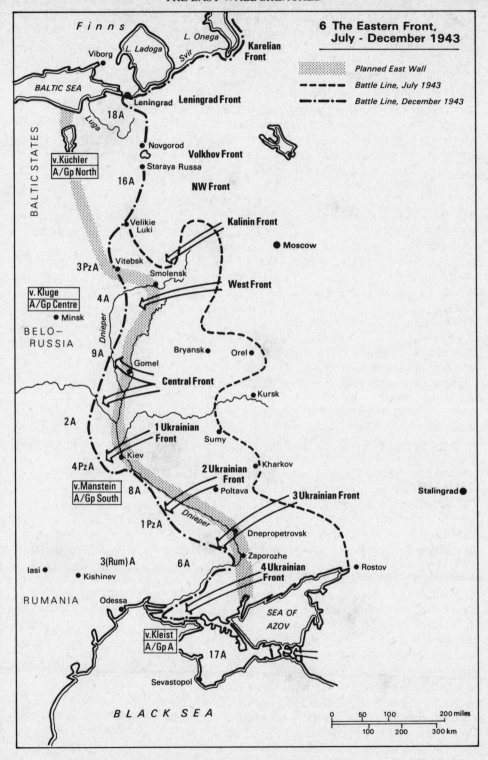

**6 The Eastern Front,
July - December 1943**

Planned East Wall

- - - - Battle Line, July 1943

-·-·-·- Battle Line, December 1943

Finns

L. Onega

L. Ladoga

Viborg

Svir

**Karelian
Front**

BALTIC SEA

Leningrad **Leningrad Front**

18 A

BALTIC STATES

Luga

Novgorod

Volkhov Front

Staraya Russa

v.Küchler
A/Gp North

16 A

NW Front

Velikie
Luki

Kalinin Front

● Moscow

3 Pz A

Vitebsk

Smolensk

West Front

v. Kluge
A/Gp Centre

4 A

● Minsk

BELO-
RUSSIA

Dnieper

9 A

Bryansk ●

Orel ●

Gomel

Central Front

● Kursk

2 A

**1 Ukrainian
Front**

Sumy ●

4 Pz A

Kiev

Kharkov ●

**2 Ukrainian
Front**

v.Manstein
A/Gp South

8 A

Poltava ●

3 Ukrainian Front

Stalingrad ●

1 Pz A

Dnieper

Dnepropetrovsk

3(Rum) A

6 A

Zaporozhe

Iasi ●

Kishinev ●

**4 Ukrainian
Front**

● Rostov

RUMANIA

Odessa

*SEA OF
AZOV*

v.Kleist
A/Gp A

17 A

Sevastopol

B L A C K   S E A

0   50   100   200 miles

100   200   300 km

the *Beutesoldaten*, civilians in the areas newly occupied by the Soviets, who were hastily armed and led, or driven, into battle by Red Army officers. Even so, it was obvious that the Germans were themselves so tightly stretched that they could hold no longer.

Von Choltitz, the Commander of 48 Panzer Corps fighting near Kiev, a very experienced leader, had come to the conclusion that he could see no sense in the continuation of the struggle, and he much surprised his staff by his outspoken and seemingly eccentric views, for he foresaw the Soviet masses closing on Germany and submerging it in a great flood. He convinced himself that the Führer could not know the conditions on the ground. So he departed for Rastenburg, apparently with von Manstein's connivance, to seek a personal interview with Hitler in order to offer his resignation and persuade the dictator of the futility of the war. Von Choltitz got no further than 'the unfortunate Chief of General Staff [Zeitzler] who, pale and saddened, listened to the report with a helpless shrug of the shoulders'. It was then, said von Choltitz, that he realized that Rastenburg was already aware of the true situation and he himself knew that the war was lost.

Meanwhile Kiev had fallen, the East Wall had been breached and Vatutin had swept on some eighty miles west of the Dnieper. For this, Hitler held Hoth, the able but exhausted commander of 4 Panzer Army, to be responsible, and he was dismissed and never re-employed. For the moment the defences in the Dnieper bend and on the land-bridge to the Crimea were still holding, but Stalin had got Kiev, the main prize. Von Manstein had been forced back on his left and this brought his northern neighbour, von Kluge's Army Group Centre, under great pressure, where the Soviet high command was intent on securing the whole of the Orsha land-bridge, as well as Vitebsk, the gateway to the Baltic States.

In early October Eremenko's Kalinin Front attacked 3 Panzer Army in the sector held by a *Luftwaffe* field corps, the offensive being so heavy that a half trained and inexperienced *Luftwaffe* division broke almost immediately, some of it running away in panic. Within a matter of hours Eremenko's men were pouring through a ten-mile gap into the rear. Göring, whose honour was involved by the failure of the *Luftwaffe* ground troops, had immediately allocated reinforcement *Luftwaffe* flak batteries and 600 aircraft to the sector and, with their assistance, the situation was temporarily brought under control. But it was obvious to 3 Panzer Army that the Red Army troops had been surprised at the ease with which they had taken Nevel and made a breach in the East Wall. Reinhardt, the Commander of 3 Panzer Army, fearing a resumption of Eremenko's offensive, begged von Kluge in vain for permission to counter-attack and regain the lost Nevel area.

At his army group headquarters in Orsha von Kluge had been beset by difficulties hardly less grievous than those suffered by von Manstein in the Ukraine. Von Kluge was energetic, hard-willed and an outstanding leader in the field but, by the German standards of the time, inclined towards caution. He had noted how the Soviet field command was much more confident, even daring, after Kursk, while he himself, worried about his declining fighting strength, became increasingly reluctant to make any counter-attack that would involve him in casualties.

Von Kluge's hands were tied at this time by the fighting on Heinrici's 4 Army sector in the area of Orsha and Mogilev a little further to the south, and he referred Reinhardt's request for permission to counter-attack back to Zeitzler. Von Kluge had much less confidence in the OKH than formerly, for he told his staff on 18 October that Zeitzler was very tired and had no further influence with

Hitler, and that in his (von Kluge's) opinion the days of the Chief of the Army General Staff were numbered. Four days before, von Kluge had written a long personal letter to the Führer, pointing out that although the morale of his fighting men remained good, they were beset by a feeling of isolation and neglect, facing as they did the massed numbers of Red Army infantry. Army Group Centre was 200,000 men short of establishment and the recent losses had been so great that the drop in the fighting strength of the formations that had borne the brunt of the attacks was frightening. The standard of such replacements as had been received, said von Kluge, left much to be desired, many of them lacking training and inner soldierly qualities. Without troops, weapons and reserves, no commander could function, however skilful he might be. Von Kluge had always been Hitler's man and was one of those generals who had accepted personal gifts from the Führer in the form of landed estates or money from his privy purse; he was, for this reason, very careful to assure the Führer of his own personal loyalty, but he stressed that 'the danger of the trend' had to be faced. He ended his letter by saying that although it was commonly assumed that the Russians had the same losses and problems, this was, in reality, not the case, because the Red Army could always obtain a numerical superiority by concentrating its forces at the point selected for attack. No answer was received to this letter. On 27 October, as a result of a motor accident, von Kluge was invalided from his post and was replaced by Field-Marshal Busch, a former commander of 16 Army.

Meanwhile Roosevelt and Churchill, with their political and military staffs, had made the long journey to Teheran to consult with their Soviet ally as to the conduct of the war during the coming fateful year.

The Americans and British, bedevilled by the lack of assault landing-craft, were again in disarray. The Americans were insistent on a maximum of forces for the Second Front that they wanted to launch at the beginning of May 1944, and they were determined to keep their British ally up to its share of the bargain. Churchill took a more flexible view in that he wanted the greatest offensive action possible in the Mediterranean before landing-craft and troops were withdrawn for France, even though this should mean delaying the Second Front until July. This, at least, is how the Americans understood him. They regarded his plan to capture Rhodes as folly in view of the humiliating defeats that the British had just suffered in Cos and Leros, and they suspected him of wanting to meddle in the affairs of the Balkans.

At the first meeting on 28 November, Stalin appeared in the uniform of a Marshal of the Soviet Union looking care-worn but unusually affable. His interventions were made in a quiet voice, without any gestures, but at the same time were direct and decided; sometimes they were so abrupt as to be rude. He left no doubt in any one's mind, according to one of those present, that he was master in his own house. In contrast to the British and American groups, each of which numbered twenty or thirty, Stalin had with him only Molotov and Voroshilov, with Shtemenko, the head of the general staff operations directorate, outside in the communication centre on a direct link with the general staff in Moscow. From time to time Stalin had whispered consultations with Molotov and Voroshilov, but Stalin was the sole spokesman; and there was never any doubt of his authority 'nor the slightest indication that he would have to consult his government'.

Stalin said that he saw no point in separate chiefs of staffs consultations, 'for that was his business [as the *de facto* Commander-in-Chief] and that was what he had come for'; only reluctantly would he agree to be represented on the military committee, for he was his own military expert and had brought no other experts with him; Voroshilov (a former Defence Minister) would, however, 'do his best'. His other comments were blunt, terse and to the point. On one occasion he capped Churchill's oratory by asking tartly whether the British were only 'thinking' of the Second Front in order to appease the Soviet Union; at another, after a particularly long speech from Churchill, he asked: 'How long is this conference going to last?'.

Brooke, the British Chief of the Imperial General Staff, was of the opinion that Stalin had a military brain of the highest calibre. Never once in any of his statements, said Brooke, did Stalin fail to appreciate all the implications of a situation with a quick and unerring eye, and in this respect, said Brooke, he stood out compared with Roosevelt and Churchill.

Roosevelt surprised and disturbed his own chiefs of staff by bringing up the possibility of a Mediterranean operation across the Adriatic through Yugoslavia into Rumania to effect a junction with the Red Army near Odessa (the very strategy forecast for the western allies by Hitler and Jodl). Naturally, Churchill supported this suggestion. Stalin then gave his opinion as to what he thought his allies should do. It was unwise, he thought, to scatter forces throughout the Eastern Mediterranean since *Overlord* (the Second Front) should be the basis for *all* Anglo-American operations in 1944; it would be better even to abandon the seizing of Rome so that the bulk of the allied troops in Italy might be used to invade Southern France. Stalin said repeatedly that he was sure that Turkey would not come into the war, as if to emphasize that the Black Sea would remain closed to Anglo-American naval forces.

Stalin had supported the United States general staff plan that all available allied forces should be landed in France, and Brooke and the leader of the United States military mission in Moscow subsequently ascribed motives of self-interest to the Soviet leader's proposals. Apart from securing an obvious diplomatic advantage in siding with the Americans against the British, Stalin wanted, suspected Brooke, to keep his western allies away from the Black Sea left flank, out of the Balkans and clear of the East Mediterranean. What Stalin was subsequently alleged to have told Shtemenko — as reported by Shtemenko after the war — would appear to support this view.

A measure of agreement was reached in that the date of the Second Front was put off until the end of May, it being recognized that this would fit in with the Russian late spring offensives. Stalin, tired of waiting, accepted this firm date with some satisfaction. Yet it was evident to both the British and Americans that this was a new Stalin, no longer nervous and tense, but confident and self-assured. Brooke believed that Stalin thought that 'the Germans had shot their bolt', while the Americans had the impression that Stalin was now indifferent to what the allies did, as long as they got on with it, and did not drag their feet or get in his way.

In mid December 1943, Stalin, back in Moscow, had recalled Zhukov and Vasilevsky to the capital to prepare, together with the general staff, the detail of the new offensive by the four Ukrainian Fronts that was to destroy the enemy salient in the Dnieper bend and take the Red Army into Galicia and Rumania. The first priority was to rid Soviet soil of the enemy, and Stalin had reversed his earlier order forbidding great encirclement operations. If the enemy would not retire then he was to be destroyed where he stood.

The weight of the German forces, particularly in armour, lay in the south where the Ukraine and the Crimea were held by von Manstein's Army Group South commanding 1 Panzer and 4 Panzer Armies and 8 Army, totalling forty-three infantry, fifteen panzer and seven panzer grenadier divisions, and by von Kleist's Army Group A made up of 17 Army in the Crimea and 3 Rumanian Army and 6 German Army in the Dnieper bend, von Kleist's army group having in all eight German infantry and ten Rumanian divisions.

On Christmas Eve Vatutin's 1 Ukrainian Front began a heavy offensive against the north flank of Army Group South, and von Manstein concluded that it was the Soviet intention to separate him from his northern neighbour, Army Group Centre. Von Manstein asked Hitler's permission to move Hube's 1 Panzer Army over to his left flank but this was refused with an empty promise that each of the three other army groups should give up a division that would be railed to von Manstein. Nor would Hitler permit von Manstein (or von Kleist) to withdraw from the exposed and vulnerable Dnieper bend salient to the south. Although Hitler maintained the semblance of good relations with von Manstein, in fact he disliked and despised him; von Manstein's proposals, and, in particular, his suggestion that he move his own army group headquarters back from Vinnitsa north-westwards to Lvov and closer to Army Group Centre, were discussed by the Führer with Zeitzler and Jodl, and the absent von Manstein was the butt of the dictator's sneers and sarcasm. The deteriorating situation soon forced von Manstein to move Hube's 1 Panzer Army over to his left, but no sooner had he done so than his right, Wöhler's 8 Army in the Dnieper bend, came under heavy attack when Konev's 2 Ukrainian Front began a new offensive near Cherkasy, aimed in the first instance at driving in 52 German Corps and 47 Panzer Corps.

Von Vormann, who had just arrived from Germany to take over the command of 47 Panzer Corps, has told of the condition in which he found his three panzer, one panzer grenadier and four infantry divisions. The divisions were hardly more than regiments and Ramcke's 2 Parachute Division, with a fighting strength of 3,700 men, had a frontage of thirteen miles. Deep snow lay everywhere and the temperature stood at minus 22 degrees centigrade. Any change of battle position on the infantryman's part, even of only a few hundred yards, meant that he had to dig new weapon pits and fresh shelter from artillery fire and from the cold, often an impossible task in the iron-hard ground. The morale of the men remained good, but, according to von Vormann, many were already a prey to doubts as to the future and the outcome of the war. Letters from home told of the devastating bombing and of the increasingly heavy police repression. Few could understand the seemingly senseless orders that came from above, apparently from the highest. Yet, in spite of this, most knew that there could be no hope of terms with Russian or with Anglo-American, and they believed that the Führer was their only salvation. To the soldier in the field Hitler was the Commander-in-Chief of the Army and in their eyes there was no other army leader of sufficient stature who could replace him.

On 5 and 6 January the artillery supporting 47 Panzer Corps alone fired off

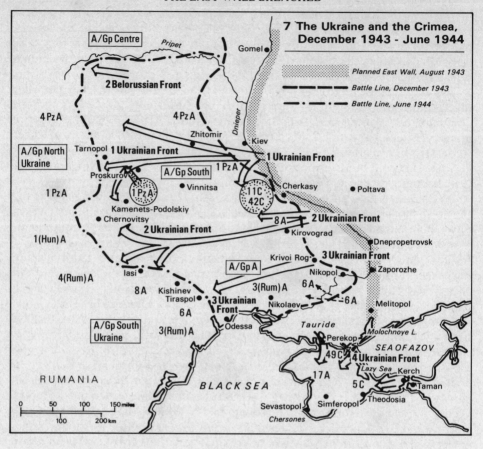

7 The Ukraine and the Crimea, December 1943 - June 1944

Planned East Wall, August 1943

Battle Line, December 1943

Battle Line, June 1944

A/Gp Centre

Pripet

Gomel

2 Belorussian Front

4 Pz A

4 Pz A

Zhitomir

Dnieper

Kiev

A/Gp North Ukraine

Tarnopol

1 Ukrainian Front

1 Ukrainian Front

Proskurov

A/Gp South

1 Pz A

1 Pz A

Vinnitsa

11 C 42 C

Cherkasy

Poltava

Kamenets-Podolskiy

Chernovitsy

8 A

2 Ukrainian Front

1 Pz A

2 Ukrainian Front

Kirovograd

Dnepropetrovsk

1 (Hun) A

A/Gp A

Krivoi Rog

3 Ukrainian Front

Iasi

Nikopol

Zaporozhe

4 (Rum) A

8 A

Kishinev

Tiraspol

3 Ukrainian Front

3 (Rum) A

6 A

6 A

6 A

Nikolaev

Melitopol

A/Gp South Ukraine

3 (Rum) A

6 A

Odessa

Tauride

Perekop

Molochnoye L.

SEA OF AZOV

RUMANIA

49 C

4 Ukrainian Front

Lazy Sea

Kerch

17 A

5 C

Taman

BLACK SEA

Sevastopol

Simferopol

Theodosia

Chersones

0   50   100   150 miles

100   200 km

177,000 rounds trying to close the many gaps in the front, and, three nights later, the corps headquarters was overrun and dispersed by a Soviet tank brigade. The heavy pressure continued for a fortnight and, on 28 January, on the very day that Hitler had called his army commanders to Rastenburg to hear a lecture on the virtues of National Socialism within the German Army, the flanks of Vatutin's and Konev's fronts completed a double envelopment and surrounded 11 and 42 German Corps, about 60,000 men in all, in the area of Cherkasy.

In Army Group South there was an immediate flurry to collect a relieving force, as it was known by experience that the longer the counter-attack was delayed the tighter would be the Russian stranglehold, and the more difficult the task of relief would be. The Führer reserved to himself all major decisions, and the battle was controlled from his desk as he set to work pulling out a division here and a battle group there. He had learned another lesson of war that contradicted everything that he had been preaching over the last year, for 'infantry', so he told Zeitzler, 'were no longer of any use unless they had tanks or assault guns behind them'. Hube's 1 Panzer Army was ordered to end its battle on von Manstein's left and move back again towards the right; Wöhler's 8 Army had to give up von Vormann's 47 Panzer Corps. Von Manstein had apparently arranged that a panzer division was to be released by Hollidt's 6 Army in the Dnieper bend, but Hitler had the division sent back again so that the troops made a round trip of 500 miles and suffered a heavy loss of more than half its vehicles abandoned in the mud, without ever coming into battle.

Wöhler had been ordered to relieve and extricate the two encircled corps but he was allowed to use no initiative and every order came down to him from above. The operation was bungled, and not before 17 February was direct contact made with the two surrounded corps. The Germans claimed to have got 30,000 men out of the besieged pocket, but the same number of men and all vehicles and equipment had been lost. Meanwhile the movement of Hube's 1 Panzer Army from the north had uncovered von Manstein's left flank once more and the right flanking formations of Vatutin's 1 Ukrainian Front moved rapidly westwards into the vacuum, finally reaching a point well inside the 1939 borders of Poland. Koch, the Reich commissioner for the Ukraine, fled from his headquarters at Rovno on the arrival of Red Army troops, and the loss of the town led to the usual recriminations by the Führer against the German Army and the threat of the death sentence on the officers in command.

The Soviet offensive was then taken up again on von Manstein's far right flank when, towards the end of February, Malinovsky's 3 and Tolbukhin's 4 Ukrainian Fronts attacked the exposed salient in the Dnieper bend, held by Hollidt's reformed 6 German Army, the main thrust coming in the area of the void left by Hube's 1 Panzer Army *before* it had started on its gap-plugging shuttle up and down the front. Nikopol and Krivoi Rog fell and the left bank of the Dnieper was cleared. The German troops in the bend were soon in full retreat, and, irrespective of the Führer's will, they were forced to abandon much of their heavy equipment and make off westwards, to avoid encirclement, in the great movement that was eventually to uncover the Crimea. The East Wall, as it extended in the Ukraine and the Tauride plain, had long since been left behind.

Soviet strategy in South Russia and the Ukraine was based on a westwards movement of Kurochkin's 2 Belorussian Front astride the boundary between Army Groups Centre and South along the southern edge of the Pripet marshes towards Kovel and Brest-Litovsk, while, immediately to Kurochkin's south, 1 Ukrainian Front, under the command of Zhukov since Vatutin's death at the hands of Ukrainian nationalist partisans, struck westwards and south-westwards towards the Dniester to push a great wedge between the army groups and outflank von Manstein from the north. Konev's 2 and Malinovsky's 3 Ukrainian Fronts were to move directly south-westwards in the direction of Iasi and Odessa on the Rumanian frontier, in order to envelop Army Group South's right flank, while Tolbukhin's 4 Ukrainian Front prepared to take the Crimea, now isolated from the rest of the German front.

The continuation of this massive offensive was not unexpected by Army Group South, for whereas Hitler was still relying on the mud and Soviet exhaustion to give him some respite, the troops in the field were well aware that the opposing Red Army troops possessed far greater mobility than they did themselves. The Soviet tank and motorized formations were better mechanized than their German counterparts, and whereas the German motorized formations were tied to the roads, the Soviet troops, using great numbers of American four-wheeled drive and six-wheeled drive trucks, were able to operate across country in all but the worst weathers. All German formations, whether motorized or infantry, suffered from a lack of motorization and a shortage of tracks and tractors, and were being worsted at the hands of a more numerous and a more mobile enemy. The retreats in the Ukraine had caused enormous losses in tanks and motor vehicles, these being abandoned for lack of fuel or because they were awaiting repair and could not be moved when the Russians overran the area. Many were lost simply because they could not be got out of the mud. Panzer divisions had become *panje* divisions, relying for supply and movement on horse-drawn carts.*

On 4 March Zhukov attacked and overran Raus's weak 4 Panzer Army on von Manstein's left wing and, a week later, was sixty miles in the German rear. On 5 March Konev's front took up the offensive to the south of Hube's 1 Panzer Army, scattering five extended divisions of a German corps there and was soon in open country moving towards the Rumanian border. Then Zhukov and Konev turned their inner flanks and joined up behind Hube's forces; by 28 March Hube's 1 Panzer Army of sixteen divisions, including six panzer divisions, was surrounded, there being between 200,000 and 300,000 men in the vast pocket.

On 19 March von Manstein and von Kleist had been called from their theatres of operations to Bavaria, merely to attend the presentation to Hitler of a declaration of loyalty, intended as an answer to the propaganda being put out through Moscow by the former German corps commander von Seydlitz-Kurzbach and the communist-sponsored Free Germany Committee. The seriousness of the situation in the Ukraine was as yet apparent to neither von Manstein nor von Kleist, but, even so, they considered that the Führer was out of touch with reality. He declined to sanction the withdrawal of 6 Army to the lower Bug (although it was in fact being fast forced back along the Black Sea coast) partly because the German Navy was insisting that Odessa was essential to supply the Crimea and partly, so he said, to sustain morale in Rumania. He was disinclined to discuss future regrouping that might be necessary should Army Groups Centre and South become separated, and he busied himself with tactical problems that took little account of the real situation.

Hitler had agreed to Hube's proposal that the encircled 1 Panzer Army should break out to the south towards the Black Sea and Rumania; this, however, was contrary to von Manstein's plan that envisaged Hube moving north-westwards in the general direction of Lvov to meet up with 4 Panzer Army and, together with Raus, provide the pivot force needed to maintain contact with Army Group Centre and close the gap north of the Carpathians. On 25 March von Manstein went back to Bavaria to see Hitler once more to get the original order rescinded. The dictator agreed reluctantly, and directed a SS corps of two divisions to be withdrawn from France to assist Hube in the break-out, but not before he had heaped upon von Manstein charges that the German Army was running away without a fight.

On 2 April an ultimatum, said to have been from Zhukov, was received at Hube's headquarters, threatening that if all armed resistance did not cease by nightfall one-third of all German troops subsequently surrendering would be shot out of hand. A second ultimatum followed immediately on the first, saying that all German officers failing to surrender immediately would be shot on capture.

The encircled 1 Panzer Army in the area of Kamenets-Podolskiy began its march, becoming in effect a moving pocket. As it was impossible to ration so large a force by air, it was ordered to live off the country, and only ammunition,

---

* From the Polish *panje* cart used extensively by German divisions, including the motorized divisions, for supply.

vehicle fuel, tank spare parts and medical supplies were flown in from airfields near Lvov by a transport force of Junkers 52 and Heinkel 111 planes diverted from its primary task of assisting in the supply of 17 Army in the Crimea. No German fighters could be spared for escorts, and, as the Red Air Force was very active by day, most supply sorties were flown by night. As the encircled pocket was continually on the move, frequent problems were to arise as to the selection and preparation of landing strips and dropping zones. Although landings were in fact made, most of the supplies were air-dropped, this meaning that, as very few wounded could be evacuated, hospital cases had to be transported with the moving pocket. Few German aircraft were lost as the Red Air Force failed to realize how important it was to destroy the German despatching airfields.

Eventually, by 9 April, the whole of Hube's force, after a march of 150 miles, joined up with 4 Panzer Army in the area of Tarnopol, but its equipment and most of its heavy weapons were lost. Nor had 4 Panzer Army been able to establish a defence line to stem the onrush of Soviet troops, and both Hube's and Raus's men were to continue to give ground immediately after joining up.

Hitler's most recent contribution to the direction of the fighting was the selection, off the map, of nodal points of road or rail traffic, and these were classed as strongholds that were to serve as breakwaters to slow down the Red flood. Each was stocked with ammunition and supplies and a commander was appointed who had to answer with his life for the holding of the place. But these strongholds and bastions had little effect on the course of the fighting since they were, in the first instance, bypassed by Soviet troops, and too much of the *Wehrmacht* was wastefully locked up in these garrisons. Tarnopol itself was such a besieged fortress, but it soon became a liability for the *Luftwaffe* transport force that had to supply it, since the Tarnopol ring became a collecting point for Red Army anti-aircraft units. Tarnopol fell as early as 15 April with the loss of its commander and most of its garrison.

On 30 March 1944 von Manstein was awakened at his Lvov headquarters by the surprising news that Hitler's Condor aircraft was about to land, with von Kleist already on board, in order to take the two field-marshals to Obersalzberg, there to be relieved of their commands. Their replacements, Model and Schörner, were both in the Führer's favour and were men of the hour, Model having gained further credit by the energy of his defence with Army Group North; Schörner had come to the Führer's notice as a corps commander in the Krivoi Rog and Nikopol battles. Schörner's enthusiasm for the Führer was such that he had then been selected as the Chief of National Socialist Guidance in the OKH. With the arrival of the new commanders both army groups were then renamed, Army Group South as North Ukraine, while Army Group A became Army Group South Ukraine. Lindemann replaced Model in command of Army Group North.

Except in the Crimea there followed a lull in operations over the whole of the eastern front as the Red Army regrouped, waiting for the ground to dry out, and prepared for the late spring and early summer offensives that were to coincide with the Second Front in Western Europe. Finland was still in the war, as it had been unable to obtain terms from the USSR that it could bear, but elsewhere the Red Army had been victorious and had closed up to the Baltic States, Poland, Czechoslovakia and Rumania, and was not far removed from the 1939 borders of the USSR.

The final in the succession of German defeats in the Ukraine was probably the greatest of them all. The Crimea continued to be held at Hitler's insistence on political and military grounds', his arguments being based on the likely reaction of Turkey and Rumania to the giving up of the peninsula, and the possible loss of air and sea control over the Black Sea that would result from this. Antonescu, the Rumanian dictator, on the other hand, opposed staying in the Crimea and had already served notice on Hitler that he wanted to withdraw the Rumanian troops there.

By April Jaenecke's 17 Army in the Crimea consisted of two German corps made up of five German and six Rumanian infantry divisions and one German flak division, with no armour except for two assault gun units. It was reckoned in the Crimea that roughly eighty days would be needed for a systematic withdrawal of Axis troops, of which at least twenty-three days would be taken in shipping out the 270,000 men, but, because of Hitler's order that the Crimea would be held indefinitely and that no contingency plans were to be drawn up for a withdrawal, no joint planning had been held between the army and navy to cover such an emergency. Jaenecke and the *Luftwaffe* commander Deichmann had, however, on their own responsibility and at some personal risk, begun parallel planning inside 17 Army and 1 Air Corps for a withdrawal to Sevastopol and an evacuation thereafter. 17 Army had for some time been supplied by air and sea without any real interference from the Red Air Force or Navy, but Jaenecke still hoped that a German counter-offensive in the Ukraine might re-establish the land-bridge.

The German troops in the Crimea had long been conscious of a feeling of isolation, and even the simplest soldier was well aware of the vulnerability of the peninsula and of his own perilous situation. The previous autumn it had been understood that the Führer intended to evacuate the Crimea, and in consequence the necessary arrangements had been made to pull back westwards from the Kerch peninsula. On the evening of 29 October 1943 the divisional commander of 98 Infantry Division had actually given out his orders for the withdrawal to begin the next day; then, a few hours later, he had been called to corps headquarters to receive counter-orders that the German force would remain where it was, for the Führer had just decreed that the Crimea would not be given up. It was, commented the divisional commander, like the 1941 winter in front of Moscow all over again, stop and go, backwards and forwards, uncertainty and doubt. And in the following April the division was still in the line.

Schörner paid 17 Army a fleeting visit — his first — at the beginning of April, and, although it was known that the Crimea was about to come under very heavy attack, he reported back to the OKH that everything was in the best of order there, with no cause for anxiety, a view that was not shared by Jaenecke or Zeitzler. By the evening of 9 April, however, Schörner had changed his mind entirely and, expressing confidence in 17 Army, he asked that Jaenecke should have freedom to act as he thought fit, *even though this should result in the giving up of the Crimea*, as Schörner now thought that it would. Hitler refused but said 'that he would send Zeitzler down to Galicia'. The next afternoon Schörner reported that Jaenecke had already ordered 5 Corps to pull back some distance from the Kerch bridge-head to a more favourable position to the rear, a decision that he, Schörner, supported to the full. In the circumstances Hitler was obliged to accept this withdrawal, but he did so with very bad grace; he ordered that there were to be no more withdrawals and that the 49 Corps, on the Perekop isthmus, was to remain where it was, come what may. That same day, on 10 April, Schörner was pressing for the complete evacuation of the Crimea without delay.

The Crimea was by then under attack by Tolbukhin's 4 Ukrainian Front attacking southwards, not only down the Perekop isthmus but also across the very shallow lagoons of the Lazy Sea, while Eremenko's Independent Coast Army, controlled directly from Moscow, broke out of the Kerch bridge-head, the Soviet force consisting of thirty-two divisions and 500 tanks, in all half a million men. On 11 April 49 German Corps had already been outflanked across the Lazy Sea, and Tolbukhin's tanks were streaming southwards, racing across the steppe for Simferopol. Meanwhile the Führer, from his distant retreat in the Bavarian Berghof, was still forbidding any withdrawal from Perekop. He could have had no conception as to the effects on the troops on the ground of his erratic war direction.

As a concession Hitler eventually permitted a further withdrawal of 5 Corps in front of Eremenko's forces, back to the Theodosia narrows. But such withdrawals could not of course be carried out successfully on snap decisions from the high command, for a decision given too late and in the absence of earlier planning for such a contingency, led, almost inevitably, to the loss of heavy equipment and guns, followed at the next defensive position by the dispersal or routing of the fighting troops who, without artillery support, ammunition or anti-tank guns, broke and ran under Soviet tank attack. To call German formations 'divisions' and 'regiments' was merely a self-deception, for a grenadier regiment of 98 Infantry Division had 200 men in the line, barely a tenth of what it had in 1941. And not many of these were infantry, since many men in the firing line were not infantry by arm of service or by training, being orderlies, clerks, drivers, signallers and artillerymen. These could not be compared with the old infantrymen, now dead or disabled, but they were in fact the hard core, the only remaining reliable fighting element. And before these fighting men could break contact and withdraw, the wounded, the Rumanians, the *Hiwis*, what could be moved of the flak and the baggage, had to go, together with every other unit not vital to the forward area.*

When, on Easter Monday the 10th April, 98 Infantry Division was suddenly told that it was to withdraw *that night*, the horses, without which nothing could be moved, were still twenty miles to the rear. There was very little motor transport available, and so it was decided that the only equipment that could be carried would be that on the man. At seven o'clock the regimental gun and heavy weapons companies destroyed their infantry guns and anti-tank guns and mortars, and marched into the darkness pursued by enemy tanks and motorized infantry. Shortly afterwards units and sub-units lost contact as many of them were routed and broken up. On 13 April one of the infantry battalions was down to fewer than thirty men, to which thirty stragglers from other units had attached themselves. A regimental heavy support company had nothing left but one heavy and three light machine-guns.

The defence had by then fallen apart and Jaenecke ordered a general withdrawal back to Sevastopol, an order that Hitler tried to countermand, saying that Jaenecke had lost his nerve. The commander of 49 Corps was dismissed by a Führer order, an order that was ignored as that unfortunate officer continued to try to collect and rally his broken troops. On 12 April Hitler had finally to agree to what was already happening, a withdrawal to Sevastopol, and he had even conceded that

---

* *Hiwis* were Russian prisoners of war who had volunteered for duty as unarmed auxiliaries with the German Army. They usually formed the labour and transport force.

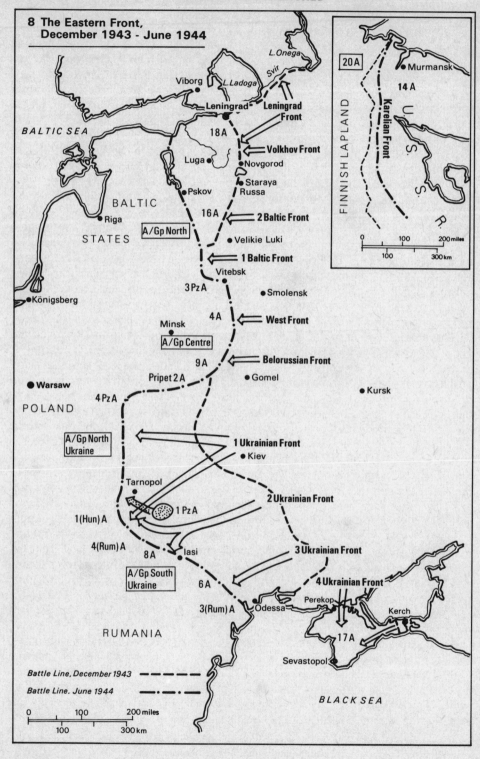

8 The Eastern Front, December 1943 - June 1944

L. Onega

Viborg   L. Ladoga   Svir

Leningrad   **Leningrad Front**

BALTIC SEA   18 A

Luga   Novgorod   **Volkhov Front**

Staraya Russa

Pskov

BALTIC

16 A   **2 Baltic Front**

Riga

STATES   A/Gp North

Velikie Luki

1 Baltic Front

Vitebsk

Königsberg   3 Pz A   Smolensk

4 A   **West Front**

Minsk

A/Gp Centre

9 A   **Belorussian Front**

Pripet 2 A   Gomel   Kursk

Warsaw   4 Pz A

POLAND

A/Gp North Ukraine   **1 Ukrainian Front**

Kiev

Tarnopol

2 Ukrainian Front

1(Hun) A   1 Pz A

4(Rum) A   8 A   Iasi   **3 Ukrainian Front**

A/Gp South Ukraine   **4 Ukrainian Front**

6 A   Perekop   Kerch

3(Rum) A   Odessa

17 A

RUMANIA

Sevastopol

Battle Line, December 1943 — — —

Battle Line, June 1944 — · — ·

0   100   200 miles

100   300 km

BLACK SEA

Inset:

20 A   Murmansk

14 A

FINNISH LAPLAND   Karelian Front   U. S. S. R.

0   100   200 miles

100   300 km

'elements not required for battle should be shipped out'. Sevastopol, however, was to be held 'for the time being'. Zeitzler was saying, quite openly, that Sevastopol could not be held and he was warning Schörner that if he did not bestir himself, then Russian tanks might be in Sevastopol before him.

On 21 April Schörner was forced to follow the path that so many of his predecessors had trod when he made the painful flight to the Berghof to persuade Hitler that the Crimea should be given up; but he was put off with the persuasive charm reserved for newcomers to high command who were temporarily in favour. He was told that Sevastopol had to be held for eight weeks until the Anglo-Americans 'had made their attempt to land in Europe'. In any case the holding of Sevastopol was of paramount importance in keeping Turkey out of the war, since the Turks were already submitting to western pressure to cut off supplies of chrome to Germany. The usual hollow promises of equipment and reinforcements followed, and Schörner came back empty-handed. Hitler was obliged, however, in response to repeated requests from Antonescu, to begin the evacuation of the Rumanian troops from the Crimea.

In Sevastopol the disorganized remnants of the divisions had been set to work on the defences. Morale was surprisingly good, even optimistic. The men were certain that when the German naval, *Luftwaffe* and administrative organization had been shipped off after the Rumanians, the German fighting troops would follow. Fourteen days should see the last man away. The troops were not worried about likely enemy interference with shipping because they were convinced that the *Luftwaffe* and the German Navy would not leave them in the lurch. On 24 April they were informed of the Führer's order that Sevastopol would be held to the last, and all of them knew that it was their death sentence. That same day Jaenecke, a survivor of Stalingrad, flew to Hitler, with whom he had two painful and stormy meetings. An angry and vindictive Führer removed him from his command.

The last Soviet offensive began on 5 May and two days later the Russians had broken into the town. The German troops withdrew westwards, covered by rearguards, on to the open Chersones peninsula, in the hope of being picked up from the sea. On 9 May the Führer changed his mind once more and ordered all German troops to be brought off, but by then nothing more could be done. On 10 May a dozen remaining *Luftwaffe* fighters took off for the last time and disappeared towards the mainland. That same day, as an exaggerated version of the latest Führer order reached the disorganized masses on the heavily bombed and shelled beaches, it was rumoured that a *Luftwaffe* group and a great fleet of ships were being sent to their rescue. Nothing came.

The permanent losses to 17 German Army in the Crimea were its total equipment and, so it has been computed, about sixty to seventy thousand men, a great loss by the early 1944 standards, a loss hitherto exceeded only at Stalingrad and Tunis. By the end of May 1944 the German casualties in the east stood at nearly one and a quarter million dead and over half a million missing; the wounded or sick discharged as totally unfit for further service amounted to another quarter of a million men.*

---

* The wounded since June 1941 totalled more than three million, although most returned to duty, and some, included in this figure, had been wounded more than once.

CHAPTER SIX

The Second Front

Hitler had decided, as early as March 1942, that the defence of Western Europe should be based on coastal fortifications, and so, during 1943, the building of the Atlantic Wall on the Channel and the Atlantic coasts had continued apace amid the glare and blare of a publicity that appeared to have been aimed at frightening the enemy and deterring him from even attempting an invasion. The scattered defences were steadily developed into a series of fortresses, strongpoints and resistance centres incorporating coastal artillery and heavily concreted emplacements, while the shores and part of the tidal beaches were mined and covered with landing-craft obstacles. The defence preparations in the fortresses were indeed impressive, but they covered only the major ports that might be of use to the enemy, Ijmuiden, the Hook of Holland, Dunkirk, Boulogne, Le Havre, Cherbourg, St Malo, Brest, Lorient, St Nazaire, and the mouth of the Gironde; the intervening areas between these fortresses were often only lightly fortified, or sometimes were not defended at all. There was a serious shortage of materials, particularly of cement, which was, from the spring of 1944, rationed by the OKW, and there was also a dearth of labour, particularly in those deserted areas where there was no civilian population that could be recruited for work.

After the war von Rundstedt, the Commander-in-Chief West, called the Atlantic Wall a gigantic bluff; there is some truth in this, although this is not exactly what he told Hitler at the time. For in his report at the end of October 1943 he explained that the Wall could not be *defended* by the troops at his disposal, but only *covered*; nor could he guarantee even to cover the Atlantic coastline south of the Loire, since he could only keep it under observation. The permanent fortifications, von Rundstedt continued, were 'indispensable and valuable for battle as well as for propaganda'; but he went on to qualify their value in that 'as a rigid German defence was impossible there for any length of time, the outcome of the battle must depend on the use of a mobile and armoured reserve'. Hitler, however, regarded the situation somewhat differently in that he foresaw the coastal fortresses and strongpoints holding out almost indefinitely, and he was, at about this time, ordering that the strongpoints should be stocked with eight months' ammunition and supplies.

The enemy in the west, with his overwhelming air and sea supremacy, had strategic superiority almost everywhere, so that Germany no longer enjoyed the so-called operative freedom that it had had in the First World War. Von Buttlar, the head of the army department of Jodl's *Wehrmachtführungsstab*, wrote in February 1944:

> We are conducting the strategic defence of Fortress Europe without, however, having any of the advantages of fighting on interior lines, in that the enemy has numerous uncommitted forces in the Mediterranean, the Middle and Near East, Africa, America, England and Iceland, all of which are ready to land directly into Europe; and meanwhile they pin to the ground a great part |sic| of our reserves.*

In truth virtually *all* the OKW forces were committed to defensive tasks and the reserves no longer existed.

The Anglo-American intelligence deception measures, mainly in the United Kingdom, had been widespread and comprehensive, laying a great deal of emphasis on the creation of an enormous radio network representing a large number of non-existent higher headquarters and divisions, in reality a handful of staff officers and wireless operators, backed up by some scattered units, detached for the purpose, together with a quantity of dummy equipment; these gave the ghost radio formations some appearance of substance in case *Luftwaffe* air reconnaissance planes should arrive over the area. By now German intelligence was badly served both by the *Luftwaffe* and by agents in the United Kingdom, who were in any case virtually non-existent, so that *Fremde Heere West*, for lack of other material, came to rely very heavily on signal intelligence, that source which, if uncorroborated, is most likely to deceive the recipient.

In consequence German intelligence and the OKW grossly over-estimated the enemy forces in the United Kingdom. There was believed to be a heavy concentration of troops around the Firth of Forth in Scotland that the Führer saw as a threat to Norway.** Force 'Anderson', under the general formerly in command of 1 British Army in North Africa, was thought to be in Essex and Suffolk, waiting to cross to the Netherlands; and later, by midsummer 1944, Force 'Patton' was believed to be forming up in Kent and about to cross over to the Pas de Calais. The 1942 Dieppe raid and operation *Starkey* of the previous autumn had served as a further pointer that the Pas de Calais and the Somme were where the allies might make their main effort.

These indicators affected, however, only part of Hitler's strategic appreciation of the defence of Fortress Europe. Political and economic factors had to be taken into account and he was often a prey to his own obsessions. The dictator thought an attack on Norway *possible*, but only as a diversionary operation, since the distance from the United Kingdom would preclude both early allied fighter cover over the area and also a rapid enemy build-up. He believed an invasion of Portugal *feasible* since it was without risk to the allies, and so he had the *Luftwaffe* draw up a plan ready for reprisal bombings on Lisbon should the Portuguese fail to resist the landings. The allies might of course seal off the Iberian peninsula by invading South-West France from both the Mediterranean and from the Bay of Biscay. But this too, so the dictator thought, would be a subsidiary to a main landing and would be designed to make the OKW disperse its forces. A landing in Jutland or the German Bight he reckoned to be unlikely at this time since it offered none of the political or economic advantages to be expected from a landing in Norway or Iberia, while militarily it would be more difficult to undertake. A direct attack on

---

* *Notiz WFStab/Op(H)* 13.2.44 (*KTB des OKW, Vol. IV I*). p.80).

**_Fremde Heere West_ identified this as 4 British Army of twelve divisions. As a result Hitler kept a force of 30 coastal U-boats at Bergen for anti-invasion duty.

105

the Atlantic coast was not probable. He believed the Netherlands to be a likely landing place, as, of course, was the French Mediterranean coast. Even more probable were Brittany and Normandy, particularly Normandy, but, even so, he was fully aware of the restrictions likely to be placed on the allies by the range of most of their single-engined fighters and by what he supposed to be their need for the early capture of ports to supply their forces after they had landed; for he was not to know that his enemies could largely overcome this latter problem by the use of artificial harbours and underwater pipelines.

According to Hitler's summing-up of the likely enemy strategy, the Anglo-Americans would first make widely scattered landings from Normandy to Norway—merely as diversionary operations prior to *the main landing in the Pas de Calais*. For the Pas de Calais, although heavily fortified and banked by cliffs and although it had no large ports, had the tactical benefit of a short air and sea haul and a weighty strategic advantage in that it opened directly into Belgium and the Reich. This prediction of the pattern of the allied invasion, that is to say one or more subsidiary landings on the western perimeter of Fortress Europe followed by the main blow across the Straits of Dover, became a not to be questioned Hitler-Jodl *premise*, fully accepted by the field-marshals in the west. This was to result in large German forces being kept idle in the Pas de Calais long after the invasion had taken place.

During 1943 the coastal defences in France had been much improved but, as against this, the real fighting strength in the west had fallen. For, after the Anglo-American landing in North Africa in November 1942 had removed the immediate danger of a Second Front in Europe, France had become the troop reservoir for the eastern front and for elsewhere. The German occupation of Vichy France in November 1942 and the internment of 4 Italian Army on the French Mediterranean coast in September 1943 had further increased von Rundstedt's responsibilities. By the end of August 1943 Army Group West had already reached the lowest point in its strength, only thirty-eight divisions in all.

By the autumn of 1943 the staff of the OKW and Army Group West were again aware of the rapidly growing threat of an invasion of Western Europe and what this would mean; the OKW diarist recorded that the fighting in Italy was in many respects tougher and more bitter than that experienced on the Russian front, and he concluded that the fighting in France would be the same. Blumentritt, von Rundstedt's chief of staff, had drawn Jodl's attention to the fact that German divisions were unfitted for a war of movement and were in no way comparable with Anglo-American divisions, since these were the finest equipped that the world had ever seen. Blumentritt included a list of the forty-seven divisions that had been removed from the west during the last year, and he pointed out the danger of a landing, in that the Pas de Calais was not 150 miles from the borders of the Reich. Blumentritt's letter resulted in absolute priority being given to Army Group West over all other theatres including the eastern front, and this had enabled von Rundstedt's forces to be built up steadily throughout the winter and spring until they reached their peak strength in June 1944. Even so, von Rundstedt had been ordered to send some divisions to the east in the spring to assist in extricating Hube's 1 Panzer Army, and for the temporary occupation of Hungary to prevent that unhappy country from going out of the war. For although Hitler, in an expansive moment, had once said that he intended to create a central mobile panzer reserve of twenty-five divisions for use in either east or west, he was never in a position to boast of *any* reserve at all. The best that he could do was to move a SS corps of perhaps two divisions from west to east and back again, but even these hardly constituted an OKW reserve since, except for periods of rail movement *en route*, they were nearly always in the fighting line. Meanwhile, although the German strength stood at about 285 nominal divisions, Jodl and Zeitzler quarrelled over the allocation of even a single division, since this was all they had to form either an OKW or an OKH reserve.

Although the Second Front was expected at any time after mid February, von Rundstedt's Army Group West presented a very untidy picture. The naval forces under Krancke, the Admiral Commanding Group West, were entirely independent of the German Army and took their orders from Dönitz in Berlin; they consisted, however, of only a few destroyers, about thirty motor torpedo-boats and about 300 minesweepers and picquet and patrol boats, and these had to hug the safety of the French coast since they were entirely outclassed by Royal Navy Channel flotillas and were frequently under air attack. The Atlantic U-boats, based on Lorient and Bordeaux, and the fifty coastal U-boats in the Bay of Biscay of *Gruppe Landwirt* intended for anti-invasion duty in the Channel, were largely independent of Krancke. Krancke did, however, control the naval-manned coastal artillery and the large shore-based installations numbering nearly 100,000 men, and these became a bone of contention between the army and the naval staffs, since the navy resisted what it considered to be army dictation on the matter of coastal defence and was reluctant to find naval ratings to take part in the ground battle under the local army command.

The flying component of the *Luftwaffe* came under Sperrle's 3 Air Fleet, whose headquarters, like Krancke's, was at Paris. Sperrle's command consisted of only 400 bombers and about 300 fighters and was responsible directly to Göring. Air defence artillery, equipped for the most part with 88 mm dual purpose guns particularly suitable in an anti-tank role, were also part of Sperrle's responsibility. The *Luftwaffe* strength was nearly 340,000 men of a *Wehrmacht* total in the west of 1,400,000, but, of this number, about 100,000 were flak troops and 30,000 belonged to the ground force parachute divisions.

Von Rundstedt was by no means master in his own house even when it came to the ground fighting. Parachute, flak and SS divisions could be allocated to him or taken away again by Göring or Himmler, although this was normally done through the OKW; these troops on tactical loan were disciplined, trained, equipped and administered by the *Luftwaffe* and the SS. The army panzer and panzer grenadier formations, although under von Rundstedt's command, had been allocated from Guderian's domain, and both army and SS motorized formations were often removed from von Rundstedt's control in that they were frozen as part of the OKW reserve and could be committed only to tasks designed or approved by the Führer, with Guderian at his side. On 5 November 1943 came the crowning indignity when, by a special Führer order, Rommel, together with his own army group headquarters, was commissioned by Hitler to make an inspection of coastal defences, firstly in Jutland and then in Army Group West—in the Pas de Calais and Somme, followed by the Cotentin in Normandy, then the Netherlands and Brittany—this Army Group West priority of inspection being Hitler's order of invasion probabilities. Rommel was to be directly under the Führer's command and was to make his inspection report personally to the dictator.

Von Rundstedt's operational command consisted of the *Luftwaffe* general

Christiansen's Armed Forces Netherlands, administered directly by the OKW, von Salmuth's 15 Army covering the Channel coast from Belgium to the Orne (in central Normandy), Dollmann's 7 Army in west Normandy and Brittany, von der Chevallerie's 1 Army covering the Atlantic coast south of Brittany, while von Sodenstern's 19 Army defended the Mediterranean littoral from Spain to Italy. A central panzer reserve, Geyr von Schweppenburg's Panzer Group West, had its headquarters near Paris. By the end of May von Rundstedt's overall command stood at fifty-nine divisions, of which ten were panzer or panzer grenadier, twenty-three were static divisions and six were reserve basic training formations.* The centre of gravity was in the north against the English Channel, the largest number of divisions having been allocated to 15 Army covering Flanders, Artois, Picardy and the mouth of the Seine.

The responsibility for the internal security of the rearward areas in the west was largely out of von Rundstedt's hands in that it was delegated to the military governors, von Stülpnagel for the larger part of France, and von Falkenhausen for Belgium and the French departments near the Belgian frontier, both being subordinate to the OKW and with responsibilities to Himmler and von Ribbentrop. The civil administration throughout the whole of France was controlled, at the German dictation, by the Vichy régime, except that the coastal twenty mile-wide belt could, at von Rundstedt's discretion, be put under military control. The costs of the German occupation were paid for by the French economy, and French industry was geared to the needs of the Reich. Over a million French prisoners of war were still in Germany, the Jewish population had been rounded up, and a half a million French citizens had been sent to Germany, many of them as forced labour.** The system of Vichy government was by direct rule, without parliamentary representation, by Pétain, the eighty-four year old State President, and Laval, his President of the Council.

The resistance movement in the old occupied zone was relatively weak compared with the nationalist movements in the former unoccupied zone; there, in the south, these nationalists made up the bulk of the Secret Army, but this did not include the communists or L'Action Franco-Anglaise directed by the French expatriates in the United Kingdom. The Secret Army was believed by the Germans to have strong links with the French labour service, with retired French ex-servicemen, and with the French police; for whereas the gendarmerie co-operated 'reasonably well' with the Germans against British agents, it was thought that 'they could have been more diligent' in unearthing resistance elsewhere.

A German counter-intelligence operation in October 1943 had rounded up 300 men, of whom thirty-four were British officers, with a great haul of weapons, but since the enemy were believed to be sending out up to 100 air sorties a night, with

---

* The deployment of the German ground forces divisions (including SS and Luftwaffe) at the end of May 1944 was as follows:

East	Finland	Norway	Denmark	West	Italy	Balkans	Total
157	7	12	3	54	27	25	285

In the west there were 23 static, 19 infantry, 1 security, 8 panzer and 2 panzer grenadier and 6 reserve divisions.

** In January 1944 the German Labour Service (GBA) had wanted to raise a further million forced labourers from France and a half a million from Belgium and Holland. Von Rundstedt, Keitel and even Himmler had recommended that this be postponed until the invasion attempt 'clarified itself', since further large scale levies would drive these people into the terrorist organizations!

fresh agents and equipment, it was reckoned in Rastenburg that the British would soon replace this destroyed network. The communists overlapped and were independent of other organizations, occupying themselves with terrorist attacks against those French thought to be friendly to the Germans, tactics later adopted also by the Secret Army and the *Maquis*, members of which, in broad daylight and in uniform, shot Vichy officials by firing squad on the market squares, attacked Gestapo convoys to release French prisoners, and even, on 8 March 1944, attacked a company of German soldiers on its way to a cinema in Clermont-Ferrand.*

Most terrorist incidents took place in Savoy, Aix, the Ardennes and, to a lesser extent, in the areas of Dijon, Avignon and Limoges. In Belgium the White Army resistance was smaller and more tightly controlled, but it was well organized and effective.

Yet the terrorist attacks by the resistance movements before May 1944 were no great security problem to the German occupation force, because few of them were directed against military targets. In this phase the resistance activity was primarily against French collaborators, about ninety attacks being recorded in the first ten days of February alone, these not including threats or attempted reprisals that victims did not dare to report for fear of further revenge. The OKW realized that the attacks represented only a tiny fraction of the potential of the resistance movements, since most of their members were lying low awaiting the more favourable opportunities that would be offered by an allied invasion in the west; the OKW diarist recorded that a successful landing would alter everything, even the attitude of the Vichy officials and the hitherto 'loyal' police. Meanwhile foreign arms were flooding into the country.

Many of the resistance networks, including those controlled from the United Kingdom, had been penetrated by the Gestapo, and the daily radio messages from Britain to the field networks were intercepted and decoded; no action was being taken for the moment against known resistance groups because of the serious loss of intelligence cover and information that would result. In March, however, the Führer was tempted to have a clean up by mass arrests, not to improve the security of von Rundstedt's forces, but, entering into the realms of psychological warfare, 'to let the enemy know the extent to which his organization was compromised and force the allies to postpone the invasion!'. It was finally decided to defer this action until immediately before the invasion in order to dismay the enemy at the very last moment. This opportunity never came, although Himmler did manage to arrest and intern a large number of retired senior French officers believed to be in contact with the Secret Army. Meanwhile von Rundstedt instructed his troops 'to be ready with reprisal measures'.

The main threat to the German defenders in the early spring came from the allied air attacks on airfields and on railways everywhere across North France and Belgium, but being particularly heavy in the areas between Rouen and Paris and between Calais and Brussels. In February, 277 locomotives were out of action, rising to 508 in March, although many of these, the Germans were convinced, had been damaged by railway workers—even by their own crews—since the drivers saw no virtue in risking their lives by moving trains to keep Germany in the war. The whole French railway system became entirely unreliable and more than ten thousand uniformed German railway supervisors were brought in from the Reich.

* The *Maquis* were Frenchmen who had taken to the hills and the woods, particularly in South-East France, to escape the forced labour call-up. They soon assumed a military organization.

Track damage could not be repaired due to the difficulty in moving materials, and von Rundstedt asked for OKW permission to withdraw 60,000 Todt labour workers from the Atlantic Wall to keep the railway bed in repair. By the beginning of May there was a blockage or backlog of 1,600 trains, and all main lines had to be reserved for German use while the French economy was relegated to subsidiary back routes. In April *Wehrmacht* troop leave had been cancelled in order to relieve the strain on the railways.

From 27 April the enemy air forces attacked coastal defences for the first time, at first from Calais, working westwards, and then all along the coast. In the six days before 21 May, fifty-three main defensive complexes were attacked between Calais and Cherbourg; in spite of the weight of the attacks the material damage inflicted was light and the military casualties numbered in all no more than 130 men.

When Field-Marshal Rommel had completed his tour of inspection the Führer made the extraordinary decision to incorporate Rommel's headquarters into the von Rundstedt command in the west, interposing Army Group B between von Rundstedt's Army Group D and 7 and 15 Armies on the Channel coast.* Although it was certainly not unknown for one army group to be under the operational control of the commander of another army group, the most unusual feature of this reorganization was that, according to the order of 15 January, Rommel was to have only *tactical* control over the two armies, his control being limited to the coastal belt that stretched from 400 yards below high water level to six miles behind the shore. Any measures that involved *operative* movement, particularly the movement of motorized divisions, could only be done through von Rundstedt, the Commander-in-Chief West. Von Rundstedt was to remain responsible for the organization, training, equipping and supply of Rommel's two armies, while Rommel 'was to keep close contact with Krancke and Sperrle, referring any difficulties to von Rundstedt'. In the same order, all motorized divisions in the theatre were put under the direct command of Geyr von Schweppenburg's Panzer Group West, whose command had the same standing as that of a panzer army and came directly under von Rundstedt. This arrangement suited the Führer in that he had injected new ideas and now had a second military opinion that could be used as a check against von Rundstedt; he had, moreover, effected yet another split in the military command.

That either of these two field-marshals should have accepted such an unorthodox and unworkable command arrangement in the first place is remarkable. Shortly afterwards, however, von Rundstedt began to complain that his authority was being restricted by Rommel's presence, while Rommel was not slow in bringing his own dissatisfaction directly to the Führer's notice. He disagreed with von Rundstedt's concept of the coming battle, for von Rundstedt, harking back to the halcyon days of 1940, intended to destroy the enemy after he reached open country by the fast moving encircling operations of his panzer reserve. Rommel was convinced that the enemy air strength would be such that the German motorized formations would be pinned to the ground by day and would have little or no

---

* Army Group D headquarters also formed Army Command West.

freedom of movement in the short summer nights; in consequence, said Rommel, the Anglo-Americans *must* be destroyed on the beaches; for if the enemy could not be held at the Atlantic Wall, then 'not only the campaign but the whole war would be lost'. For this reason Rommel wanted the panzer formations allotted to his control and sited right forward near the coast where they could come into action within hours of the first enemy soldier coming ashore. After Hitler had heard his complaints in an interview at Klessheim on 20 March, the dictator was temporarily won over to many of Rommel's views and he concluded that Rommel must be allotted part of von Rundstedt's armour, but Hitler added a surprising postscript that Rommel should also be given some responsibility for 1 and 19 Armies (on the Atlantic and Mediterranean coasts) in matters of coastal defence. This bad compromise completely undermined von Rundstedt's position, and was still not enough for Rommel, who continued to press for the whole of the armoured reserve to be sited in the forward areas.

This brought remonstrations from von Rundstedt once more, and the Führer then went back on his previous ruling, deciding this time in favour of the Commander West, in that the *Panzer Gruppe* and *AOK 1* and *AOK 19* were not to be put under Rommel, although it was understood that Rommel 'should have an inspector's brief there'. But the best was yet to come when Hitler decided that 'Rommel should take overall command where the enemy landed'—and if the enemy should first land in South France then 1 and 19 Armies would immediately become Rommel's command, *leaving von Rundstedt to command in the north.** The OKW diarist added what appears to be an understatement that 'some confusion and duplication in command appears unavoidable because of this arrangement, but this has been taken into account'. Meanwhile Rommel was instructed to show himself publicly in the south of France, and numerous formation billeting parties were directed into 1 and 19 Army areas to earmark accommodation for troop movement that was not intended and for formations that did not exist. The object, once again, was merely to hide the lack of troops in the south and frighten off the enemy.

All this was little to von Rundstedt's liking, and he countered by suggesting a new headquarters for the south to exercise tactical control over the two armies there, and *Armee Gruppe Blaskowitz* came into being.** For the moment, however, this did not alter the very confusing high command arrangements for the west.

Meanwhile Rommel continued his whirlwind tours of inspection, improving the beach defences with a new mining and beach obstacle programme, and he did much, so it was believed at the OKW, to improve the morale and self-confidence of the defenders. At the beginning of May the Führer was of the opinion that the enemy would not make a wide landing along the breadth of the Channel coast but would seize only a limited beach-head 'in Dieppe fashion', and, if it failed, the enemy 'would call it a raid'. The dictator first came to believe that this landing would be near Brest or Cherbourg, but afterwards decided, with an intuitive eye, that the *first* enemy landing would be in 7 Army area on the Cotentin peninsula. The Commander-in-Chief West was instructed on exactly how this area was to be reinforced and he was ordered to dig everything in there, including the horses. By

* OKW war diary entries 2 and 3 April 1944.

**An *Armee Gruppe* is not a *Heeresgruppe* (army group) but is a headquarters intermediate between an army and an army group.

the end of May it had come to Rommel's knowledge, presumably from an air photograph, that the enemy's landing exercises were no longer taking place on the flood-tide but on the ebb-tide, and this reinforced the defender's need to site obstacles even lower than at the low water level mark. Time was not to allow this, however, and on 6 June the German defences rarely stretched for more than 400 yards below high water mark, and then only in a few selected areas.

Rommel himself was of the same opinion as the Führer in that he regarded von Salmuth's 15 Army sector as the most likely for the main landing, and he presumably agreed with Hitler that the Cherbourg peninsula landing, if made at all, would be only a diversion, an attempt by the enemy to draw German reserves into Normandy before making the main landing in the Pas de Calais that would cut off Army Group West from its supply base in the Reich.

Rommel had succeeded in extracting from von Rundstedt three panzer divisions (21 Pz., 116 Pz. and 2 Pz.) to form his own army group reserve, and these were deployed along the 15 Army sector between Caen and Amiens, about twenty to thirty miles back from the coast. The only other motorized divisions remaining in the north (1 S S Pz. Corps with 17 S S Pz. Gren., 12 S S Pz. Gren., the *Panzer Lehr* and 1 S S Pz.) remained in the second line and about fifty miles from the coast, and were scattered across the front from the Lower Loire to north of Brussels; these divisions, part of Panzer Group West, had been removed from O B West and were in O K W reserve, so that von Rundstedt was left with no armoured reserve under his own hand in the early hours of 6 June.*

The night of 5 June was one of heavy seas and strong winds and, as the German meteorological stations had no distant Atlantic weather stations, it was wrongly believed that the bad weather would continue over the next few days. Yet the radio intercept of resistance messages from the U K indicated that an invasion was imminent and picquet boats could hear the engines of Royal Naval minesweepers offshore; then, after midnight, the landing of enemy parachutists was reported in the rear areas. As against this, the French population and its resistance organization was entirely quiet, and the naval reconnaissance that put to sea from Cherbourg returned some hours later to report that they had found no enemy activity or presence at sea. Not until the landings began 'between 0300 and 0330' on the ebb-tide, supported by the heavy gunfire of enemy naval units, was it accepted that an invasion had begun.** Rommel was at his home in Swabia that night and a number of other formation commanders were away from their posts on leave or on detached duty.

The allied invasion of Normandy was carried out by a naval landing force of 1,200 warships, of which nearly eighty per cent were British and Canadian, together with 4,200 United States built landing-craft, of which seventy-five per cent were British crewed. Against this armada the Germans could bring to bear twenty-three heavy coastal batteries, together with field artillery, thirty fast E-boats, fifty coastal U-boats and a handful of destroyers. Allied air power consisted of 6,000 United States and 5,500 British aircraft, to be used mainly in tactical support of

---

* *Armee Gruppe Blaskowitz* in the south had 9 and 11 Pz. Divs and 2 S S Pz. Div.

**At 2 a.m. von Rundstedt, Krancke and Sperrle were confident that no invasion was imminent.

the landings, and 3,500 gliders; to combat this force the *Luftwaffe* would be fortunate if it could get two hundred fighters into the air.

The allied invasion plan embraced the assault landing of two armies, Dempsey's 2 (British) Army to the east on both sides of the Orne, and Bradley's 1 (US) Army further west on both sides of the Vire and on the east coast of the base of the Cherbourg peninsula. The ground command of both armies went to Montgomery's 21 Army Group, under Eisenhower as the Supreme Commander of all the allied forces engaged. The three airborne and five infantry divisions that spearheaded the assault were to be built up as rapidly as possible to twenty-four divisions, Crerar's 1 (Canadian) Army joining Dempsey while Patton's 3 (US) Army was eventually to be passed through Bradley's men as they broke out of the beach-head. When Patton's army came into action, Bradley was to hand over his 1 (US) Army to Hodges and assume overall command of both American armies as the Commander of 12 (US) Army Group. Montgomery, however, was to continue to control the two army groups until Eisenhower took over from him the responsibility for all ground operations; 21 Army Group would then revert to commanding the British and Canadian armies only.

The second phase objective of *Overlord* was to occupy North-West France between the Seine and the Loire rivers by breaking out of the Normandy beach-heads, fanning out on divergent axes, with Patton's 3 Army moving westwards from Avranches into Brittany while Hodges protected Patton's flank by thrusting southwards. The British and Canadians meanwhile were to advance eastwards and south-eastwards to the Seine, which was to be reached on D + 90.

No further allied landings were intended other than that in Normandy, except that the Anglo-Americans were still debating and contesting among themselves whether or not they would land a further force on the French Mediterranean coast. It was not until 2 July, nearly four weeks after the Normandy invasion had taken place, that the Combined Chiefs of Staffs issued the agreed directive for *Anvil-Dragoon*, a three division assault from the Mediterranean, building up to ten divisions, with a target date of 15 August.

The day for the Normandy landings had been set provisionally for 5 June, but when, on the morning of 4 June, the allied meteorologists presented their reports to Eisenhower, they forecast low cloud, very high winds and formidable seas that would make landing hazardous, air support impossible, and naval gun-fire inaccurate. By then part of the invading force had already put to sea. Montgomery wanted to land notwithstanding; the airman Tedder, Eisenhower's deputy, disagreed; Ramsay, the naval deputy, thought he could cope either way. Eisenhower, happily, postponed the invasion. Early the next morning the meteorologists forecast a slackening of the storm and relatively fair weather for a short period of thirty-six hours. The invasion was then set for the early hours of 6 June. Two days before, on 4 June, the Americans, having joined up with the Anzio beach-head, had entered Rome and the German front in Italy had begun to disintegrate.

When the allied landings were made on the Normandy coast they achieved complete surprise almost everywhere.

The German Navy in the west was powerless to intervene in allied operations, for the attacks of the light surface craft and the *Landwirt Gruppe* U-boats were soon

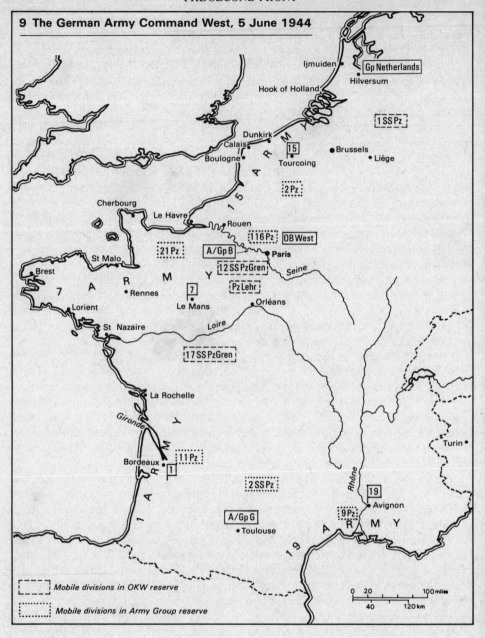

9 The German Army Command West, 5 June 1944

Ijmuiden

Gp Netherlands

Hilversum

Hook of Holland

1 SS Pz

Dunkirk

Calais

Boulogne

15

Brussels

Liège

Tourcoing

2 Pz

Cherbourg

Le Havre

Rouen

116 Pz

OB West

21 Pz

A/Gp B

Paris

St Malo

12 SS Pz Gren

Seine

Brest

7 ARMY

Rennes

7

Pz Lehr

Lorient

Le Mans

Orléans

St Nazaire

Loire

17 SS Pz Gren

La Rochelle

Gironde

Turin

Bordeaux

11 Pz

1

2 SS Pz

19

ARMY

Avignon

A/Gp G

9 Pz

Toulouse

Rhône

1 9 ARMY

┌- - - -┐
└- - - -┘ *Mobile divisions in OKW reserve*

┌·······┐
└·······┘ *Mobile divisions in Army Group reserve*

0 20   100 miles
40   120 km

defeated. The fire support of the allied fleets standing off shore, pouring an enormous weight of shells on the defensive emplacements and field works and on the movement of German reserves, was one of the most telling battle-winning factors, not only on the beaches in the first few hours but on the whole tactical battle during the coming weeks. The effect of this fire was a most frightening experience.

Sperrle's *Luftwaffe*, too, was without any tactical, let alone strategic, significance, since it was entirely outclassed and outnumbered. As against an allied 14,000 air sorties on D day (6 June) Sperrle reported 400 *Luftwaffe* sorties on D + 1. Losses of German aircraft were heavy, in the air, by bombing on the ground and by accidents attributed to the inexperience of pilots. The allied air bombardment, particularly the attacking of panzer concentrations, the destruction of railways and of all the Seine bridges, and the stopping of all road movement, completed the process started by the ships' guns in the area of the beach-heads.

The allied landings made against the eastern flank of 7 Army sector were steadily enlarged. Meanwhile von Rundstedt was having difficulty in getting his own motorized formations released back to him from the OKW frozen reserve, while Rommel's panzer reserve had already received a battering during its twenty mile approach march to the beach-head. German military commentators in post-war times have contended that the battle might have gone very differently if Hitler had not delayed by several hours the release of von Rundstedt's armour from OKW reserve; but this argument ignores the long approach march of anything between fifty and 150 miles that the divisions had to make before they could be brought into battle. Other apologists have said that if *all* the armour had been handed over to Rommel for siting close to the forward beach defences, roughly in the area between the Orne and the Vire where the Anglo-Americans in fact landed, the battle might have gone badly for the allies. And so it might. But it begs the question of how Rommel or von Rundstedt or indeed Hitler, defending a coast line of thousands of miles in length, were to know that the invasion was to be made where it actually came, in a sector hardly fifty miles wide. Surprise, and naval and air attacks defeated Rommel and von Rundstedt in the first instance; Hitler's overriding control, deadening though it might have been, confusing and out of touch though it certainly was, had little to do with the early beach-head defeats. For, as early as 8 June, the OKW diarist was recording that 'our own panzer counter-attacks are immediately strangled (*erstickte*) by enemy air attacks that destroy headquarters and all communication networks', while daylight movement became all but impossible. The commander of 21 Panzer Division said that he lost over fifty tanks out of a total of 124 by air attack on the road up, while the *Panzer Lehr* lost over eighty armoured vehicles on the open road for the same reason. Admittedly peremptory orders to 7 Army from the OKW to 'drive the British into the sea' and to 'destroy the enemy bridge-head by that evening', when the necessary panzer formations were still two days march away, did not help.

The panzer formations gave of their best, and the static divisions and infantry divisions near the coast, often poorly equipped, partially trained and sometimes of low category troops, put up the toughest resistance. But the final outcome, in spite of some small and local allied reverses, could never have been in doubt. The terrain was very different from that of Italy and not particularly favourable for defence, for it was without much cover from the air and, in the hinterland, when they had reached it, eminently suitable for allied motorized movement. If the German divisions had all been first-class field formations, even considerably increased in their numbers, they would still have been defeated in the end, for no ground troops could fight effectively in such adverse air conditions. On the other hand, if the allies had attempted to land against Dollmann's 7 Army as it stood on 6 June, but in conditions of German air supremacy, then the invasion would surely have failed.

Geyr von Schweppenburg's *Panzer Kommando West,* with three panzer divisions under command, had been ordered to take over the sector south of the British beach-head between the Orne and the Vire, being made responsible to Dollmann. It was soon found that this spelt the end of the mobile striking force. Every tank was needed in the line to check the rapidly growing British and Canadian pressure southwards, and, once committed to this role, the critical situation did not allow the withdrawing of panzer formations to reserve. Meanwhile, as early as 9 June, American armour was forcing a gap westwards 'with a possible threat to Cherbourg'. A day later the British and Americans had joined up their separate beach-heads. Yet, so the OKW believed, 'there were distinct indications that the allies were about to land in Belgium' and 1 SS Panzer Division was ordered to close up to the Belgian coast. Then Geyr von Schweppenburg's headquarters was virtually destroyed by air attack and had to be replaced temporarily by Hausser's 1 SS Panzer Corps headquarters. The Führer sent further reinforcements from the Reich and ordered Dietrich's 2 SS Panzer Corps of two panzer divisions to abandon its planned offensive against the Russian-Polish border town of Kovel and return post-haste to the west. Meanwhile, so Hitler told his OKW staff, he confidently 'awaited a second invasion between Calais — Le Havre, or between the Schelde and Dunkirk', together with another possible diversionary landing in Brittany.

In a situation report to the OKW dated 12 June von Rundstedt explained his failure by crediting the enemy air activity with 'up to 27,000 sorties a day', and by describing the terrible effectiveness of the allied naval guns; the enemy airborne troops, too, had been particularly troublesome: the Anglo-Americans had, he concluded, already gained the strategic and tactical initiative. But he sweetened this unwelcome news by emphasizing that 'the [German] troops continued to fight with bitterness and outstanding devotion to duty'. Then he played back to Hitler and to the OKW Hitler's own theme, quoting figures and suspected enemy intentions that he could only have received from the OKW, 'that the enemy still had twenty to thirty field and four airborne divisions uncommitted and ready for a second invasion that would come either in the Somme [Pas de Calais] or Belgium'. Meanwhile, continued von Rundstedt, tension was mounting in South France since seventy enemy transports were said to be lying off North Africa. There had been an increase of terrorism in Central France, though not as bad as had been expected, and meanwhile, said von Rundstedt, the population had been warned that the resistance forces would be regarded as non-belligerents (Freischärler), an announcement that the Germans regarded as sufficient authority to shoot prisoners or suspects out of hand.* So as to give substance to this threat, the Waffen SS, on 10 June, murdered inhabitants of the French village of Oradour in a so-called reprisal action.

Inside the OKW, only Jodl voiced any disagreement with von Rundstedt's appreciation, for, although Jodl did not consider further landings at all unlikely, he now believed that the OKW should reinforce the Normandy area immediately, if necessary by taking troops out of Italy. This contemporary OKW record gives little support to post-war accounts, canvassed by some German generals, that von Rundstedt wanted, from 7 June onwards, to transfer his forces from 15 Army to 7 Army, but was forbidden to do so by Hitler and the OKW.

The Führer meanwhile had elbowed both von Rundstedt and Rommel aside and had taken complete control of the tactical battle, conducting this off the map,

---

* The Freischärler was a guerrilla unprotected by the normal conventions of war.

as he had so often done in the east, giving out his orders by teleprint and telephone. Dispositions, axes, tactics and timings down to the level of individual divisions were ordered by him. The Führer plans and orders for counter-attacks were unrelated to the rapidly deteriorating battle situation so that von Rundstedt, unwilling or unable to convince the dictator of the truth, asked that Jodl should visit the OB West headquarters; Jodl was to be the go-between. Hitler decided, however, that he would go himself and take Jodl with him, and the celebrated meeting with von Rundstedt and Rommel took place at Margival near Soissons. Although some of what von Rundstedt and Rommel were subsequently said to have told the Führer appears to be unsupported by the written record, it is certain, however, that the two field-marshals did warn Hitler about the enemy's growing strength and the imminence of a general offensive, and that they made representations about the lack of *Luftwaffe* and naval support. Nothing that was said changed the Führer's style of command, and part of the conference time was taken up with Hitler giving out detailed orders as to the defensive measures to be adopted, the types of mines to be used, the forbidding the use of 77 Infantry Division 'in a stopping role' and the strengthening of Cherbourg. And, according to the war diary, von Rundstedt declined to put before the Führer Rommel's request that all troops be withdrawn from the Channel Islands 'because he knew that the Führer was against it'. The only action taken on this conference was that Dönitz was required to 'destroy or at least neutralize the enemy naval forces, particularly his capital ships'. On 20 June von Rundstedt was given a new Führer plan for a grand offensive by the four SS and two army panzer divisions 'to destroy the American forces at Balleroy — after the British had been annihilated east of the Orne'.

By the end of the month there were wide differences of opinion between Hitler and the two field-marshals over the projected counter-offensive. They saw the *Schwerpunkt* of the battle as being on the Anglo-Canadian sector in the east, particularly near Caen, and they thought that any thinning out of German tanks there would, to say the least, be risky *(bedenklich)*. The Führer, on the other hand, had come to a new conclusion, contained in a teleprint issued at the end of the month, that 'the offensive should be made where the enemy is weak, against the scattered and disorganized American forces west of the Vire, not where he was strong and compact'. Immediately afterwards Cherbourg was lost, in spite of frantic Führer plans to reinforce it 'with a regiment airlifted or taken in by sea'.

Both field-marshals had been called to Berchtesgaden on 28 June for another inconclusive Führer lecture. On 1 July von Rundstedt at last presented the unvarnished truth to the Führer, even though he did this by forwarding the written views of the commanders of 7 Army and Panzer Group West, together with his concurrence. The Caen bridge-head, they said, must be evacuated and the line straightened and drawn back 'in order to get out of the range of the ships' guns and prevent the panzer formations from burning themselves out'. Geyr von Schweppenburg had added that 'the choice was either patchwork cobbling *(Flickarbeit)* that meant defending every foot of ground and leaving the initiative to the enemy, or elastic and fluid operations that, at the best, *might* allow some initiative to the German forces for part of the time'. In this judgement the army commanders had experienced, and had condemned as a failure, *Rommel's* concept of winning the battle by close coastal defence. They now wanted to revert to von Rundstedt's earlier plan. On this document Jodl, on 1 July, wrote his own commentary for the information of the Führer. This appreciation, said Jodl, was 'a final acceptance that the enemy

117

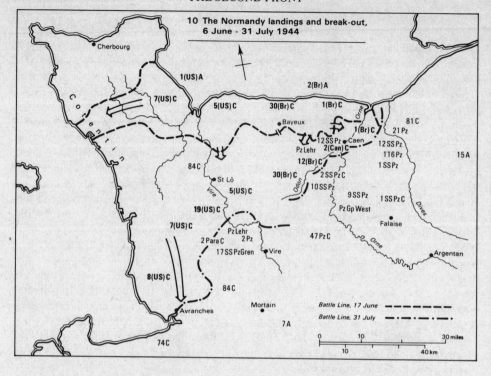

10 The Normandy landings and break-out, 6 June - 31 July 1944

landing would never be defeated, although the Anglo-Americans had so far brought to bear hardly one-third [*sic*] of their available forces; it [the continuance of a Second Front] also signified a committal of large-scale German forces and heavy German casualties that, in the long term, could not be replaced'. This situation, continued Jodl, really called for the evacuation of France, because there were only two courses of action possible for Germany, throw the enemy into the sea or get back as quickly as possible to the shortest line of defence, behind the West Wall on the frontiers of the Reich.

That day, on 1 July, Panzer Group West reported that, if a decision were not given immediately, four panzer divisions would be so burned out that they would be of no further use. Rommel then committed the unforgiveable when, on his own initiative, he put all *Luftwaffe* and *Kriegsmarine* units in his area under the command of the German Army.

The Führer's reaction was one of fury. On 2 July von Rundstedt was replaced by von Kluge, still convalescing from his motor accident injury; Geyr von Schweppenburg was relieved by Eberbach: Dollmann had just suffered a heart attack and was replaced, on Hitler's order, by SS General Hausser; Rommel's order was rescinded by the dictator and Rommel's days of favour were ended. On 3 July Hitler said that all troops would remain where they were, 'for any form of elastic defence could not be risked because of the air situation'. Four days later he issued a *Weisung* containing ten disjointed military generalizations, most of which were impossible to follow even as guide-lines: panzer divisions in the line were to be replaced by fresh infantry divisions; *Panzer Gruppe West* was to mount a counter-offensive to split the beach-head and 'the experiences of 5 Army in 1914 would be followed in using night attacks without fire preparation'; a strong reserve should be kept behind 15 Army, and 19 Army should be reinforced; infantry divisions should be taken out of the line in rotation and rested; Seine shipping should be used for movement instead of the railways; in all, it was a collection of disconnected and irrelevant thoughts.

Von Kluge had spent a fortnight with Hitler and Jodl and had been briefed on the spirit of defeatism of the commanders in the west, so that he arrived in Paris optimistic and determined to put some backbone into his new command. A lightning tour of the forward areas rapidly changed his mind, however, and on 10 July he was asking OKW approval for a limited withdrawal in the area Marécageuses — Angeville, and this was agreed. A second withdrawal request was ignored. On 17 July Rommel was badly injured when his car was shot up by an enemy fighter, and von Kluge took over the command of Army Group B in addition to his own appointment of Commander-in-Chief West. From then onwards von Kluge argued daily with the OKW, often about the employment of a single division that he wanted to use in a counter-attack. Everything had to be referred to the Führer, although the situation was changing so rapidly that the OKW agreement was no longer relevant by the time it was received. On 24 July von Kluge reported the German losses in the five weeks of fighting as over 2,000 tanks and 340 aircraft and 113,000 men; as against this loss only 10,000 reinforcements had arrived. Meanwhile the enemy's losses were 'immediately replaced'. Von Kluge credited the allied strength as forty divisions 'with a further fifty-two divisions in the United Kingdom'. But he was the first senior German commander to doubt that the Anglo-Americans would in fact make a second landing across the Channel, 'this becoming even more improbable in view of the steady enemy advance to the south'. For the moment these thoughts went unheeded if the OKW.

On 20 July the unsuccessful bomb attempt was made by officers of the general staff on the life of the Führer at his Rastenburg headquarters, and Hitler's counter-terror finally destroyed both the army general staff and what was left of the army command organization. Henceforth the German Army structure was demolished and made entirely subordinate to the SS who took over the control of the raising, equipping and training of army formations (the *Volkssturm* home guard being entrusted to Nazi party officials). The remnant of the OKH and what served the purposes of a general staff was policed by SS stalwarts with powers as far-reaching as Stalin's secret police at the time of the purges, for senior army officers of the highest rank and in the most responsible positions were arrested, suffered SS interrogation and were imprisoned at will, almost at whim, even on unfounded suspicion of what was said to be treason.

The conspiracy had gained momentum and adherents, particularly from the winter of 1941 onwards, and, with each successive defeat, elements of the general staff had become more determined to find a way out of the war and break the personal oath of allegiance that bound the armed forces to the dictator. A successful Second Front landing in the west, would, they knew, finally spell Germany's complete defeat. Numbers of civilians were also involved in the plot, but the majority of the members and the responsibility for action belonged to the German Army, for the *Luftwaffe* and the *Kriegsmarine* were kept in ignorance. Following the failure of the attempt, many generals, both serving and retired, were executed or imprisoned. Yet some of those close to the Führer who had knowledge of the *existence* of a counter-Nazi conspiracy escaped. Rommel, who had had some contact with the conspirators, was murdered at Hitler's orders, and von Kluge, for the same reason, had already become a man wanted by the Gestapo.* Like many others, von Kluge awaited the expected telephone call from Keitel, recalling him to Germany 'for consultation or reposting', the last journey that some of these generals ever made. In order to ensure conviction and an appropriate punishment of those suspects who were brought to trial, Hitler convened special Military Courts of Honour, presided over by von Rundstedt and including Keitel and Guderian among the members, designed to remove the accused from the German Army and hand them over to the jurisdiction of the People's Courts.

Zeitzler, another suspect, had been summarily dismissed as Chief of the Army General Staff, and his duties, but not his appointment, were taken over by Guderian, the Inspector-General of Panzer Troops. Guderian was to exercise even less authority than Zeitzler, and he served merely as the Führer's spokesman for the command of the eastern theatres. Fromm, the Commander of the Replacement Army, was imprisoned and later executed; the same fate awaited Fellgiebel, the Director of the OKH/OKW Signals. The OKW itself was otherwise largely unaffected, except that Himmler's SS organization had, some weeks earlier, absorbed what had been Admiral Canaris's *Abwehr,* a principal political and military intelligence agency. Himmler was now given the command of the Replacement Army.

Politically, the bomb attack confirmed to Germany's remaining allies what they already knew, that Germany's defeat was certain and not far away. The assassination attempt and the purge shook the German Army to its foundations, and the party propaganda machine saw to it that its remaining hierarchy lost the respect and confidence of the German public and of the formations in the field. The purge had been carried out with a vindictiveness intended to crush not only any vestige of resistance but also any remaining independence and initiative of all military commanders, so that, from the highest to the lowest, they would, mindful of the retribution that attended failure, do exactly what the Führer ordered.

The regimental officers, the rank and file, and the German public at large, had had no opportunity to observe their Führer at close quarters and they knew virtually nothing of him. And they remained entirely loyal because they believed that national unity and the solidarity of the Nazi régime was the only hope against the great flood of Red terror, barbarity and bestiality that threatened to submerge the eastern territories of the Reich.

At the end of July, in order, according to the OKW war diary, 'to counter a landing near Dieppe', there were as many divisions of 15 German Army still standing against the beaches as had been there on the day of the invasion. Only after Canadian forces had appeared in strength in Normandy did the seven German divisions in reserve begin to filter over from 15 Army to 7 Army.** Some infantry

* Rommel was ordered to take poison as the price of the safety and welfare of his family.

**The OKW had long assumed, somewhat irrationally, that 1 Canadian Army would be landed near Dieppe.

divisions had, however, already been removed from the mouth of the Gironde so that 1 Army was now much weakened: 19 Army on the Mediterranean coast still remained virtually untouched, with a strength of one panzer and seven infantry divisions.

In those last days in July Bradley's 1 (US) Army launched its offensive against 7 Army between St Lô and the coast, and, bursting the front wide open, passed Patton's 3 (US) Army into the hinterland and the entrance to Brittany. The main attack fell on von Choltitz's 84 Corps near Avranches.

Hausser, commanding 7 Army, and von Choltitz, commanding the corps, were at loggerheads and were giving contradictory orders. Von Kluge himself, on another whirlwind tour, was with the *Panzer Lehr* on 28 July, where the commander had reported his formation completely destroyed, and at 7 Army headquarters on 30 July, where he found the set-up 'farcical, a complete mess, the whole army putting up a poor show'. The chief of staff and von Choltitz were removed from their posts, but not SS General Hausser. Hausser, describing the situation in a private letter, said that up to ten of his divisions had disintegrated, leaving small leaderless groups of men roaming the countryside, many without weapons, equipment or headgear, all living off the land. Their morale was badly shaken. A not inconsiderable number, he thought, were disappearing at the hands of terrorists and the civilian population; the *Luftwaffe* paratroops were particularly unpopular with the French.

Meanwhile Bradley and Montgomery had agreed that Patton should use one corps only to secure Brittany, the remainder of 3 (US) Army striking south and south-east to the Loire, then turning eastwards in the general direction of the Seine. By 1 August it was obvious to the OKW that this movement must open the way to Paris and threaten to envelop the rump of 7 Army from the south. With part of Hausser's army shattered, the Führer agreed that the emergency justified von Kluge taking ground elements of the *Luftwaffe* and *Kriegsmarine* under his command, and moving panzer divisions from Panzer Group West to 7 Army; but he would not allow him to withdraw an infantry division from the Channel Islands.

The battle of the Falaise pocket that resulted was one of the great allied victories of the war, and it destroyed nearly half of the men and most of the equipment of Eberbach's and Hausser's forces — this was admitted within the OKW at the time. On the other hand the OKW were to congratulate themselves on their success in extricating so many German troops from what could and should have been the total destruction of two armies. Western analysts have subsequently been critical of both Montgomery and Bradley for failing to close the gap between Falaise and Argentan, the gap through which part of the encircled enemy eventually escaped. But the great double envelopment of the Falaise pocket was certainly not planned by the allies as a master-stroke, however neat the great pincer movement may have appeared in retrospect: the battle simply developed the way it did, largely because each enemy side misread the other's situation and intentions.

Montgomery had hoped, at the best, to pin part of the enemy force against the lower Seine, since this was without bridges, for he thought that as soon as the enemy front was broken the Germans would inevitably have to withdraw eastwards. In the circumstances this is what he himself would have done, and if von Kluge had been left to his own devices he would undoubtedly have done so too. But the Anglo-Americans, although they did not realize it until after the war, were not pitting their wits against the formal military training of the German general staff, unorthodox though this might have been by the British standards of the time; they were wrestling instead against the master-mind of a very desperate man, whose control was absolute, and who by now *could be counted upon to reinforce failure*.* If Montgomery and Bradley had known the enemy side of the picture, Montgomery would probably have been bolder, more far-sighted and precise in his orders; Bradley, too, would have been more daring, at least in that he would not have placed a brake on Patton, forbidding him to continue northwards beyond Argentan. But, contrary to what the allied commanders and intelligence staffs might have thought, Hitler had no intention of abandoning the fight deep in the pocket against the base of the Cherbourg peninsula.

Ignoring the fact that a whole American army had passed through the Avranches gap and was streaming south-eastwards, Hitler was determined on a massive panzer counter-offensive of five panzer divisions that was to close the gap and restore the front; when this was done Patton's forces in the German rear were to be liquidated. But, on 3 August, von Kluge reported that 'although he was in agreement with the orders given to him, Panzer Group West was finding it difficult to pull out of the line the panzer divisions [needed for the offensive] as they were pinned by the enemy in front of them'. The next day von Kluge reported that he had 'closed the gap to 7 Army and formed a new front', adding somewhat ruefully, however, that 'this had not prevented the Americans [Patton] from streaming on to the south and south-east'. On 5 August the Americans had already reached Laval and Mayenne 'having stronger forces than we thought'.

Von Kluge began to collect armoured remnants together for the offensive ordered by the Führer on Mortain and Avranches—including tanks turned out from the equipment depot at Mailly le Camp. Von Kluge decided that the attack should be commanded by Funck, the commander of 47 Panzer Corps, under the overall control of *SS Hauptgruppenführer* Hausser: this offensive, the field-marshal thought, should be mounted as quickly as possible before the enemy should get wind of the intention and break up the formations from the air. The Führer, however, would not agree. The offensive was to wait until the last available tank could be mustered; Eberbach, an experienced armoured man, was to command the force, not Funck, and Eberbach was to give up his own Panzer Group West to the temporary command of SS General Dietrich; and Hitler sent General Buhle from the OKW, armed with detailed written instructions on how the offensive was to be conducted, to see that his orders were carried out. Von Kluge, however, had not waited, and in the early hours of 7 August Funck attacked into Mortain, where the offensive shortly came to a halt 'under unendurable attacks' of fighter-bombers of a fury never known before. With failure everywhere about him, Buhle reported back to the Führer guardedly that 'a quick success could not be counted upon'.

The Führer never forgave von Kluge his initiative, and afterwards repeatedly harked back to this failure, 'made too early and too weak when the weather was favourable to the enemy air force'; Hitler was later to infer that von Kluge's disobedience had cost the dictator what might have been victory in the west. Von Kluge was told to prepare for a resumption of the offensive with '*Alarmeinheiten*

---

* On 7 August, Hitler, unmindful that he was talking to one fresh from the disastrous scenes in Normandy, told von Choltitz that 'he was about to hurl the enemy into the sea'. Von Choltitz could only conclude that 'the man was mad'.

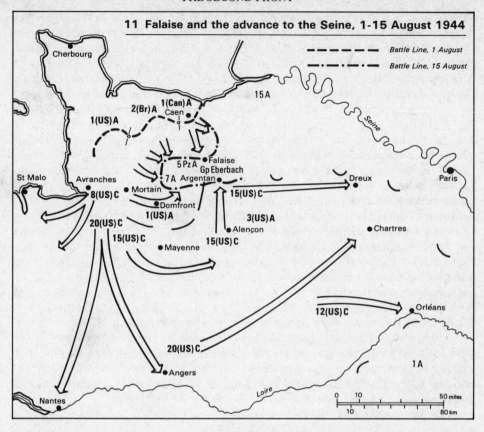

11 Falaise and the advance to the Seine, 1-15 August 1944

and the infantry divisions coming up from 15 Army being added to the assault force'.

By the evening of 10 August von Kluge had noted that Patton had changed direction again, first eastwards and then northwards towards Alençon, this being in reality Bradley's immediate riposte to the Hitler offensive against Mortain, with the intention of catching the German thrust in its southern flank. As it so transpired, this movement was to turn into something much larger, as von Kluge quickly foresaw, for, when he relayed the information to the OKW, he said that Patton's northward move was 'obviously a double envelopment, together with a Canadian thrust from Falaise, aimed at 7 Army and 5 Panzer Army' (formerly Panzer Group West). But von Kluge did not care to suggest to the dictator that the preparations for Hitler's offensive in the depth of the great pocket should be cancelled, or advise a general withdrawal to the west: instead he asked permission 'to deliver a short sharp tank attack against the Americans coming north, and so secure a firm base' for the Führer's coming offensive in the north-west corner of the pocket. But von Kluge did warn that this resumed offensive towards Avranches—Domfront 'could not now take place before 20 August'.

It was not until the next day, on 12 August, that von Kluge had summoned up the courage to put the true situation to the Führer, and then he put the words into Hausser's mouth, giving Hausser's opinion, with which he concurred, that 'an

123

attack towards Avranches was no longer possible' and that the situation was deteriorating hourly.* The Führer reluctantly agreed that 7 Army should for the moment remain on the defensive on the west flank of the pocket, while 5 Panzer Army held back the Anglo-Canadian force in the north. Meanwhile Eberbach's scratch panzer force was to attack the flanks of Patton's thrusts from the south.

On 15 August von Kluge, touring the area in the western mouth of the pocket, went missing for several hours and could not be reached by radio or telephone, and it was believed that he might be in enemy hands. Hitler had little doubt that he had gone over to the allies to escape retribution for his connection with the bomb plot conspirators, and the dictator ordered Kesselring to report to him from Italy and Model to come back from the eastern front; one of them was to take over the post as Commander-in-Chief West. Meanwhile Hausser was to be the temporary commander of Army Group B. Then, in the early hours of the morning of 15 August, von Kluge was reported to have turned up at Eberbach's headquarters. In a teleconversation with Jodl, von Kluge reported that it was impossible to carry out Hitler's orders: nor could he dislodge Patton's forces in the south since Eberbach's tanks were short of fuel; it was only then, on 16 August, that Hitler admitted defeat and sanctioned a withdrawal from the pocket. Von Kluge, however, was ordered to move out of the threatened gap, now only twelve miles wide, and 'to conduct operations from 5 Panzer Army headquarters' where the Führer would know where he was and where he could get his hands on him.

That day Model arrived unannounced to take over command from von Kluge, who was to return to Germany. On the way, the field-marshal, fearful of the fate that might await him, committed suicide. Von Kluge had sent a personal letter to Hitler advising that the dictator should end the war since Germany was at the end of its resources, a letter from the grave so ingratiating and fulsome in its praises of the Führer, that Schramm has marvelled that the man should, even in death, have felt such a missive necessary, Schramm likening it to Paulus's radio message immediately before the Stalingrad surrender. But Professor Schramm's wonder takes too little account of the reality of the deadly threat of *Sippenhaft*, the imprisonment and death of close relatives for the fault or omission of the principal. Von Kluge left a family behind him in Germany and a son in the Falaise pocket.

The German 1 Army facing the Bay of Biscay had already been ordered to fall back north-eastwards towards Fontainebleau and the Seine to form the new left flank of Army Group B. But there were a large number of administrative troops in South-West France and these were, by the Führer's order, added to 1 Army's 64 Corps, which itself commanded only a reserve recruit training division and an Indian regiment of renegade prisoners of war. In all 100,000 German troops and 200 women began the long march to the north-east, for the most part on foot, running the gauntlet of resistance guerrillas that were now openly under arms; 35,000 Germans never made it to the Seine, though it was hoped and believed in the O K W that a half of these must have struggled the shorter distance to the Loire trying to gain the safety of the American prisoner of war cages.

On 18 August the Canadian-American pincers had closed at last, encircling about six divisions of 7 Army, two divisions of 5 Panzer Army and some elements of *Panzer Gruppe Eberbach*. Shortly afterwards Hausser, in command inside the pocket, was seriously wounded. Meanwhile 2 S S Panzer Corps with two panzer

---

* An S S military opinion in the latter part of 1944 always carried more weight with the Führer than one from the German Army.

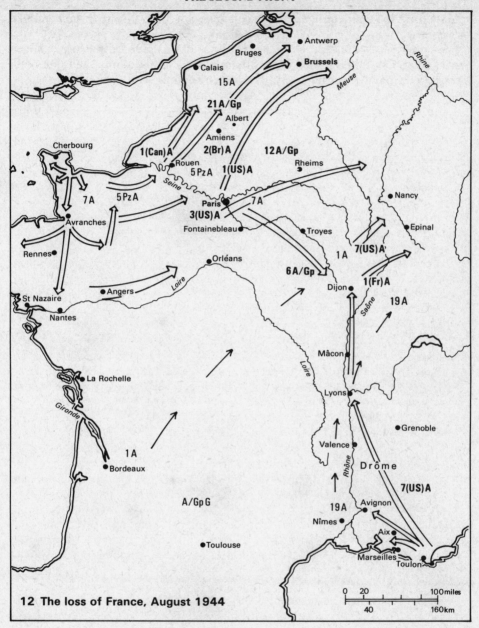

12 The loss of France, August 1944

divisions stood immediately east of the ring. Reports that American forces, those troops detached further eastwards on the initiative of Bradley and Patton, were already on the Seine heightened the German alarm. Three days earlier, on 15 August, American and French troops had begun landing on the Mediterranean coast, and, on 16 August, Blaskowitz's *Armee Gruppe G* headquarters and 19 Army, except for the garrisons in Toulon and Marseilles, were ordered to withdraw northwards up the Rhône valley, assailed by resistance partisans as they went, to form the connecting link between the open Army Group B flank and the Swiss border.

The complete evacuation of France had begun in which only two weakened armies, 15 and 19, still retained some organization and discipline; the remainder, 7 Army, 5 Panzer Army and 1 Army had been routed.

CHAPTER SEVEN

Hitler's Secret Weapons

German rocket development, and indeed the United States and Soviet guided weapon arsenals that have come into being since the Second World War, owed their origin to a Society for Space Travel formed by a number of space travel enthusiasts in Breslau in 1927. In 1930 the group was joined by Wernher von Braun and by a serving German Army officer, Captain Walter Dornberger, who arranged for the society to receive a small subsidy from German Army funds. At about this time the old military training field in Berlin-Reinickendorf was taken over for rocket-testing. Two years later von Braun was hired by the German Army Ordnance Department and continued his experiments on liquid propellant rockets at the artillery centre at Kummersdorf.

In 1934 two A-2 rockets were launched from the North Sea island of Borkum, and, although these reached an altitude of only 8,000 feet, they were reckoned to be successful according to the standards of the time; two years later the artilleryman von Fritsch, the Commander-in-Chief of the German Army, witnessed a static firing of an A-3 at Kummersdorf and was sufficiently impressed to support the enlargement of the missile programme. Göring, however, wanted to be associated with it and so a joint German Army-Air Force development centre was set up on the northern tip of Usedom island at Peenemünde, of which Dornberger's army section became a separate department. The *Luftwaffe* began developing rocket and jet aircraft while the army concentrated on the missile rocketry.

The A-4 experimental rocket missile, designated by Hitler as the Reprisal Weapon 2 (V-2), was successfully launched by the Dornberger-von Braun team on 3 October 1942. By then Dornberger was a major-general. Its series development for operational use was seriously delayed, however, by allied air attacks beginning with the RAF 600 bomber raid on Peenemünde on 17-18 August 1943, so that on December of that year the mass production of the A-4 missile was transferred to a subterranean plant near Nordhausen in Lower Saxony. The A-4 (V-2) liquid oxygen and alcohol propelled projectile was the most successful weapon produced at that time, for it had a range of about 200 miles and an altitude of sixty miles, delivering a high explosive war-head of about a ton at an impact velocity of 1,750 miles per hour. It was a ballistic missile, without guidance after its initial programmed turn in the direction of its target, and was not very accurate; except that its war-head was subject to premature explosion it eventually proved to be a reliable weapon for area destruction. Its arrival before impact was at the rate of twice the speed of sound and there was virtually no possibility of the enemy getting prior warning in the target area, and since the flight took only a matter of four to five minutes and the strike could not be forecast with any degree of accuracy, the British could have no defence against it.

Although Hitler's choice of the method by which the missile would be launched was to prove an unhappy one, there appears to be no real evidence that he did in fact delay the production of the V-2 in any stage of its development, for the dictator was very enthusiastic about it and made the most exaggerated forecasts of what it would do to the enemy. The destructive effect of the war-head was, however, no greater than that of a 2,000 lb bomb, and a bomber could achieve greater accuracy than the missile. But the Lower Saxony works had been designed to produce 900 V-2s a month and Hitler boasted that by using the missiles as area weapons he would make a desert of London in the space of three weeks. The dictator counted, too, on the moral effect of a missile that arrived without warning and against which there was no defence creating a panic among Londoners that would force their government to come to terms with Germany.

The large scale production of the new V-2 missile was already under way when there arose a dispute within the high command as to how it should be launched, from mobile field launchers or from fixed base concrete installations on the north coast of France. Hitler, against the advice of Dornberger's technical staff, decided to use heavy concrete bunkers to be constructed at Watten, near Calais. But when American bombing raids on the fixed sites made further development impossible, the German Army then had to revert to the use of road surfaces, a rock or log-bed or even hard level ground as a missile launching-pad, so that a battery could set up its equipment, launch its missile and be gone within thirty minutes; this of course reduced the missile team's vulnerability to counter-battery air strike. Its relatively short radius meant, however, that as soon as the Pas de Calais and the coast of Belgium had been cleared of German troops then London was no longer within range of the missile. The V-2 weapon system depended very much, too, on liquid oxygen supplies provided from French industry.

The other main reprisal weapon, the V-1, developed mainly by the Fieseler aircraft works and sponsored by the *Luftwaffe*, took the form of a small pilotless and subsonic pulse-jet aircraft carrying a high-explosive war-head of between 1,600 and 2,000 lbs in weight and having a cruising speed of about 300 m.p.h., later increased to nearly 400 m.p.h. It was launched under its own power from a metal ramp and its range was from 150 to 220 miles.* It flew at a relatively low altitude being guided by automatic built-in pilot controls that proved, however, to be so faulty that hardly a quarter of the missiles that were launched arrived near the target. This pilotless plane was to have been ready for use at the beginning of 1944, but the existence of this weapon and of the V-2 became known to the allies through Polish and French workers employed on the sites, and, in consequence, the repeated Anglo-American bombings of the development and launching areas delayed the first V-1 firing until June 1944. Numbers of subsonic V-1 planes were destroyed in flight over the south of England by anti-aircraft artillery and by high performance fighters. Like the V-2, the V-1 was cheap to produce but, because of its inaccuracy, could hardly be compared with the manned bomber for effectiveness.

The V-1 and V-2 research and development programme eventually came under SS supervision, and, by January 1945, *SS Obergruppenführer* Kammler was made

* According to Schramm (*K TB des OK W*, Vol. IV (1), p. 971) the *Kriegsmarine* also had a hand in the sponsoring. The V-1 could be launched from a parent aircraft, so increasing its range, and this was done after German troops had been forced back to the Rhine.

responsible for the control of all V weapon firings, as directed by the Führer through the OKW. Before the end of the war Kammler was appointed the ground defence commander for the Nordhausen factory complex.

Piloted jet aircraft were being designed side by side with the reprisals weapons, and these took the form of kerosene-burning pure jet aircraft, or of planes that took their propulsion from dry or liquid rocket fuels. The first experimental flights were made in 1941, and maximum speeds were claimed for Me 163 rocket aircraft of about 580 m.p.h. Various prototypes were developed, but the most successful, the Me 262, that had passed its trials in mid 1942, was delayed in going into production by interdepartmental frictions and by a Führer ban on putting new aircraft types into service. At the end of 1942 the Me 262 was viewed and approved by Hitler, but series production was again delayed as the dictator wanted the aircraft used as a high-speed bomber and not primarily as a fighter, for he was still obsessed by what he saw as the need to retaliate against the Anglo-American bombing of the Reich. Not until the end of 1944 did the aircraft come into operational use, and, of the 1,600 machines produced, hardly 600 were ever airborne. The remainder stood unused, in the period of Germany's collapse, awaiting armament, ancillary equipment or fuel. The other main model, the Arado 234, a turbo-prop night-fighter and light bomber, with a speed of 550 m.p.h. at 30,000 feet, only came into service at the end of the war. Probably less than 200 ever flew. The rocket-propelled Me 163 single-seater fighter proved to be very fast and had a remarkable rate of climb, but its limited endurance prevented its widespread use.

Although German scientists had been experimenting to produce an atomic weapon there was no atomic bomb in Germany in *any* stage of development. The research had been cut back severely in August 1942 by Hitler because the scientists could not commit themselves to promising any results within two years. By then, the Führer reckoned, the war would have been decided one way or the other, and no part of the dwindling German potential could be expended on anything so uncertain. What remained of the effort was virtually put out of business by the allied attack on the Norwegian *Werk Rjukan*, for, thereafter, heavy water could not be produced in sufficient quantities to continue the project with much hope of final success.*

The other of the Führer's wonder weapons, on which he pinned such extravagant hopes, was a new range of submarines. Hitler had once promised that German U-boats would roam the South Atlantic, the Indian Ocean and the Pacific, at will, being replenished by surface tankers and supply ships or by giant supply submarines; but the sinking of these depot vessels by the allied navies soon made such an undertaking impossible.** Then came the failure of the standard Atlantic U-boats. These craft, the VIIA and VIIC, with a displacement of about 700-1,000 tons and speeds of sixteen knots on the surface and seven knots submerged, had a very limited endurance under water due to the short energy life of the propelling batteries. The U-boat had to surface in order to recharge the electric batteries, using its diesel motors for which fresh air was essential. When a craft was submerged it was slow, sometimes slower than the convoys it was trying to intercept; when

* German physicists had a complete though theoretical understanding of the atomic bomb but could not translate the theory into the manufacture of a working reactor: because they mistakenly rejected graphite they turned to heavy water as a moderator, and this was available only at Vemork in Norway.

**A few *Milchkuh* giant supply submarines had been in service in the southern hemisphere.

not below the water the submarine was very vulnerable to surface and air attack. Dönitz had tried unsuccessfully to redress the balance and improve their range, speed and effectiveness, by ordering U-boats to operate in packs and, where practicable, to keep on the surface as long as possible, even when attacked from the air and even though this should mean fighting off the attacking aircraft with anti-aircraft weapons. A lot of enemy aircraft were indeed shot down, but even more U-boats were lost, and the Dönitz order had to be rescinded.

The close convoy system, the extension in the range of allied aircraft patrolling over the Atlantic, the invention of a sensitive short wave radar for both air and naval craft, and the introduction of a new Royal Naval radio signal code that German cryptographers could not break, all sounded the defeat of Dönitz's U-boat forces. More and more U-boats failed to return and in May 1943 no fewer than forty-one U-boats were lost. This allied victory in the late spring of that year was as decisive in importance as the 1940 air battles over Britain. Dönitz fully admitted the extent of his defeat to Hitler and, by March 1944, virtually all U-boats had been withdrawn from the Atlantic until the projected new types of submarine could come into service.

In the summer of 1943, trials had begun in the Baltic with a ventilating tube that would allow fresh air to be taken in to a U-boat submerged at a depth of about twenty feet and, at the same time, expel exhaust gases, so that the batteries could be recharged and the diesel motors operated without the submarine being forced to the surface. The development of this *Schnorchel* was delayed by the loss of two U-boats during trials, but, eventually, the new device was perfected so that it could be used both by the existing old pattern VIIA and VIIC U-boats, and by the new fast ones about to come into service. The Germans feared at the time that the *Schnorchel* mast, when exposed, might have been vulnerable to detection by the allied 10 cm radar (and for this reason it was treated with materials to reduce its echo effect to a radar signal), and that the exhaust smoke might have been visible above the surface; in practice, however, this does not appear to have been the case for the *Schnorchel* mast proved to be very difficult to detect. Yet the U-boat force made little use of the *Schnorchel* in the closing year of the war.

The new German wonder submarines on which Hitler and Dönitz were to pin their hopes were the XXI and the XXIII, the first being a very large vessel of 1,600 tons (1,800 tons submerged) propelled under water by very powerful electric motors that gave it an underwater speed of seventeen knots, two knots faster than its diesel surface speed. This vessel was a true submarine and not merely a submersible, since its underwater range was 285 miles and, with the aid of a *Schnorchel*, the diesel engines could be used when the vessel was lying eighteen feet below the surface. First commissioned in June 1944, 118 of these vessels were built in all. The XXIII, similarly, was also an 'electric' U-boat, but being only 250 tons displacement and with a submerged speed of twelve knots, was designed for coastal waters; it only went into service just before the end of the war. The third type was the tiny Walther V80 submarine, propelled by a turbine that got its power from a chemical reaction of hydrogen-peroxide, this attaining the remarkable underwater speed of twenty-eight knots. It remained, however, an experimental vessel.

These new submarine designs had little effect on the subsequent course of the war, in spite of the fact that the U-boat operational strength reached its peak in March 1945 when there were, in all, 463 boats fit for service. The *Schnorchel* proved difficult if not impossible to detect by sight or by radar, and the presence of submarines could be traced only by Sonar/Asdic and then usually only when the U-boat had attacked or was in position and about to attack. The new high speed U-boats, if they had been available much earlier in the war and in large numbers, would have caused the allied navies the greatest of anxiety; Dönitz would, in all probability, have won back the initiative at sea.

The same was not necessarily true of the air war. The *Luftwaffe* would have required enormous numbers of jet fighters and fighter-bombers to have regained the superiority in the air that it had lost in 1940, together with trained pilots and the industrial potential to cover maintenance and wastage. And Germany had only a tiny fraction of the oil resources available to its enemies. Moreover there appears to be little reason for doubt that the western allies, at any rate, after some initial set-back in the air, would, in a very short space of time, have produced their own jet aircraft equal or superior in performance to those of the *Luftwaffe*.*

The invention of the V-2 was one of the most important scientific developments of the war, ranking only after the atomic bomb. Yet the V-1 and V-2, at their stage of development in 1944, were probably the weakest of Hitler's wonder weapons. The weight of explosive carried at their operating range was no greater than the bomb load of a German medium bomber, and a heavy bomber could have dropped three times that weight. The unreliability of the V-1, and the inaccuracy and restricted range of both the V-1 and the V-2, and the lack of numbers of weapons available, detracted from their value. Of the 9,000 V-1 firings against London in the three months after June 1944, a quarter of the total did not cross the coast and only a further quarter got near the capital. Only 1,000 V-2 firings were made against London since the tide of battle soon put it out of range, but a further 2,000 V-2s were launched against Belgium. The casualties caused by the V weapons from June 1944 until the end of the war were put at 32,000 civilians killed or seriously wounded in the United Kingdom, and 27,000 on the continent.

In using these weapons Hitler relied on indiscriminate and mass destruction and on what he expected to be the terror effect on the enemy civilian population. The V weapons certainly caused a mass exodus from London and an evacuation of those whose presence was not necessary in the capital. But the effect, from the German point of view, was disappointing. The weapons could never have affected the course of the war because of their poor performance, lack of numbers and very limited range, and, most important of all, because they had been introduced too late. The war was nearly over. The Londoners knew, as Hitler did too, that the successful Second Front landing must shortly spell the end of Fortress Europe and the Greater German Reich. And as German commentators were later to remark, these reprisal attacks could only spur the islanders on to greater efforts, knowing that final victory could not be long delayed.

* Whittle's British jet aircraft had made its first flight in 1941.

CHAPTER EIGHT

The Collapse in the East

After the German failure at Kursk, Finland had sought peace once more, but the Soviet offer of terms in July 1943 had been entirely unacceptable to Helsinki. By the autumn of 1943 Finland still had 350,000 men under arms, all of high quality, opposing 180,000 second grade Soviet troops, while Dietl's 20 German Mountain Army in North Lapland, with a strength of 180,000 good combat troops, also outnumbered that part of the Soviet Karelian Front facing it by two to one. Finland had already suffered heavy casualties in the two wars since 1939 and, knowing that the war was going to be decided elsewhere than in Finland, had now determined upon a policy of inactivity for itself and for the German troops on its soil. Fret though they might about what they considered to be Finnish indecision, the Germans were not in a position to force the Finns to do anything; and without Finnish permission and support Dietl could not attack by himself.

On 28 September 1943 Hitler had ordered that 20 Mountain Army should continue to hold on to Finnish Lapland and the Petsamo nickel mines even if the Finns should go out of the war. In reply, Dietl told Jodl that the OKW orders were unrealistic since he was sure that he could not survive in such an exposed position; and, as the neutrality of Sweden could no longer by relied upon, he feared that his whole army would be stranded in the far north. In February 1944 the Finns sent delegates to Moscow, but once again negotiations broke down. Hitler retaliated by restricting arms and grain shipments to Finland.

Stalin had already agreed at Teheran, in response to a request by Roosevelt and Churchill, that Finland should retain its national independence, but he had made up his mind to settle with Finland before he undertook the great offensives that were to coincide with the Second Front in Western Europe; this led him to reinforce the Soviet Karelian and Leningrad Fronts. Stalin had originally planned to attack 20 German Army on the Arctic coast before turning on the Finns, but the unexpected success of an offensive by Govorov's Leningrad Front against the Finnish defences north of Leningrad that began on 9 June, three days after the Normandy invasion, made him change his mind; Meretskov, commanding the Karelian Front, was ordered to support Govorov and mount a rapid offensive against the Finnish south-east flank, since the Finns had been forced to move troops from this area over to the sector of the Leningrad Front. The Finns held on desperately throughout the summer without German help, for Hitler was, in any event, unable to spare them any; 20 German Army, under Rendulic since Dietl's death, remained idle and isolated in the far north.

Although Stalin failed to overcome Finland before starting his great campaigns into Central Europe, he had weakened the Finnish forces and had driven them back northwards away from Leningrad. The next blow against Fortress Europe was to fall on the eastern frontier of the Reich, in Belorussia and in the German *General-Gouvernement* of Poland.

The first Red Army general staff plan for the Belorussian operation had been completed in Moscow by 14 May. A week later it formed the basis of a series of presentations given to Stalin by Antonov, the Deputy Chief of General Staff, in the presence of Zhukov, Stalin's military deputy, Vasilevsky, the Chief of General Staff, and the front commanders Rokossovsky, Cherniakhovsky and Bagramian, together with their politico-military councils, and arms and air representatives. This new great offensive was aimed at the complete destruction of the German Army Group Centre, once commanded by von Bock and von Kluge and now under Field-Marshal Busch. The Soviet operation was to be called *Bagration*, after the Russian prince and general, the descendant of the *Bagratidae* of the royal house of Georgia, for Stalin loved the old imperial names. The date of the offensive was set provisionally as 19 June.

The *Bagration* offensive was to begin over a 450 mile wide sector with six assault thrusts, all widely dispersed at first so as to cause the German enemy to separate and to dissipate his reserves. The concept was that of a double envelopment intended to pinch out virtually the whole of Army Group Centre; the northern pincer, consisting of Bagramian's 1 Baltic and Cherniakhovsky's 3 Belorussian Fronts, destroying 3 Panzer Army in the area of Vitebsk and then moving rapidly 200 miles westwards to the area of Minsk, where it was to join up with the southern pincer of the double envelopment formed by Rokossovsky's 1 Belorussian Front. This vast encircling movement was intended to annihilate 3 Panzer and 4 and 9 German Armies, and bring the Red Army to the borders of the Baltic States and East Prussia. All the fronts had been specially reinforced and 124 divisions, totalling 1,200,000 men, over 5,000 tanks and 6,000 aircraft, are said to have taken part in the offensive. Busch's Army Group Centre comprised thirty-eight infantry and two panzer divisions.

The great offensive was eventually launched on 22 June, the third anniversary of the start of the war and two weeks after the Normandy landings. The Soviet success was both widespread and immediate.

Reinhardt's 3 Panzer Army was panzer only in name, for its total strength stood at nine infantry divisions forward and two in reserve, of which total four were committed by the order of the Führer to the static defence of Vitebsk. In spite of the bad flying weather, low cloud and rain storms, the Red Air Force bombing and machine-gun attacks were so violent as to be described as murderous, and von Greim, the commander of the supporting air fleet, when visiting 3 Panzer Army headquarters on 25 June, said that 'with his limited resources there was nothing that he could do about it'. Heidkämper, Reinhardt's chief of staff, was aghast at the unexpectedly rapid successes of the Red Army troops, and, on the evening of 23 June, there began the first of a number of difficult and outspoken meetings when Reinhardt demanded from Busch that Vitebsk be evacuated immediately. Busch refused point blank. Nor would he permit Reinhardt to move his own reserves until he (Busch) had received the agreement of the OKH.

The situation was so threatening that, early in the morning of 24 June, Zeitzler arrived in Minsk to be briefed by Busch, after which the Chief of the General Staff of the Army flew to Bavaria to report to the Führer. That same afternoon Zeitzler telephoned Reinhardt from Obersalzberg and was told that, as Vitebsk was in imminent danger of being encircled, this was the last opportunity to withdraw 53 Corps from the area. When Zeitzler replied that Hitler was against giving up Vitebsk because of the loss of equipment that it would entail, Reinhardt emphasized to him that the loss of nearly five divisions was at stake. Reinhardt was told to hold the line while Zeitzler scurried off to talk again to the Führer. But, after a seemingly long and anxious ten-minute delay, Zeitzler returned to the telephone with the curt message that 'the Führer has decided that Vitebsk will be held'. A few minutes later a radio message received by 3 Panzer Army from 53 Corps in Vitebsk, told of the road west from Vitebsk being threatened by the enemy; this message was relayed to Busch with yet another request for permission to withdraw. Within the hour Busch repeated the request to Hitler and was told that Vitebsk would be held and that, should it be necessary, the road into the town was to be reopened by counter-attack. Two hours later, at 1830 hours, to the surprise and consternation of 3 Panzer Army, a radio mesage was received from the Führer that '53 Corps should fight its way out of the encircled Vitebsk, but that one division should be nominated to remain and hold the fortress'. Heidkämper could not understand the logic of the order, since, if a corps could not hold, the sacrifice of a division was absolutely to no purpose.

During the afternoon of 25 June, Reinhardt, anxiously following 53 Corps attempts to break out, was surprised and irritated to receive an order from the suspicious Führer that he, Reinhardt, should have an officer of the general staff parachuted into Vitebsk, for the sole purpose of handing personally to the commander of the remaining division a written order commanding him to fight to the very end.*

In any event everything was too late. On 27 June a last radio message was received from the corps saying that it was trying to fight its way westwards but was still only ten miles out of the town. Thereafter there was silence and the corps and 35,000 men simply disappeared.

While Busch, like the Führer, was repeatedly insisting that orders be sent time and time again to the division already lost in Vitebsk, Army Group Centre was falling apart. Reinhardt had lost a second corps and only two of his original eleven divisions remained to him. The larger part of a German Army had been encircled near Bobruisk in the south. In the centre von Tippelskirch's 4 Army, pressed back by Zakharov's 2 Belorussian Front, was in danger of being cut off by enemy tank columns, deep in its rear, moving rapidly towards Minsk.

Meanwhile, however, Hitler's views had not changed. All that was required was to hold firm up front. He had not agreed with Busch withdrawing from Vitebsk or from anywhere else because of the appalling impression that it would make on the Finns who, he said, were fighting desperately near Ladoga for their very existence as a nation. On 26 June, the day before the loss of 53 Corps, Busch went to the Berghof to plead the seriousness of the situation, but he received little understanding; Orsha and Mogilev had to be held as bastions until the very end. And so another two German divisions were destroyed. The next day, however, the dictator,

---

* Reinhardt, in reply to the OKH, said that he refused to lose another man, but, if the Führer insisted, he (Reinhardt) would go himself. The matter was then dropped.

realizing for the first time that the front had been torn open, left the problems of the Normandy fighting and flew from Bavaria to Rastenburg. That same night he attempted to solve the difficulty by drawing a line across the map from Polotsk to Lepel and the Berezina and ordering Army Group Centre to hold it. Busch, in his turn, sat at his map planning counter-offensives in the old grand style. Where the troops were to come from no one knew.

The Führer then ordered each of the other army groups to give up a division, although the total of the four divisions to be transferred, even if they had been readily available, could not have had any effect on the situation. He reluctantly agreed to the withdrawal of 4 and 9 Armies to the new line, although by then it was in doubt whether they could disengage or escape the enveloping armoured pincers. The three armies no longer existed as cohesive formations, and the battle was being fought by parts of divisions, engineer and police battalions, rear echelons and baggage men, alarm units and the para-military labour organization. On 28 June it was reported that Red Army tanks were already over the Berezina and to the west of Lepel and Hitler's chinagraphed map line.

The usual crisis pattern reshuffle of commanders followed. It was inevitable that Field-Marshal Busch should be removed, although like his predecessors and fellows, being allowed no initiative, he had done only what the Führer had instructed him to do. The newly promoted Field-Marshal Model replaced him, but still retained his post as the Commander of Army Group North Ukraine. Nor was the Führer satisfied with Army Group North, for its commander had become very nervous on account of the deep wedge driven by Bagramian's 1 Baltic Front between Army Groups North and Centre and wanted to pull back his southern flank. Zeitzler had supported this request, particularly since such a withdrawal might have allowed him to create a small reserve, and he had suggested that Estonia might be evacuated. Hitler was so far from agreeing that he ordered Army Group North not only to remain where it was but also to attack south-eastwards in support of Army Group Centre. Lindemann, the Commander of Army Group North, being unable to do so, was immediately replaced by Friessner.

Model was in the fortunate position of commanding two army groups and was one of the very few senior army generals who had the Führer's confidence, and for these reasons he did not await the divisions promised by Hitler. Instead he began to move panzer divisions from one army group to the other and the loss of this armoured force was to be sorely felt when Army Group North Ukraine itself came under heavy attack a few weeks later. By the end of June Model had come to realize that the Soviet objectives were more ambitious and far deeper than he had hitherto imagined and included the land-bridge gaps carrying the road and railway through the Nalibocka forest belt and marsh near Molodechno and Baranovichi. There never had been any possibility of holding Hitler's Berezina line. On 2 July Model had to admit that he could not hold Minsk or save many of the encircled troops of 4 and 9 Armies, and he told the O K H that he must have more formations to bring the enemy to a halt. Vilna itself appeared to be threatened and Model joined forces with Zeitzler in advising the Führer to withdraw Army Group North to the west of Riga.

The few divisions sent to Army Group Centre hardly affected the situation. The motorized troops were suffering from a serious shortage of fuel, so that long road moves were out of the question; at the same time the railways were slow and uncertain because of attacks by the Red Air Force or by partisans, for the great woods and marshes were the home of irregulars and brigands. Endless columns of artillery, anti-aircraft guns and motor and horse transport crawled slowly back towards the Berezina bridge, only to find that it had been put out of action. Few German aircraft were to be seen and the continuous enemy air attacks caused many casualties, including the deaths of three general officers.

On 4 July the Red Army took Minsk, and most of 4 German Army and part of 9 Army, in all about 100,000 men, were trapped in the great cauldron. Between 5 and 11 July the Soviet high command began to destroy these German pockets without halting the rapid movement of its tank formations to the west. About twenty-eight divisions of Army Group Centre had been lost as fighting formations, and the total casualties were put as high as 300,000 by the OKW diarist at the time. The three week *Bagration* offensive was undoubtedly one of the greatest victories of the whole war, and for Germany the defeat, in summer and close to home, was more disastrous than that of Stalingrad. The German people had heard for so long of the military genius of the Führer, the superiority of the German soldier and the inferiority of the Slav, that they had come to believe it; such a defeat could, in their view, be explained only by treachery, the treachery of the German generals and the general staff. Such views appeared to be confirmed by the bomb plot of 20 July and the activity of the communist sponsored German officers' committee in Moscow. The embers of suspicion were deliberately fanned to flame by the Nazi Party's propaganda machine.

On 6 July General Burrows, heading the British Military Mission in Moscow, had been taken by the Russians on a three day visit to 3 Belorussian Front, the Soviet intention, so Burrows reported to London, being to impress on their allies the magnitude of the victory. Vasilevsky, the Chief of General Staff, who had been responsible for co-ordinating the fronts in the northern pincer (while Zhukov commanded those in the south) was unusually communicative; he told Burrows that the Soviet success had been due to the artillery and the Red Air Force, but he had detected a deterioration in the fighting value of the Germans, and what he called 'a blockhouse mentality'—the very mentality in fact that had been inculcated into them by Hitler.

The Soviet high command had no intention of halting its offensive in Belorussia but intended, if it could, to enter the Baltic States, East Prussia and Poland before the enemy could mend the breach, for Soviet troops were already within fifty miles of the Rastenburg headquarters on the East Prussian border, so near in fact that the Führer's personal guard troops were rushed off eastwards to help plug the gap. On 9 July, Model, who had been in command of Army Group Centre for only twelve harassing days, flew with Friessner, who was in his fifth day of office, to persuade the dictator to pull back the line and evacuate Estonia. This was refused once more, partly because of the effect that it might have on the Finns and partly, Hitler said, because Dönitz was opposed to giving up the Estonian naval bases.

On 18 July Model and Friessner returned once more to the Führer, Model begging that the Lithuanian gap be closed between the two army groups, and, as he had not the troops to do it, suggesting, much to Friessner's indignation, that Army Group North should find the necessary forces. Friessner, too, had his difficulties. The threatened separation from Army Group Centre would result in the encirclement of his forces if the Red Army should break through to the Gulf of Riga; on the other hand the extension of his southern frontage to cover the disappearance of much of the old Army Group Centre, together with the growing

Soviet pressure on his own front, meant that he needed every man that he could muster to prevent himself being driven into the Baltic. Friessner had taken over his army group with energy and enthusiasm, determined to support Model by a rapid counter-offensive to the south-east, in accordance with Hitler's orders, but a few days of the realities of command had shown him that such an offensive was impossible.

In the third week in June the Soviet high command had completed plans for a third offensive to be made following those in Finland and in Belorussia, aimed at occupying Poland and destroying Army Group North Ukraine (formerly Army Group South), the same army group that Model had taken over when he relieved von Manstein in the spring of 1944. Model still commanded this army group through his deputy Harpe, in addition to Army Group Centre immediately to the north.

The new Soviet offensive into Central and Southern Poland was to be made by Konev's 1 Ukrainian Front, together with the left flank of Rokossovsky's 1 Belorussian Front. But on 8 July Stalin appeared to have been uncertain whether Konev should be reinforced by formations taken from the Finnish and the Belorussian theatres or whether to mount a second all-out offensive from Belorussia in a determined effort to occupy East Prussia and encircle Friessner's Army Group North against the Baltic. His military advisers were in favour of this latter course, but Stalin eventually decided in favour of the Konev offensive into Poland, partly because he did not want to become bogged down in East Prussia should there be a stiffening of German resistance as soon as the battle was taken into the Reich, but more particulatly since he intended to gain an immediate advantage, *vis-à-vis* his western allies and the London Polish Government-in-Exile, by the speedy occupation of ethnic Poland. He ruled, therefore, that Konev's offensive should be reinforced and go ahead as planned. Zhukov was to leave the Belorussian theatre to Vasilevsky and was to co-ordinate Konev's and Rokossovsky's fronts. Konev was to launch what was to become known as the Lvov-Sandomierz operation directly against Army Group North Ukraine across Ukrainian Galicia and South Poland, while Rokossovsky was to thrust against Harpe's left flank into Central Poland towards Lublin and Warsaw.

Model meanwhile toured his two army groups keeping up a display of fanatical energy as he conducted his whirlwind visits, livening up his divisions and leaving a trail of disorder behind him, losing some of the confidence and respect of his subordinate commanders by a wanton interference in details that were none of his concern. For no German general, unless it were Schörner, was more attuned to the demands of the Führer and the party, even to the extent of being an enthusiastic supporter of the system of Nazi military commissars. Model was extraordinarily active, both mentally and physically, he knew no fear and he wanted to see everything—and do everything—for himself; he had a very good understanding of tactics that was partially nullified by the lack of a sense of what was practicable; he over-estimated his own ability and that of his troops and demanded the impossible; he was erratic and inconsistent, an excellent improviser, with few social graces, inclined to curry favour with the rank and file at the expense of the officers. Model shared in fact many of Hitler's characteristics and he continued to enjoy the dictator's highest regard, particularly for the way in which he had 'brought the enemy Belorussian offensive to a halt'. Yet, for all that, he was most able.* But the price of Model's temporary success in Army Group Centre was about to be paid for in Army Group North Ukraine.

Army Group North Ukraine consisted of thirty-one German divisions, of which four were panzer, and twelve Hungarian brigades. The Hungarian Army was grouped with 1 Panzer Army to form Group Raus, Raus having been transferred from 4 to 1 Panzer Army in April on the death of Hube in an air crash. Raus in his turn had been replaced by Harpe in command of 4 Panzer Army, but Harpe was, at the beginning of July, also acting as the deputy commander of the army group, so that, at the time of Konev's offensive, both the army group and 4 Panzer Army were controlled by absent commanders.

Konev's offensive was not unexpected by Army Group North Ukraine, for the Russians had been bringing up troops within a radius of 250 miles. Although much of the enemy movement had been done by night it was impossible to conceal the concentration of a force said to number over 800,000 men, 1,600 tanks and 2,800 aircraft. On the German side there was a general stand-to on 6 and 7 July, after which the troops were stood down again. Then, on 12 July, the first Russian probing attacks began, at first only limited, but developing during the next two days into a full offensive. Once again the defenders were surprised at the intensity of the enemy artillery bombardment and the overwhelming power of the Red Air Force that, for the first time in the experience of many of the troops fighting there, had an absolute and unchallenged air supremacy over the battlefield. Near Koltov the Soviet enemy soon punched a hole through the defences three miles wide and ten miles deep, and through this narrow gap there poured a great column of men and vehicles as two Soviet tank armies emerged into the open. Hauffe's 13 German Corps of 40,000 men, part of 1 Panzer Army, was encircled near Brody and, by 22 July, virtually destroyed.

The Soviet armoured advance continued rapidly westwards, at first bypassing to the north the defended area of Lvov. On 24 July the German garrison there began to evacuate the city and fell back to the south-west on Sambov, and three days later the great town of Stanislav was given up. On 30 July Konev was across the Vistula, having covered 130 miles in nineteen days. Meanwhile further to the north Rokossovsky's advance had been even more rapid. On 18 July, a few days after the start of Konev's offensive, the left wing of Rokossovsky's 1 Belorussian Front, supported by about 1,400 aircraft, moved westwards on a broad front along the southern fringe of the Pripet marshes, with the intention of separating Army Group North Ukraine from Army Group Centre. The Bug was crossed in three places and the left wing of 4 Panzer Army was driven in. The Army Group North Ukraine was already fully extended by Konev's offensive in the south and it had already lost its only panzer reserve when it was transferred by Model to Army Group Centre to dam the breach in Belorussia.

From 20 July, the day of the assassination attempt on Hitler, the eastern front was in danger of disintegrating and it seemed that the Army Group Centre disaster in Belorussia would be repeated in Army Group North Ukraine. Rokossovsky was well into Poland and, having left the Pripet behind him, was shortly going to be in a position where he could unite the north and south parts of his 1 Belorussian

---

* It is of interest that Model told Boldt in July 1944, when he was still on the eastern front, that 'the war was lost'.

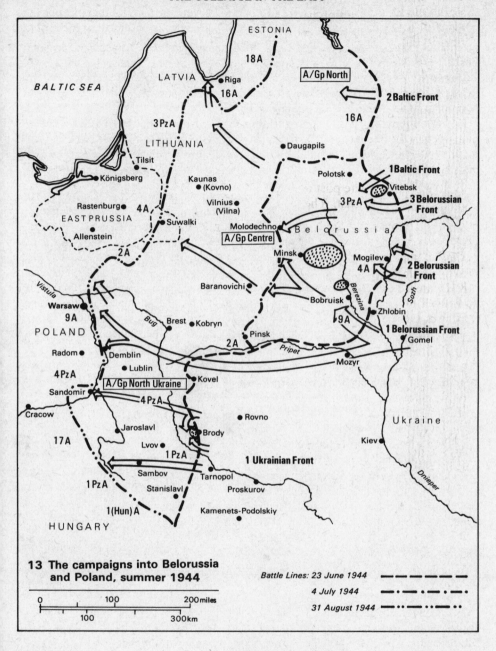

13 The campaigns into Belorussia and Poland, summer 1944

Battle Lines: 23 June 1944	— — — —
4 July 1944	— · — · — ·
31 August 1944	— ·· — ·· — ··

Front. Weiss's 2 German Army, the right flank formation of Army Group Centre guarding the Pripet in the area Brest-Kobryn, was now threatened on three sides. Lublin fell on 23 July. The Führer had forbidden any withdrawal, but the course of events made his orders of little consequence for the enemy was across the Vistula near Demblin on 25 July, well to the rear of 4 Panzer Army. Weiss attempted to stand at Brest-Litovsk but this fell only three days later. Meanwhile Rokossovsky was moving rapidly down the Vistula, reaching the outskirts of Warsaw on 31 July. A little further to the south Konev was advancing on Cracow and nearing the Carpathians and the Czechoslovakian border, while in the far north Bagramian's 1 Baltic Front had succeeded in driving a wedge between Friessner's Army Group North and Model's Army Group Centre and had reached the Baltic shore, isolating Friessner from the other battle fronts. The overall situation in the east would appear to have been beyond salvation.

Hitler meanwhile had begun hunting down army officers suspected of any disloyalty to his person and régime; an anonymous complaint, sent in by an other rank with a grievance, could be sufficient to imprison, remove or reduce an officer to the ranks. The German high command and military organization were in this way destroyed from within at the time of the greatest crisis of the war: Germany's war production had begun to decline and the terror bombing of the home front was growing heavier month by month; the front had been broken in Italy, while in France Hausser's 7 Army had disintegrated and Army Group B could no longer stave off defeat; in the east much of Army Group Centre had disappeared and Army Group North Ukraine appeared to be in danger of collapse; Army Group North had been encircled and the existence of 20 German Army in Finland was threatened. The army and SS losses for June and July of that year had totalled 85,000 dead, 200,000 wounded and 340,000 missing. Only the Balkans and Army Group South Ukraine on the borders of Rumania seemed to be secure. Zeitzler had gone and his deputies Heusinger and Stieff had been removed, so that nobody remained responsible for the eastern front; Guderian, ordered to assume the duties of the former Chief of Army General Staff as well as filling the appointment of Inspector-General of Panzer Troops, was a tactician not a strategist and was no more fitted for the task than Zeitzler had been, except that Hitler had eroded the status of the post to that of an executive between the dictator and the army groups in the east. There remained to the Chief of General Staff not a vestige of authority or initiative.

When Guderian arrived in Rastenburg he found the general staff offices of the OKH almost deserted. Most of the staff had been sent back to the main headquarters at Zossen and many of the departmental heads had been taken away by the Gestapo. Guderian, undaunted, set to work in a flurry of energy, exactly as Zeitzler had done before him, in spite of the fact that the Führer had only just before categorically and forcefully refused to allow him to issue any orders on his own authority. For the Führer had done away with the Commander-in-Chief of the Army, and the OKH, and he saw no reason to retain the designation and function of Chief of Army General Staff. To him, even the general staff was an anachronism.

Differences arose immediately between Guderian on the one hand and Model and Friessner on the other. Friessner wanted all his troops out of Estonia and Model wanted to cover his open south flank by withdrawing Weiss's 2 Army from the area of Brest and concentrating what he could behind the Vistula. Guderian, however, had entered the unreal world of the Führer when he professed to believe that the situation could be restored by removing a few divisions from Rumania. On 24 July Hitler issued an order committing Army Groups North and Centre to remain where they were. And he instructed Friessner to exchange his post with Schörner, the Commander of Army Group South Ukraine in Rumania and the other firm favourite of the Nazi régime. Friessner, by way of consolation, was advanced in rank to colonel-general and was sent off to what was considered to be a quiet theatre of operations.

The first three weeks of August saw a slackening off of pressure on the three battered German army groups between the Baltic and the Carpathians, mainly because the Red Army had outrun its supplies and was preparing another great offensive elsewhere. On 10 August, 4 Panzer Army, now under Balck, with three panzer divisions transferred from 1 Panzer Army, delivered a short and successful counter-attack on Konev's bridge-head west of the Vistula; further to the north, Rokossovsky's forces had come to a halt in front of Warsaw. But in the area of the Baltic Schörner was having no greater success than his predecessors Lindemann and Friessner, and, like them, he advised the Führer to evacuate Estonia. Hitler, however, continued to insist that every inch of Baltic territory was to be held, in spite of the fact that it was known that Finland was again seeking terms. Schörner was himself under heavy attack in the north-east from Govorov's Leningrad Front, which had moved the main weight of its forces southwards away from the Finnish front, and in the east from Maslennikov's 3 Baltic Front. Meanwhile Bagramian, to Schörner's south, was trying to widen and strengthen his hold on the Baltic coast.

The Führer carried out once more a further exchange of senior commanders in what was increasingly becoming a game of musical chairs, in that, if the general did not commit suicide, get murdered or imprisoned in the interim, he might eventually find himself back in command, or even in the same command from which he had been dismissed a few months before. On 16 August, Model was removed to the west to replace von Kluge, so that he might patch up the situation there as he had already done in Army Group Centre. Model was replaced in command of Army Group Centre by Reinhardt, whose vacancy in 3 Panzer Army (part of Army Group Centre) was filled by Raus. Harpe was confirmed in his post in command of Army Group North Ukraine.

At this point Hitler launched a new counter-attack, devised by himself, to be made by Raus's 3 Panzer Army, reinforced by two panzer formations removed from Rumania that had formed Friessner's only armoured reserve. This force was to attack north-eastwards from its concentration area in Lithuania and restore the land communications between Army Groups Centre and North; it was then to strike south-east on Kaunas in a raid across the rear of 1 Baltic and 3 Belorussian Fronts. The attack began on 16 August and, after some initial success that re-established a narrow land link between the two army groups, came to a halt; the link offered the last chance to withdraw Army Group North by land from the north Baltic States with all its heavy equipment. Hitler, however, had found a substitute for Finland when he maintained that an evacuation would have a disastrous effect on the attitude of Sweden; and so he moved another two divisions from Army Group Centre to Army Group North.

On 25 August the Americans and the Free French were in Paris and the Anglo-Americans were rapidly advancing on the undefended western frontiers of the Reich. The Führer then came to the conclusion, immediately after the failure of his Kaunas raid, that the main war effort must be switched to the west and he decided to collect within the homeland a mobile striking force that would deal the Anglo-Saxons a crippling blow west of Germany's frontiers; he would then turn eastwards to face the oncoming Red Army. For it was part of Hitler's dilemma, being under constant counter pressures from easterners and westerners, that he was forced continually to change his mind as to which to deal with first. The tensions, between Jodl on the one hand and Zeitzler and Guderian on the other, had reached such a pitch that the dictator would only hear the representations of the one side in the presence of the other. Meanwhile he turned a deaf ear to Guderian's pleadings to evacuate the Balkans, Finland, Norway and part of Italy, all of which were, of course, the executive responsibility of Jodl's *Wehrmacht-führungsstab*.

Guderian had turned his attention towards the raising of home defence units to protect the frontier areas in the east, and he began measures to build fortifications around Königsberg, Danzig, Glogau and Breslau, these being mainly of earthworks thrown up by volunteers, women, children and old men, the only labour available. Guderian gave orders for the raising of a hundred infantry battalions and the same number of artillery batteries from convalescents and low medical category soldiers, but most of these, Guderian complained, were seized by Jodl and dispatched to the west, to be followed by a reserve of guns and heavy equipment that Guderian had hoped to deploy in the east. Even the last drafts of combat troops that Himmler's Replacement Army produced were destined not for the defence of the east but for an offensive in the west.

The raising of the part-time volunteer citizen units for regional defence had been entrusted to the party and the measures taken were dilatory and ill-considered, but eventually the *Volkssturm* was born. The new organization had been publicized and recruited to such an extent, however, that insufficient leaders, instructors or arms were available to make it in any way an effective force; meanwhile it was receiving equipment that was urgently needed by the regular forces. Only in the final stages of the war and, in particular, on the Oder, did it become a fighting element of any importance.

When the Red Army entered Poland the political and ideological differences between Stalin's Soviet Union and the western allies could no longer be concealed. In 1939 and 1940 Stalin, no less than Hitler, had purposefully destroyed the Polish clergy, aristocracy, and *bourgeoisie*, in an effort to stamp out all Polish nationalism by mass murder and deportation. By midsummer 1944, there were all the signs that these Soviet purges were to be resumed. On 17 July, near Vilna, after many expressions of friendliness and gratitude, the local leaders and staff of the Polish national resistance movement (the Home Army or AK), were invited to a staff conference with Cherniakhovsky, the Commander of 3 Belorussian Front: none of them returned. The Soviet attitude was what might have been expected in the circumstances, and its intentions were confirmed when Poland was occupied and the communist sponsored and Moscow directed Lublin government came into being. Leading elements of the AK, and those Poles who were connected with the Polish Government-in-Exile in London, either disappeared or were rounded up for Siberia.

The final act of the drama that was to seal Poland's unhappy fate was being fought out in the streets of Warsaw, while Rokossovsky's troops remained halted near Praga on the east bank of the Vistula. On 1 August the Polish resistance movement in the city had taken up arms against the German occupation troops, the people showing the greatest of heroism as they fought not only to rid themselves of the old invader, but also to safeguard their future as a nation against the coming of the new. For its part, Moscow, well understanding the mentality and the aspirations of the Polish government in London, and being mistrustful of the British, hardly wished the uprising well. If Rokossovsky had been ordered, and had been able, to support the insurgents with all the means in his power, and had succeeded in occupying Warsaw during August, he would have been faced with a patriot army, estimated at about 35,000 strong, armed mainly with German weapons, a citizen force that would have been an acute embarrassment and threat to the new communist Lublin government.

At this time the Kremlin was unwilling to involve the Red Army in fighting Polish patriots, nor was it yet ready for an open trial of strength with the Anglo-Americans as to the future of Poland. Stalin therefore pretended, at first that there was no rising in Warsaw, then that the Home Army was allied to the Germans, and finally, in a remarkably brazen *volte-face*, said that the Polish A K leaders were both criminal and irresponsible in needlessly sacrificing Polish lives. Stalin used these arguments as excuses for inaction, and meanwhile refused a British and United States request for air landing facilities on Soviet soil so that the insurgents might be supplied by air with arms, ammunition and medical equipment.

It is said that Hitler refused to entrust the German Army with the quelling of the uprising but gave the task to Himmler whose S S troops committed indescribable atrocities on the Polish population. Meanwhile the patriot Home Army continued to fight on in the cellars and sewers through the whole of August and September, the remnants not surrendering until 2 October.

These dissensions between his Soviet and his western enemies, many of them real, some of them imagined by the German dictator, were seized upon by Hitler, who confidently expected an early break up in the enemy coalition. The dictator reasoned that, in the final outcome, the Anglo-Americans, England in particular, would soon be ready for peace in order that Nazi Germany might remain as Europe's bulwark against a Stalin imposed communism. Some of Hitler's senior generals had more sanguine expectations, in that they believed, even as late as May 1945, that the Anglo-Saxons would join what was left of the *Wehrmacht* in a joint effort to drive back the Russians to the east.

———————

During the summer, and largely as a result of the unacceptable demands made earlier by the Soviet Union during the peace negotiations, Finland had been forced back into the German camp, and President Ryti had signed an undertaking with von Ribbentrop that Finland would not make a separate peace; this undertaking was in exchange for German arms and the loan of a single German infantry division and a brigade of about thirty assault guns, all that Hitler could spare at that time. By the end of July, however, the German material assistance had dried up entirely and Hitler was asking for the return of his infantry division.

Germany's defeat in Belorussia and the Baltic and its failure to repel the Normandy landings quickened Finland's fears that Germany was sinking fast, and there was much bitterness that Berlin was failing to keep its part of the Ryti-von Ribbentrop bargain. On 4 August Mannerheim, the Finnish Commander-in-Chief, succeeded Ryti as President, and this permitted the Finns to repudiate the agreement; then, immediately on hearing that fighting had broken out near the Black Sea between

German and Rumanian troops, Finland, on 25 August, asked the Soviet Union for peace terms once more. Moscow agreed to resume negotiations on the prior undertaking that Finland should break off relations with Germany and that 20 German Mountain Army should be out of Lapland by 15 September.

The Austrian Rendulic, the commander of German troops in North Finland, was a firm Nazi supporter who was on very good terms with Hitler. According to Mannerheim, Rendulic called on him to deliver 'a threatening hint' that Finland should not submit to Soviet pressure to take up arms against the Germans.* Germany had frightened Europe in 1940 and 1941 and could count on a respectful audience in Italy and Rumania in 1943, but in Finland any suspicion of heavy-handedness had a hollow ring since the Finnish troops in that northern theatre were, in the main, superior to the German, and the isolated 20 German Army, outnumbered by two to one, could not be reinforced.

Rendulic began to withdraw towards Norway but it was obvious that his troops could not be out of Finland by mid September without abandoning most of their heavy equipment. Moscow meanwhile showed little interest in trying to pin the Germans with Red Army troops. The relationship between German and Finn remained quite good, however, until the German naval staff persuaded Hitler to seize the Finnish Baltic naval base at Suursaari. The attack was made on the morning of 15 September and was repelled by the Finns with considerable losses to the Germans. By attacking Suursaari Hitler played into Soviet hands and let the Finns out of an embarrassing situation, for they there and then demanded that Rendulic quit the country immediately. There was some scattered fighting between Germans and Finns, but in the main the withdrawal was orderly and without major incident.

So ended the Finnish War, a war that cost Finland about 200,000 casualties, of which over a quarter were killed. In addition it lost heavily in territory and economic resources and was oppressed with a crippling reparations debt. Yet Finland was fortunate to have remained a near independent nation and for this it had to thank its own courage and sturdy resolution, its closeness to the sea and the deep emotional interest taken in its future by the United States and Britain.

———————

Peace talks between Rumania, the USSR and the western allies had already taken place unknown to Germany, being broken off by Antonescu on 15 May 1944 since the proposed conditions were unacceptable to him. But the Rumanian nobility, intelligentsia and other opposition elements were determined to get out of the war, whether Antonescu agreed or not. Reassured by Moscow promises, they began to plot Antonescu's removal and the break with Germany, although for many of them liquidation or the slow death of the Soviet concentration camp was to be their fate.

The German-Rumanian relationship that had deteriorated so much during 1943 had shown no improvement in 1944. The inter-allied situation was very different from that in Italy in the summer of 1943 in that Antonescu now insisted on equality of command and would not allow German troops to be interposed between Rumania formations unless they were put under Rumanian control; and

---

* Rendulic subsequently denied this in a letter to the author.

17 German beach defences in Holland (1944)
18 German defence boom on the Channel coast

19

19 A Nazi press photo showing Rommel inspecting coastal gun emplacements (1944)
20 German beach obstacles in Normandy, photographed on 7 June 1944, the day after the invasion
21 German Army cycle mobility in the west

20

21

22 Part of the invasion fleet shortly bound for South France (August 1944)
23 American and French airborne troops landing behind Nice and Marseilles (August 1944)

24 Railway sidings at Vire, Normandy, after Allied bombing (June 1944)
25 A German dual-purpose 88mm gun used hastily in an anti-tank role

26 A V-1 pilotless winged jet missile photographed in flight (1944)
27 A V-2 rocket leaving its launching pad (1944)

28 United States tanks passing through part of the West Wall near Aachen (September 1944)
29 A captured German Panther (MkV) tank with a British crew on the 2 (Br) Army sector (January 1945)

30 Red Army troops attacking near Königsberg in East Prussia (February 1945)
31 The city of Kiel after Allied air bombing (May 1945)

the Germans were forced to accept it. There were other difficulties. Rumania wanted German equipment for which it could not pay and which Germany could no longer provide, and the friction with the Germans was hardly lessened by the presence on Rumanian soil of twenty German divisions, 125,000 *Volksdeutsch* refugees from Transdniester, and other foreign *Osttruppen* and *Hiwis*. The German troops were becoming increasingly impatient of Rumanian indolence, inefficiency and corruption, but the Führer had been unwilling to let his military commanders put pressure on their allies in case this should result in a further deterioration in his relations with Antonescu.

The German military command in Rumania was of a complicated pattern. As elsewhere, the *Luftwaffe* air and ground troops, including two flak divisions protecting the Ploesti oilfields, were responsible to Göring and the OKL, but local command in Rumania was entrusted to the air attaché and head of the air mission. Similarly all German Army troops inside Rumania, mainly training missions and base installations, came under the army attaché and head of the army mission in the capital; but this army attaché was responsible not to the OKH but to Jodl and the OKW, since Rumania, Hungary and the Balkan countries had been OKW theatres since 1941. But the OKH eastern front was now retiring on to these OKW commands, so that the army control within Rumania came to be split between Jodl and Guderian, for Friessner's Army Group South Ukraine in North Rumania remained responsible to the Führer through the general staff of the OKH.

Control was further bedevilled by the innovation of the Rumanian insistence on equality in command; the days when higher Rumanian formations could be coupled with and be put under the command of relatively subordinate German headquarters were long since past. Friessner was obliged to accept that a Rumanian army commander (Dumitrescu) should exercise command over two armies on the right, one of them German, in order that a German commander (Wöhler) should have command over a Rumanian army on the left. For the first time in the war German corps and divisions were under real instead of nominal Rumanian command. This division of responsibility, with the advantage to the Rumanian host, was extended throughout the rear areas, so that when the Soviet offensive began and Rumania suddenly changed sides, the whole of the German command was paralysed.

When Friessner was exchanged with Schörner and sent to Rumania to what was described in the OKH as a quiet front, he was to find that the German officers under his command had feelings of grave disquiet because of the new and strange attitude of their Rumanian comrades-in-arms. Bessarabia and Moldavia were untouched by the war, and the Rumanian authorities, even after due allowance had been made for corruption and incompetence, were taking no steps to put the country on to a war footing. The effect of Antonescu's earlier mobilization measures was half-hearted, and it was obvious that his orders were no longer being obeyed. The Germans were often ignored, an event that would have been considered impossible only two years before, and many of the newly appointed Rumanian commanders were thought to be hostile, not only to the Germans but also to Antonescu. There were grounds for suspicion that some of these commanders were preparing to come to terms with Russia, while others, preferring the west to the east, were hoping to secure Anglo-American support. These fears and suspicions were relayed by Friessner to Rastenburg.

The Führer, however, had received entirely contrary intelligence through the OKW and German foreign office. The Bucharest missions, the ambassadors and

Jodl's roving military representative, all reported favourably on the Rumanian support for Antonescu and the determination of the people and government to stay in the war. Friessner's misgivings were regarded as baseless, the head of the *Luftwaffe* mission telling Göring that if there should be a *coup d'état* in the Rumanian capital he was quite confident that he would 'quell it with a *Luftwaffe* flak battery'. Surprisingly, only von Ribbentrop was unconvinced, and he asked Hitler to station a panzer division in the capital as a pledge for the security of Antonescu's government. Guderian had not one to spare, but as he and Jodl freely offered each other's formations, and as the acting Chief of the Army General Staff rightly regarded Bucharest as an OKW responsibility, he suggested that the fully motorized SS police division in Yugoslavia would be eminently suitable. Jodl demurred, and there the matter was left.

In Bulgaria, too, the Germans experienced a feeling of uneasiness, and the head of the German military mission in Sofia reported to Guderian that the morale and behaviour of the Bulgarian troops indicated that something was going on under the surface. On 2 August Turkey had broken off diplomatic relations with Germany and there was a possibility that the German troops in Rumania might be attacked in the rear.

When Friessner had arrived in Rumania he found that his new command had been used by Hitler, Göring and Guderian as a pool from which other army groups were reinforced. A *Luftwaffe* group had already been transferred to Latvia, and of the nine panzer divisions originally available to his predecessor, Schörner, only one panzer and one panzer grenadier division remained.

Army Group South Ukraine consisted of two German armies and two Rumanian armies, tactically organized in two groupings. The Dumitrescu group in eastern Bessarabia was formed of 3 Rumanian Army and Fretter-Pico's 6 German Army on the line of the lower Dniester. Further to the west was the Wöhler group in Bukovina and Moldavia consisting of 8 German Army and Racovitza's 4 Rumanian Army. The total strength of Friessner's force was the equivalent to twenty-three German and twenty-three Rumanian divisions numbering over 800,000 men, of whom 360,000 were German.

The real strength of the two German armies could not, however, be measured in numbers for their battle readiness was by no means satisfactory. The commanders and chiefs of staff of the army group and 6 Army were new to their posts. The infantry divisions were actually up to strength, since they had been heavily re-inforced in the previous two months; but only fifteen per cent of the old battle experienced infantry remained. The standard of the reinforcements left much to be desired, for quite a number were over-age for front line duty and many of the others had been combed out from the administrative services and rearward depots; although these in due course might have made useful infantry, too many of them, officers included, were newly arrived and without any experience of action. Shortages of guns, mortars and ammunition were widespread, and obsolete German and captured Red Army artillery and mortars had been taken into use; although the Soviet guns were of good quality, they lacked prime-movers and ammunition. There was very little motor transport, and nearly all horse transport and services were in the hands of the *Hiwis*. Army Group North Ukraine did have 280 assault guns, but the most serious of Friessner's deficiencies were in tanks and aircraft, for of the 120 tanks fit for battle more than a half belonged to the Rumanians. The air corps forming the air element of Dessloch's 4 Air Fleet had only 300 aircraft, of which about fifty were first-class fighters; of the two flak divisions one had no experience in engaging tanks or ground targets and half of its gun crews were Rumanians.

Antonescu had suggested some time before that the Axis forces should evacuate Bessarabia and withdraw southwards into Transylvania on to the Carpathians, lower Sereth, Focsani, Galatz and the Danube estuary. In Antonescu's view the existing line was long and vulnerable because of the grain of country, and because, in particular, the valleys of the Sereth and Pruth ran south-eastwards, from the Soviet positions north of Iasi through 4 Rumanian Army area, so offering the enemy easy access to the rear of 6 German Army on the lower Dniester. This proposal, though supported in turn by Schörner and Friessner, had been rejected by Hitler; the rejection was to cost the Germans dearly. Friessner, more disturbed by the political and security situation to his rear than by the immediate Red Army threat to his front, asked Hitler that he should be given command of all the O K W, O K L and O K M controlled forces in Rumania, and that in future he should not be called upon to provide formations to reinforce other army groups. The dictator, however, gave no credence to Friessner's fears and had Keitel tell the army group commander 'to concern himself with his battle front and not with his rear'.

At the beginning of the summer Hitler and the O K H had believed that the main Soviet offensive would be made in the Balkans rather than in Belorussia. But when events had proved them wrong and the main offensive fell on Army Group Centre, with a second offensive on Army Group North Ukraine, it was generally and erroneously believed — yet again — that the Red Army had exhausted its strength. A fresh and major campaign into the Balkans in late August, on the heels of the other offensives, was certainly not expected.

The Soviet onslaught into Rumania was to be made by Tolbukhin's 3 Ukrainian Front, nearest the Black Sea, and Malinovsky's 2 Ukrainian Front, further inland, attacking side by side on a 250 mile wide frontage, their operations being co-ordinated by Timoshenko. The total Red Army strength was said to total ninety rifle divisions, together with six tank and mechanized corps of 1,400 tanks, supported by 1,700 aircraft. Since it had been arranged during the Soviet-Rumanian conspiracy that the Rumanian formations would not resist the Russian offensive, the Red Army strength was to be directed towards the destruction of the German armies.

Although Friessner was aware on 19 August of the imminence of a Soviet offensive, he had no idea of the true extent to which he was threatened. The main offensive began on 20 August and, by the evening of the next day, Russian columns had already isolated 6 German Army from the Rumanian army of Group Dumitrescu; it then became obvious to Friessner that most of the Rumanian formations were giving way without a fight. There were also alarming reports of the disarming and arrest by Rumanians of German liaison staffs and troop detachments, the cutting of German telephone lines and the refusal to obey any German orders. Some Rumanian formations said they had been demobilized and had left the line. One German mountain division was attacked by troops in Rumanian uniform who showed such resolution that they were suspected of being Red Army men.

The joint Axis defence had already disintegrated and, although the German defenders were as yet unaware of it, Soviet troops had penetrated many miles to the rear. Friessner made a frantic effort to cut all Rumanians out of the command system and to withdraw German formations detached to the Rumanian armies, but it was already too late. Red Army tank and motorized groups had launched a great enveloping movement, taking in the right flank of Group Wöhler through Husi, just west of the Pruth, then moving, as Antonescu had earlier warned that they might, along the grain of the country down the few good roads that ran along the river valleys; in this way they occupied much of the west bank of the Pruth about forty miles in the rear of 6 German Army before the German withdrawal was really under way. By 24 August six corps headquarters and the main element of twenty German divisions were encircled in a great pocket between the Dniester and the Pruth, 6 German Army headquarters still remaining outside the enveloping pincers. Having lost the bulk of his troops, for only seventy assault guns and forty tanks remained to him, Friessner was faced with the triple task of attempting to extricate the encircled army, and, since the enemy continued to move southwards and south-westwards, of evacuating the numerous German military and civilian organizations in Rumania; thirdly, he had to form a new front to hold the Soviet advance towards Hungary.

On the evening of 23 August, having reported to the King of Rumania to brief him on the war situation, Antonescu was arrested, by the King's orders, together with the Ministers for War and for the Interior. That night the King broadcast to the country that the war was at an end and that Rumanian troops should stop fighting.

The night was one of orders and counter-orders from the Führer and his two headquarters, the OKW and OKH. At 11 p.m. Friessner telephoned Hitler to tell him that he, on his own initiative, had taken over the command of *all* German troops in Rumania, an action that the dictator readily confirmed. When Friessner suggested an immediate retirement out of Rumania to Hungary, Hitler came up with a proposal that Friessner should arrest the King and what he called 'the traitor clique', and set up a suitable Rumanian general as the head of the government. The Führer's air of unconcerned detachment left an impression on Friessner that the urgency and seriousness of the situation was not at all understood. In reality Friessner commanded nothing, because the heads of the air and army missions, together with Göring and Jodl, ignored him and went their own way, making recommendations to the Führer and giving orders as they thought fit. Gerstenberg, the air attaché in Bucharest, made light of the affair to the OKL and suggested a *Stuka* bombing attack should be made on the capital of Germany's ally followed by an occupation by one of the flak divisions from Ploesti. Göring relayed this information by word of mouth to the Führer, who apparently thought the situation could be mastered by a few energetic measures similar to those taken when the Italians had been disarmed in September 1943. Jodl, still ignoring Friessner, issued appropriate instructions through the army attaché and instructed von Weichs, the Commander of Army Group F, to send a mobile group from Belgrade to Bucharest. The Rumanians, however, showing a good deal more energy and resolution than the Italians had ever done, occupied, or laid siege to, all German installations in the country.

On 25 August a 150 sortie bombing attack was made by the *Luftwaffe* on Bucharest, and this gave the Rumanians the pretext they had been waiting for to declare war on Germany.

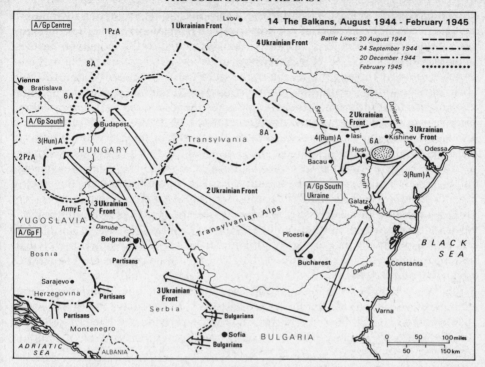

14 The Balkans, August 1944 - February 1945

Friessner forbade Fretter-Pico, the commander of the encircled 6 German Army, to join his beleaguered troops who had been ordered to break out as best they might, and Friessner set to work to scrape up a new force for the defence of Hungary. The army group and army headquarters were rapidly driven westwards by the approaching Red Army and soon lost radio contact with the pocket. Meanwhile the Führer attempted to control the battle from his desk and, being entirely out of touch with the true situation on the ground, ordered new defence lines that had already been overrun by the enemy.

From 22 August 6 German Army and a corps of 8 Army trapped in the cauldron began to withdraw in sweltering heat, the dust and haze making observation difficult; road and tracks were repeatedly bombed by the Red Air Force but, except for an occasional reconnaissance plane, the *Luftwaffe* was not to be seen. Overall control was virtually impossible as 6 Army headquarters was beyond radio range and there was no co-ordinating headquarters inside the pocket; in any event since no tables of speech and key frequencies had been issued since before the offensive, radio intercommunication became a haphazard business and increasingly unreliable as distances grew greater. Divisional commanders had to gain their intelligence by listening to the sounds of battle around them and by visiting their neighbours, if they could be found. Many divisions had no idea that they were surrounded, in spite of the fact that ammunition and ration supply had ceased some days before. Control and order rapidly broke down and regiments soon split into small groups, so that Tolbukhin's 3 Ukrainian Front parlementary, who appeared in the pocket under a white flag, was to report back that he could find no German general in overall command or with any real authority. Some

German troops threw away their weapons and surrendered, but most were determined on escape. Few, however, did so, and nearly 200,000 men disappeared without trace, only part of 29 Corps headquarters and elements of the panzer and the panzer grenadier division reaching Hungary.

The loss of 6 German Army and part of 8 Army in Rumania was in some respects a greater catastrophe than the disaster that had overtaken the earlier 6 Army at Stalingrad. Paulus's army had fought for two and a half months in the bitter Asiatic cold, whereas Fretter-Pico's force lasted only nine days in the hot Rumanian summer. There were many reasons for this rapid defeat. The political, strategic and indeed the real tactical direction lay with Hitler, who, on 25 August, was ordering *Luftwaffe* forces so badly needed for the support of the encircled troops to bomb Bucharest. A day later he was still instructing Friessner to establish a defensive line that had already been lost. Nor could Göring, Jodl or Guderian escape censure. Friessner's decision not to return Fretter-Pico to the pocket was probably a wrong one in the circumstances, and, since a successful withdrawal was out of the question, 6 Army might have done better to remain where it was. This is, however, being wise after the event. In the final outcome it would have been destroyed whatever its course of action.

On 30 August Soviet troops took Ploesti and the next day seized Bucharest, capturing most of the Germans in the capital. The remainder of Rumania was then rapidly occupied together with Bulgaria, which country, on 8 September, declared war on Germany. The Bulgarian armed forces, just under half a million strong, were then taken under Soviet command and used, together with the purged Rumanian forces, to continue the war in the Balkans. Von Weichs's Army Group F and Löhr's Army Group E in Yugoslavia, Greece and the Greek islands were now in mortal danger.

The weight of the German occupation forces in the west of the Balkan Peninsula lay in Croatia, to the north of Yugoslavia, and there were few troops in Greece, except on the islands. Nor was the active partisan resistance in Greece itself widespread, compared with the fighting that was going on that summer in Yugoslavia, and there was no liaison between Tito and the Greek guerrilla leaders. The Greek resistance to the German occupation centred on the communist EAM (with its fighting organization the ELAS), and the nationalist-royalist EDES. According to the contemporary German intelligence estimates, the British supported both movements, the ELAS, however, 'with some reluctance'. The EDES was only a third of the size of the ELAS, but it was by far the better trained and equipped. These movements were more interested in fighting each other to improve their chances of seizing power after a German withdrawal than they were in destroying the occupation troops. Zervas, the nationalist leader, had long been courted by the Germans in the hope of securing an armistice with his forces.

In mid July Zervas suddenly attacked the Germans from his bridge-head at Previza — Agrinion: two days later the ELAS south of Epirus also began to threaten German installations, and the German intelligence came to suspect some co-ordinating action by the British. On 2 August Turkey had broken off diplomatic relations with Germany and, fifteen days later, the Bulgarians had given formal notice that they were going to withdraw all their occupation divisions, some of which had for months past been indifferent both to German orders and to the deteriorating local security situation. Hitler would have willingly ordered the occupation of European Turkey and the Asiatic littoral bordering on the Dardanelles and Bosphorus — for which OKW plans already existed — but even he was forced to admit that not a man could be spared for the task. Von Weichs, the Commander-in-Chief South-East wanted to destroy Zervas and, even as late as 29 August, Hitler was intent that he should do so; but this operation had to be abandoned, too, because of lack of means and the threatening situation in Rumania. On 26 August, following the Rumanian collapse, von Weichs was ordered to withdraw to a line Corfu—Joannina—Kalabaka—Olympus and to begin the evacuation of the islands, 'contracting the German forces towards the centre of the Balkans'. It was originally intended that the evacuation should be carried out piecemeal and by stages, without undue haste, some priority being given to the salvaging of equipment at the expense of men; coastal artillery batteries that could not be dismantled were to remain *in situ*, fully manned and with infantry protection, these tiny strongholds being written off in Rastenburg as lost to the enemy. Thomale, the acting Inspector-General of Panzer Troops, went to Nish in Serbia, to try and recover the many German manufactured tanks still in Bulgaria.

At first an attempt had been made to conceal the intention to withdraw, even from the German troops themselves, and the removal of men back to the Reich was explained to the men 'as an increase in the leave quota'. Although the task of withdrawal would appear to have been a daunting one — there were nearly 70,000 troops in Crete and another 23,000 on Rhodes and the Aegean islands, most of whom were to be moved by air and at night to the Greek mainland — the evacuation continued without haste or alarm. In the early days there was virtually no British interference with the movement, so that it began to be assumed in Rastenburg that London had realized that it was in its own interests to leave Army Group E where it was, unharried and untouched, in order to serve as a counterweight to the ELAS. On 15 September, however, there was a heavy Anglo-American air raid on Athens airfields that destroyed half the Junkers 52 aircraft standing there, and thereafter the German air and sea movement frequently came under attack. German losses were nevertheless regarded as 'bearable', and the evacuation was not halted. On 21 September came British landings in Greece at Kythira to be followed by others at Araxos and Kalamato.

More serious, however, was the position to the north. Following the Bulgarian declaration of war, it was surprising to the Germans 'how the Soviets managed to turn the [hitherto despised] Bulgarian divisions into an effective fighting force'. Von Weichs was under pressure to give up the Albanian and Montenegran coastline because of Tito's rapidly growing strength, but he could not do this too soon since he had to keep the withdrawal routes open for the troops in the south. Before the end of September Tito was moving on Belgrade from the west while Soviet troops of Tolbukhin's front threatened it from the east. After the loss of the railway route through the capital, Löhr's Army Group E had to take the march route, mainly on its feet, living off the country as best it might, moving northwards steadily and covering about fifteen miles a day. All superfluous units, auxiliaries and dependents had already been withdrawn earlier by the OKW, and so the movement of the main bodies took place in an orderly fashion, very differently, said the OKW diarist, from the progress of 19 Army when it had evacuated the south of France a month or so before.

On Crete there remained 16,000 Germans and Italians, with a further 6,000 on Rhodes, and all remaining German naval vessels had been scuttled in the Gulf of Salonica. There was little interference from British ground forces in Greece against the withdrawing German troops, and by the end of October the last German soldier had left the Greek peninsula on his way northwards.

The Russians had no interest in the German occupation forces in Greece and appear to have had very little in those retiring northwards through Yugoslavia, for Tolbukhin, swinging to the south in a great arc through Bulgaria, had by then turned northwards again, and, moving astride the eastern Yugoslavia frontier, had skirted Belgrade and was advancing into Hungary. Stalin was content to leave to Tito and the Bulgarians the clearing of Yugoslav territory of the enemy, for he regarded Hungary as the worthwhile prize — the strategic centre of Europe. This was not known in Rastenburg, however, and part of von Weichs's Army Group F — 2 Panzer Army and the troops forced out of Serbia and, later, Army Group E (downgraded from November as Army E) — were handed over to Friessner in order to hold the Russians back east of the Croat border. By the end of October Army Group F held only Croatia, Slovenia and Herzegovina, the north-west corner of Yugoslavia covering the Ljubljana Gap.

During the month of August alone the German armed forces had, on all war fronts, suffered a total in casualties of 64,000 dead, 407,000 missing, and about 170,000 wounded, although a large number of these wounded could be expected to return to duty. In France, German casualties since the invasion until the beginning of September were nearing the half million mark. The total German casualties in the *Wehrmacht* and Armed S S since the start of the Second World War until the end of August 1944, not including the wounded, stood at 1,510,000 dead and 1,319,000 missing. Such blood-letting could not continue for much longer.

CHAPTER NINE

Between the Rhine and the Vistula

On 18 August, less than two days after he had assumed command in France, Model gave as his opinion that further withdrawals eastwards *would* be necessary in view of what he called 'the enemy's absolute air superiority', and he proposed that he should reform his front so that it ran roughly on the line of the Seine, with 7 Army holding from the coast to Laigle, then 5 Panzer Army in position between Laigle and Paris and 1 Army from Paris along the upper Seine; the troops, continued Model, were absolutely burned out, and he urgently needed reinforcements, transport and supplies.

The OKW had feared at the time that part of Patton's 3 Army might have thrust vigorously northwards down the Seine valley towards the Channel, in a deeper secondary envelopment outside the pincers surrounding the Falaise cauldron, so putting the German troops escaping from the pocket, as well as the relieving 2 SS Panzer Corps, in great jeopardy. The tension was relieved, however, when it was seen that the enemy in the south appeared to be more interested in making ground towards Paris and the middle Seine than in completing the destruction of the German troops in Normandy.

The Führer had readily agreed that Army Group B should get behind the Seine, since he reasoned that, with the bridges down, the front could not be supplied across the river anyway; yet, on 22 August, he was still ordering that Paris be held as 'it was the key to the Channel coast and the V weapon sites'. But although the British pressure against Model in the north was not, for the moment, at all heavy, the American thrusts in the south were so vigorous and rapid that the relief felt earlier in the OKW (that many of Patton's troops had turned away from the Falaise battle) gave way to even deeper concern when it was realized that the Americans had driven 1 Army out of Fontainebleau and had actually reached Troyes: a continuation of this movement might mean that the enemy would soon be in Dijon astride 19 Army's withdrawal route from the Mediterranean.

On 24 August Model was ordered by the Führer to hold Paris at all costs in order to keep the east-west communications open, the dictator directing that the Paris bridges should be ringed with flak artillery and prepared for demolition; terrorist leaders were to be publicly executed and areas of resistance within the city were to be flattened by the *Luftwaffe*. But even as these orders were being issued there was a sudden outburst of heavy fighting south of Rouen that drove back 7 Army and surrounded *Gruppe Fick*, while enemy troops 'supported by the resistance and the communists' broke into Paris as far as La Place de l'Etoile. Paris was then surrendered by von Choltitz, the German commandant in the capital.

Meanwhile the OKW was urging 19 Army to increase the speed of its march northwards. Except for those divisions left in Marseilles and Toulon, it had been ordered on 16 August to withdraw to 'a position to be prepared on the line Sens — Dijon — the Swiss frontier', the movement up the Rhône valley being covered by the only panzer division it had. Meanwhile, however, resistance insurrections broke out in the areas of Aix, Avignon, Valence and Grenoble, with a general *Maquis* uprising near the Swiss frontier. The situation looked so serious that Model was ordered to put troops into Dijon, while Kesselring, using his own resources from the Italian theatre, was instructed to secure the passes and put a reserve regiment into Grenoble. Nothing more was heard of this reserve regiment after its arrival in the city until *Luftwaffe* air reconnaissance reported that it had fled from the resistance fighters that had laid in wait for it. The danger to the rear was much greater than that in front, and, as the resistance barred all northwards routes east of the Rhône, the movement of 19 Army had to be made up the west side of the river; even so it could not escape running the gauntlet on the Drôme and at Lyons. On 4 September the advanced guard finally arrived in the *Armee Gruppe G* area but the columns were still strung out as far back as Mâcon. By 22 September Blaskowitz reported that over 200,000 men were withdrawing, but that, at the moment, he had only 130,000 men (from both armies) concentrated and ready for duty: the remainder were either still *en route* northwards, had been driven eastwards into Italy, or were casualties or stragglers in hiding; more than 35,000 men had been left behind in Toulon and Marseilles. *Armee Gruppe G* now became responsible for forming the link between Army Group B and the Swiss frontier.

Model had, on 30 August, suggested an entirely unrealistic idea, proposing that he should thrust north-westwards into the American flank, roughly south of the Ardennes between the Aisne and the Marne, using three motorized divisions and two panzer brigades.* Such a proposal was meaningless, for virtually no tanks remained to him and his troops were in full flight over the whole of France, the intermediate withdrawal positions marked on the map from the Seine to the West Wall having been overrun by the enemy's rapid advance before preparation or occupation had been possible. But Hitler seized on the idea and, from the first week in September, began to formulate his own plans for the preparation of a grand counter-offensive in the style of the 1940 Ardennes breakthrough.

On the very same day that he had proposed this counter-offensive to Hitler, Model asked for permission to retire behind the Somme by the night of 31 August, should this be necessary, and he sweetened this request by assuring the Führer that counter-attacks would be put in by him, whenever possible; but in any case, Model continued, 'the developing and improving of the West Wall [guarding the frontier of the Reich] should now be put in hand as a matter of urgency'. The day after Model made this report, Montgomery's 21 Army Group attacked with a totally unexpected violence, reached Amiens, crossed the Somme and made for Albert towards the Belgian frontier, scattering 7 German Army yet again and enveloping 15 German Army from the south-east against the coast of the Pas de Calais. Eberbach, who had only recently taken over the command of 7 Army, fell

---

* Independent panzer brigades had been in existence throughout the war but the numbers increased towards the end. The organization and strength varied widely. At Kursk some had over 200 tanks, but more usually they numbered about 70 tanks, with a single battalion of armoured infantry, this interim organization being the 'Panzer Brigade 44'.

into British hands. On 3 September the OKW war diarist recorded that 'terrorists had gained the upper hand in Brussels'. The following day British armoured troops had taken Antwerp with its docks and installations largely intact: 15 German Army was surrounded.

The Führer decided that yet another change was necessary in the field command. Model, who had performed what the dictator called 'a miracle' in Belorussia, had not been able to transform the near disastrous situation in the west in the short twelve days that he had been in command. The dictator had come to believe that the responsibilities were too great for one man to shoulder. Model should therefore remain in command of Army Group B with a new chief of staff, Krebs, to replace Speidel.* But the appointment of Commander-in-Chief West was to be taken from Model and given to von Rundstedt, who was recalled from the reserve to resume the post that he had, as the price of failure, been ordered to hand over to von Kluge only two months before; von Rundstedt was to have a new chief of staff, Westphal instead of Blumentritt. Blaskowitz's *Armee Gruppe G* was to be raised in status to that of a full army group.

Whether von Rundstedt was any improvement on Model is a matter of doubt. Both, in different times and in other circumstances, might have been regarded as very able. But whereas Model was the very picture of a modern and loud-mouthed National-Socialist general, brimming over with interfering and destructive energy, von Rundstedt was taciturn, reserved, and indolent, practised in decentralizing his responsibilities, and with all the dignity of the old Prussian school.** Yet the difference between them was only in the outward form, for Hitler could rely implicitly that both would do exactly what he told them. Hitler was in command, not the Commander-in-Chief West, and the whole war, down to its tactical detail, was controlled from the dictator's desk. Yet this was not known by the Anglo-Americans at the time, for 21 Army Group intelligence staffs began to attribute subsequent German successes to von Rundstedt's efficient handling of the troops under his command.

On 31 August Hitler interviewed Westphal and Krebs before they took over their new appointments and he did not fail to lay the blame for his misfortunes on Rommel and von Kluge. Rommel had become a fair weather soldier, a man who, 'in spite of his many qualities', was not a stayer, a pessimist in adversity, 'who had tried to seek non-military solutions'. Hitler knew, he said, that von Kluge and his former Army Group Centre staff were involved in the 20 July conspiracy, and von Kluge had personally tried to get in touch with the British during the Falaise battle, 'though this must remain a secret so that it brought no shame on the *Wehrmacht*'. The dictator no longer spoke of the heroism, the achievements, or the trials of the *Wehrmacht* and of the German people, for his megalomania had developed to the stage of the everlasting *Ich-Kult*. The war, he said, had not been very pleasant for *him*; for five whole years he had cut himself from the world, had not attended a theatre, concert or seen a film. All the victories and gains of former years had been *his* doing, the defeats and losses being the fault of the generals and of the general staff. With two more panzer divisions that the conspirators of 20

---

* Speidel, like Rommel and von Kluge, was suspected of being involved in the 20 July conspiracy. He was arrested on 7 September on Himmler's orders.

** According to Kesselring, von Rundstedt rarely visited the fronts or kept in close radio or telephonic touch with his subordinates. Like von Hindenburg in the old OHL, his work was done in the old fashioned way through his chief of staff.

July had somehow cheated him out of, *he* would have prevented the American break-out at Avranches, so that the situation in France would have now looked very different. It was naive and childish, he told the two generals, to think of a peace settlement with heavy German military defeats everywhere; his diplomatic hopes were based on the break-up of the enemy coalition for which history provided the example of the withdrawal of Russia from the Seven Years War, and, like the Great King [Frederick the Great], *he* would fight on until one or other of his accursed enemies tired of the struggle and gave up.

On 1 September the last V-1 was launched towards London; a week later the first V-2 was ready for firing.

Although Bradley had assumed the command of 12 United States Army Group shortly after the break-out from the Normandy beach-head, the overall command of all the British, Canadian and the United States ground forces continued to be vested in Montgomery. On 1 September, however, Eisenhower assumed direct control over Montgomery's 21 Army Group and Bradley's 12 Army Group, together, in mid September, with Devers's 6 Army Group that had arrived in the Vosges and the Belfort Gap from the Mediterranean. Montgomery had two armies, Crerar's 1 Canadian and Dempsey's 2 British, Bradley had two, Hodges's 1 (US) and Patton's 3 (US) Armies, to be increased at the end of September by the arrival of Simpson's 9 (US) Army after the capture of Brest (an operation that had lasted nearly six weeks). Devers had two armies, Patch's 7 (US) Army and de Lattre de Tassigny's 1 (French) Army. A substantial part of Crerar's Canadian Army had been detached to destroy the German fortresses and strong points on the Channel coast.

Both Montgomery and Brooke, the British Chief of the Imperial General Staff, disagreed with Eisenhower's decision to halt for resupply and regrouping and then attack into Germany on a broad front almost from the Dutch to the Swiss frontiers. They would have preferred a rapid thrust on Berlin made on a narrow front across the North German plain or, if an American army group was to undertake it, a drive south of the Ardennes through Leipzig and then on to the German capital. It was Brooke's opinion at the time that Eisenhower's broad front strategy would lengthen the war by three to six months.

Since we are concerned more with the situation inside Fortress Europe, any lengthy assessment as to whether Eisenhower was right or wrong would be out of place here. Some allied leaders believed at the time that Germany was near political and military collapse and that the fighting was virtually over, an optimism that was not, however, shared by Roosevelt or Churchill. Yet the allied command in those heady September days apparently gave little thought to the urgency of opening up the Schelde estuary to Antwerp and much of 15 German Army (82,000 men and 580 guns) was allowed to escape into Walcheren across the Schelde. Less than a fortnight later, a British corps made slow going against spirited German resistance in its progress to relieve a spearhead airborne division that was fighting for its life at Arnhem. Elsewhere allied successes were small and local. Some might say that this lack of success underlined the correctness of Eisenhower's decision to stop and regroup; others on the other hand might use the same factor to argue to the contrary, that this allied inertia was the natural result of spreading the forces too thinly. The allied problems of replenishment due to the shortage of ports and of transport and to the extended lines of communication were undoubtedly very acute, yet there was a lack of a sense of vital urgency, perhaps even some complacency, among both American and British commanders and staffs, a trait that had not existd before. Eisenhower's forecast that he might not be ready to cross the Rhine until the following May caused not a little dismay in London.

To von Rundstedt, who had reassumed command only a few days before, the situation looked very differently, however. The enemy, according to von Rundstedt's estimate, had about fifty-four divisions, almost equally split between 21 and 12 Army Groups, and von Rundstedt put 12 Army Group armoured strength at 2,500 tanks; 6 (US) Army Group had not yet arrived near the frontier but he estimated that it probably had from nine to twelve divisions. The enemy's linear deployment along the frontier without any reserves to the rear surprised von Rundstedt, and he could only imagine that further allied formations were expected from abroad. There were in North America, according to what von Rundstedt had gleaned from *Fremde Heere West*, a further thirty-nine divisions, of which five were already on their way to Europe, while another nine divisions of 14 (US) Army were being despatched from the United Kingdom to the continent. There was yet another American reserve of five infantry and four airborne divisions in Britain, making eighteen United States divisions there in all. 'Yet to be accounted for were the fourteen [phantom] British divisions forming part of 4 British Army in the United Kingdom', and von Rundstedt agreed with the intelligence staffs that this army would be likely to land in the German rear, either in North Holland or on the German North Sea coast. Although the British and American forces were originally in equal strength, it was obvious, he thought, that eventually, as the reinforcement divisions arrived, the Americans must outnumber the British. Meanwhile the enemy's air forces remained in complete mastery of the skies.

Against this imposing enemy array von Rundstedt, in a series of appreciations and reports written between 3 and 9 September, listed his assets. On 7 September over the whole of the west front he had only 100 tanks fit for battle; Model's request for three panzer divisions from the east front had just been refused by the Führer. On 4 September Model reported that 15 Army, including all available troops of the Commander of the *Wehrmacht* in Holland but not those already lost to the fortresses, totalled the equivalent of only four divisions: 7 Army had less than one panzer and two infantry divisions: 1 Army, by now far the strongest, had three motorized and just over four infantry divisions. In all, von Rundstedt reported on 6 September, he had nine infantry divisions and three much understrength panzer divisions fit for battle: eleven divisions were reforming: the remainder of what had been forty divisions were disorganized remnants, largely without equipment and leaders. Between the Maas and Liège 7 Army was trying to hold on to its positions, but to the south there was only a very thin line, less than eight battalions covering a seventy mile front; in practice, said von Rundstedt, the enemy already had full freedom of manoeuvre right back to the West Wall. Of the two divisions that were supposed to be fighting a delaying action in front of the West Wall, 'one had not arrived and the other would not come until after 12 September'. 'For 7 Army', continued von Rundstedt, 'it was now or never'. As for 15 Army, it must have three infantry divisions and a panzer division immediately otherwise it would suffer another defeat as it had done south-west of Brussels, but the next time it would not escape. In the south the withdrawing 19 Army was in grave danger and only 1 Army showed any improvement in its fighting power.

On the night of 8 September, von Rundstedt spoke on the telephone to Keitel, telling him that the position of 7 Army was very serious and that it could no longer hold in front of the West Wall and must be withdrawn. He complained also of the lack of reinforcing formations, saying that he must have properly organized divisions and not the stream of independent and hastily thrown together battalions—men with rifles—that were arriving on the West Wall from the interior of the Reich. Model was asking for twenty-five fresh divisions and a reserve of five or more panzer divisions for the Albert Canal—Maas—West Wall area, and a further ten infantry and five panzer divisions for the exposed north-west flank, 'otherwise the doorway to North Germany would be wide open'. Model might just as well have asked for the moon, for nothing came of this conversation except for a sharp Führer order to von Rundstedt, telling 7 Army to remain where it was, and, on 9 September, a list of the reinforcements that von Rundstedt *might* expect to receive: twenty *Luftwaffe* field battalions and eleven machine-gun battalions; then, perhaps a fortnight later, fourteen artillery batteries, six garrison battalions and twenty-five cadre artillery troops, some tank and anti-tank equipment and six march reinforcement battalions. On 14 September von Rundstedt was told by the OKW that he would get nothing thereafter; instead of reinforcements he received, two days later, a general directive on how to raise the fanaticism of the troops under his command.

At the end of August Hitler had ordered the preparation of defensive works along the northern coast from the Danish to the Dutch frontiers, the responsibility having been given to the *Gauleiter* of the coastal areas and to the *Marineoberkommando Nordsee*. On 1 September Himmler, as the Interior Minister and the Commander of the Replacement Army, was made responsible for western static defences and the development and manning of the West Wall, in collaboration with the *Gauleiter* and the military districts in the west. Some 130 Labour Service battalions were ordered there for frontier duty.

Wherever possible the old 1939 defence line was taken into use once more, but much of it was in disrepair and much wanted modernizing. The barbed wire had been removed and could not be replaced because it was not available, and mines and anti-tank weapons were in short supply. A civilian work force of 200,000 was soon enrolled, in addition to the Hitler Youth and Labour Service, but even so it was estimated that six weeks would be needed to improve the defensive works. As von Rundstedt's troops were already fast falling back on to the West Wall, on 11 September the command of the western defences was transferred to him from Himmler. A few days before, von Rundstedt had been vested with the direct command of all *Wehrmacht* troops in his area, a necessary step since his infantry and artillery contained many *Luftwaffe* and naval units. The defence of the Albert Canal on Model's right flank had been entrusted to Student's newly formed 1 Parachute Army, to be made up of elements of three parachute divisions, elements of two army divisions and forty flak batteries. Hardly any of these troops were, however, in position in September.

The troops falling back on the West Wall were beaten, disorganized, without equipment and often without leaders; the best had gone. The reinforcements from the Reich were too old, too young, without organization, equipment, training, experience, or war leaders, without vehicles or heavy weapons or administrative support, called battalions but being in fact groups thrown together from the army rear areas, the *Luftwaffe* and the *Kriegsmarine*. The losses in equipment in the west, east and south-east were by now gigantic, and even rifles were in short supply; vehicle fuels were strictly rationed. The German state railway was entirely disorganized and still under heavy bombing; and since, with the loss of France and Belgium, early air raid warning was no longer possible, the bombs were being dropped before the German fighters could get into the air. Von Zangen, the commander of 15 Army, in an army order of 7 October, said that all his troops must be made to realize that if the Schelde were to be lost 'the English would be in a position to land great masses of material [in Antwerp] and deliver a death blow at Berlin before the onset of winter'.

From late September there was yet another comb-out of German manpower and foreign labour, some foreign workers being given special ration cards to encourage productivity. German women born in the years 1919-1928 were required to register for war duties and the school holidays were extended indefinitely so that those children of above twelve years of age could be engaged in industrial work or be taken into the flak artillery as part time auxiliaries. All these measures, together with a drastic manpower reduction in all *Wehrmacht* headquarters and static installations and the extending of the conscription ages to the sixteen and fifty year olds, enabled Hitler to throw together a reserve of about twenty-five *Volksgrenadier* divisions.*

From the beginning of September until 16 December the Anglo-American enemy retained an initiative that he did not use, except for the Arnhem operation in mid September. For he no longer attempted to storm forward but, according to the OKW chronicler, 'groped his way cautiously and painfully often bringing on himself heavy casualties by doing so'. It remained inexplicable to the German command that was itself in no condition either to mount or to repel a heavy offensive in those early days, why the enemy did not mass his forces in any one place and break in. Instead of this 'the allies were sufficiently kind to the German leadership as to split up their own forces, distributing them evenly over the whole front from the English Channel to the Burgundian Gate', when 'every day of bad weather was a day of grace' to the frantic German defenders.

The allied airborne operation *Market Garden* had been designed to put two American airborne divisions down in the areas of Eindhoven and Nijmegen and a British airborne division further north near Arnhem, nearly sixty-five miles from the allied forward localities, in order to secure crossings over the Waal and the lower Rhine, its primary strategic object being to outflank the West Wall from the north. These three airborne divisions were to be reinforced by a Polish airborne brigade and a British air-landed division.

The operation, starting on the afternoon of 17 September, was certainly not an unqualified success, and the British, in retrospect, blamed the bad weather that caused the delay in flying in the Polish brigade and the cancellation of the committing of the air-landed division; they also thought that the close air support of 2 (RAF)

* *Volksgrenadier* divisions were the new pattern formations raised after 20 July (about 50 in all) by Himmler's Replacement Army, the name emphasizing the propaganda link with the people. They were disciplined and administered by the SS, not by the army. Regiments had only two battalions and there were three (sometimes two) regiments to the division (one of the battalions being on bicycles).

Tactical Air Force was inadequate, that the British airborne troops had been dropped too far and too scattered from their bridge objective, and that the British airborne communications and control were at fault. The planning for the ground link-up depended largely on the use of a single south-north road that was to be used by as many as 20,000 vehicles. According to one American airborne divisional commander who attended the order group of the corps responsible for the ground link-up, he thought that he could discern a lack of a personal and close control at the top.

The landing took the German command completely by surprise but it was immediately appreciated that the allied aim was the cutting off of 15 German Army to the west and opening the way to Münster and to North Germany. The supply route to 15 Army was not threatened by the enemy as the route through Utrecht was still open, but the precaution was taken of replacing all Dutch key railway personnel by Germans. Meanwhile the Führer would not allow more troops to be drawn away from 15 Army towards Eindhoven for fear that the enemy should seize the mouth of the Schelde. The *Luftwaffe* was immediately alerted and two fighter corps brought into the area, three *Luftwaffe* flak battle groups were formed for ground use and nine fortress battalions were ordered to join 1 Parachute Army. Only one infantry division was available on the ground but another infantry division was expected to join it on the following day. In the first twenty-four hours of the fighting the German forces on the spot held on to Arnhem and Nijmegen and succeeded in taking back the Arnhem bridge from the British.

The British account is apt to stress the presence of the two S S panzer divisions of 2 S S Panzer Corps that happened to be refitting in the area, particularly since these were committed to battle in the area of Arnhem town. In the O K W war diary record, however, these S S formations are infrequently mentioned since the O K W attention was concerned more with the effects of the operation on 15 German Army and with the attempted destruction of the whole airborne and part of the relieving force by a double pincer movement in the flanks from east and west, in the area of Uden and Veghel, by German army and *Luftwaffe* parachute formations.

By 22 September von Rundstedt reckoned that there were more than eight enemy divisions within the land salient occupied by the link-up force, but they still could not reach the beleaguered British airborne division. By 26 September all the forward British positions had been overrun, the war diarists recording the capture of 6,500 prisoners and the count of 1,500 dead. The British official figures admitted to 1,300 dead, 1,700 wounded and 3,800 missing.

Von Rundstedt reported to the O K W that, in his view, the British had failed not because they had selected a target too far in advance of the main defensive line, but because they had scattered their drop both in space and in time; they might have succeeded if they had landed in a compact area and had been reinforced immediately by a second and a third airborne division. Von Rundstedt thought that 'the enemy should have learned his lesson and the next time would do the thing properly', landing in strength *even further ahead* of a new sea landing or a ground thrust. As against this, he was very surprised that all the British airborne prisoners of war seemed to hold the credo, even regard it as an unalterable fact of military life, that 'no airborne formation could hold out on its own for more than three to four days without link-up and relief'. If this belief was really held by the airborne planners, said von Rundstedt, then British airborne forces would be unlikely to be used again in the near future *over* the West Wall.

The Commander-in-Chief West still regarded the open area to the *north* of the West Wall as being the most vulnerable, and he considered that the enemy would make this his main route into Germany's industrial area. But the Führer sharply disagreed, saying that the enemy *Schwerpunkt* would be made into Holland, where he could be easily reinforced from England, possibly in conjunction with further sea landings near Emden and Wilhelmshaven, and with a diversionary offensive in the Vosges,where enemy forces were already in position. The German plan must therefore be to hold Holland at all costs so as to protect the Ruhr and allow time to extend the West Wall. In this way the holding of Holland came to be accepted as a corner-stone of German strategy in the west, not only after the Schelde estuary had been cleared, but right up until the closing days of the war when the enemy had left the West Wall far behind and was in the very centre of the Reich.

Even during the withdrawal in France, the Führer and Model had dreamed of launching an armoured blow from the south that would catch the advancing allies a shattering blow in the flank. At the beginning of September 5 Panzer Army, which, together with 1 and 19 Armies, was still part of Balck's Army Group G, had been ordered to prepare such an offensive from the area of Epinal in the south, with what was to have been two panzer divisions, three panzer grenadier divisions and six panzer brigades.* Von Rundstedt had actually given out detailed orders, as passed to him by the O K W, to this effect, all formations having been ordered to be ready for action by 12 September. But before 10 September it became clear, even to the O K W, that there were not the troops, the equipment or the M T fuels available to launch an offensive of any sort. The Führer reluctantly agreed with Jodl's assessment that no major offensive could be launched until after 1 November. Meanwhile, however, the enemy pressure against Army Group G began to restrict the area in the south, making it problematical that 5 Panzer Army could ever begin its concentration and offensive from near Epinal; for the moment therefore the panzer army was given the alternative task of being ready to counter-attack in the flank the imminent American thrust towards the Vosges.

The Führer then changed his ideas once more, reverting to the suggestion made earlier by Model of an attack to be launched from the Ardennes, which area was only lightly held by the Americans. For such an offensive the dictator proposed to use his newly raised strategic reserve, much of it being held back inside the Reich during the preparatory period as part of 6 Panzer Army, a new headquarters under Dietrich.** Then, on 24 September, after von Rundstedt had reported that the American strength between Metz and Epinal had made any projected offensive by 5 Panzer Army so far to the south completely out of the question, Hitler earmarked 5 Panzer Army for removal northwards to the area of Aachen to join 6 Panzer Army for the grand new counter-offensive later in the year. Since this

* Blaskowitz lost command of Army Group G when the city of Nancy was given up without the Führer's permission.

**The extension of the age for conscripted military service, together with the manpower economy measures, had brought another 700,000 men to the colours.

increased the strength of Model's force to five armies and fifteen corps, at von Rundstedt's suggestion a new Army Group H under Student was inserted to the north of Army Group B, covering from Breskens on the Schelde estuary to Venlo, and commanding 15 Army, 1 Parachute Army and *Wehrmacht* Netherlands. This new army group was meant to lighten Model's responsibilities so that he could devote more time to the preparation of the coming Ardennes offensive; it added nothing to the actual German strength in the north, where, shortly afterwards, the Canadians succeeded in opening the Schelde as far as Antwerp.

The steady American pressure near Aachen and the Franco-American attacks in the far south towards the Rhine in the area of the Saar, the Vosges and Alsace, were forcing the defenders back into the West Wall. Von Rundstedt appealed in vain to Hitler for new formations for Army Group G; but he was told that every available man was to be earmarked for Army Group B. Instead, Himmler, the *Reichsführer SS*, was given the overall command of all *Wehrmacht* and *Volkssturm* forces on the upper Rhine between Bienenfeld and the Swiss frontier, directly under the Führer's orders; von Rundstedt's command in the south was thereby restricted to the narrow strip of the West Wall, and Army Group G was ordered to hand over one of its two armies to Himmler's command.*

Hitler reasoned that the allies had only seventy divisions deployed forward and that these were insufficient to cover the frontage in any great strength; it should be easy for the Army Command West to achieve a numerical superiority at any point on the front, so winning a success that would change not only the course of operations in the west but also, so Hitler said, the outcome of the whole war. It was essential to do this quickly in a period of bad winter weather in the shortest days of the year, in order to escape enemy air interference. A quick victory was necessary in the west, the Führer said, 'before the French should begin to conscript their manpower', for he seemed to think that the war was going on for ever and that, in September 1944, he had merely returned to the *status quo* of five years before, ready, as it were, for the second round.** Meanwhile Hitler had ordered the old 4 and 6 Army general staff appreciations and orders covering the 1940 Ardennes offensive to be unearthed from the archives at Liegnitz, so that they might be restudied and used again. All planning, preparation and orders remained, as the OKW diarist noted, closely under the hand of the Führer, even to the extent that he was to make the daily decisions as to the supply of vehicles and horses to the individual divisions making up the attacking force.

Several possible courses of action were considered, but eventually it was decided to attack through the Ardennes in the area south of Aachen through Luxembourg to Liège, and then, swinging north-westwards, thrust on Antwerp and the coast, so enveloping the whole of 21 British Army Group and that part of 1 (US) Army that was in the Aachen area, this great movement to the sea being completed, 'in the best case', within seven days.*** All the enemy north of the line Antwerp—Brussels—Bastogne would then be destroyed. Model was to have the theoretical command

---

* Himmler as Commander-in-Chief Upper Rhine commanded 19 Army, *Wehrkreis V*, and 14 and 18 SS Corps. 19 Army was not returned to Army Group G until Himmler's command was disbanded in the first week of February 1945.

**This is again a parallel with the Verdun offensive of 1916 when the Germans tried desperately for a decision before the effect of British conscription should be felt.

***9 (US) Army, to the north of 1 (US) Army, was, from December onwards, temporarily part of 21 Army Group.

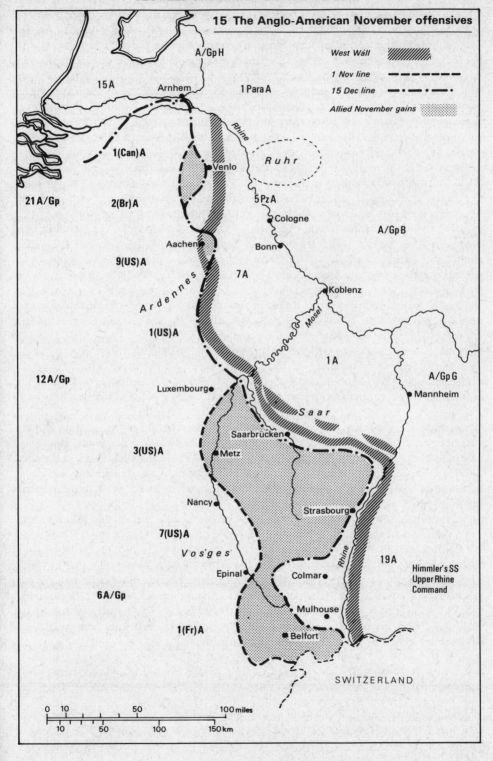

15 The Anglo-American November offensives

West Wall
1 Nov line
15 Dec line
Allied November gains

A/Gp H

15 A

Arnhem

1 Para A

Rhine

Ruhr

1 (Can) A

Venlo

5 Pz A

21 A/Gp

2 (Br) A

Cologne

A/Gp B

Aachen

Bonn

9 (US) A

7 A

Koblenz

Ardennes

Mosel

1 (US) A

1 A

12 A/Gp

Luxembourg

A/Gp G

Mannheim

Saar

3 (US) A

Saarbrücken

Metz

Nancy

Strasbourg

7 (US) A

Vosges

Rhine

19 A

Epinal

Colmar

Himmler's SS
Upper Rhine
Command

6 A/Gp

Mulhouse

1 (Fr) A

Belfort

SWITZERLAND

0 10   50   100 miles
10   50   100   150 km

163

over the whole operation with Dietrich's 6 Panzer Army on the right, von Manteuffel's 5 Panzer Army in the centre and Brandenburger's 7 Army on the left. As the movement gathered momentum Student's Army Group H was to attack in the north, this converting the manoeuvre from a single to a double envelopment. In what was almost an apologia, Jodl wrote to von Rundstedt that 'the daring concept of the aim was unalterable, an aim that, looked at from a purely technical point of view, seemed out of keeping with the forces allotted: none should be daunted on this account, however, and all must be staked on a single card'. Such sentiments expressed the spirit of the Third German Reich, and, as Jodl said after the war, the whole offensive was indeed an act of desperation.

Both von Rundstedt and Model had reservations. Von Rundstedt feared that he would himself be attacked in the southern flank and for this reason both field-marshals would have favoured a more modest envelopment that would have taken Army Group B from Aachen to Liège (this coming to be known as the *smaller* solution), rather than the *greater* that was supposed to take them to Antwerp and the sea. The field-marshals also asked to be allowed the basic freedom to be able to prepare their own plans and take such decisions that would probably have to be resolved at very short notice, such as when the offensive was to begin. Hitler's reaction was sharp and he was not prepared to discuss the matter. The detailed planning and preparations were already complete and there could be no question of any further change; and as for the selection of D day for the new offensive, 'the weather and he would decide that'.

Neither von Rundstedt nor Model appear to have given Hitler their firm opinions that the offensive must fail, for they seem to have regarded the offensive as Hitler's affair; when Model heard of objections from his subordinates, he sent his subordinates direct to Hitler; such an attitude was common among German generals in the highest command, for many were unwilling to offer, let alone press, their resignations. On 3 November, when von Rundstedt was asked for his reaction to the plan that had been presented to him, he reported 'no basic differences of opinion except for some fears about the flanks', and, having taken the ground and the relative strengths into consideration, he thought 'that more forces should be made available' to him, together with the strongest air support. This appears to have been the extent of his remonstration.

By the autumn of 1944 von Rundstedt's position, like that of his fellows, had been reduced to that of a bureaucrat or army official, forwarding to the OKW carefully trimmed and cautiously worded appreciations and reports. Army group figures could not be easily refuted by the Führer, nor, in giving details of his depleted strength, could von Rundstedt necessarily be dubbed a defeatist, for he left it to the reader to draw his own conclusions, the figures speaking for themselves. On 19 October von Rundstedt reported that his front of 625 miles was held by forty-one infantry divisions (including *Volksgrenadier* divisions) and thirty motorized divisions, but these had a real strength of only twenty-seven infantry and six panzer divisions. The enemy had actually in contact forty-two infantry and thirteen armoured divisions and eleven tank brigades (those brigades having virtually the same tank strength as an armoured division). Between 1 September and 15 October the German Army in the west had received 152,000 men as part of new formations, but the casualties over the period had totalled 150,000. In addition von Rundstedt had had to give up 86,000 men, so he was in fact 84,000 men worse off. On 2 December, a fortnight before the great offensive, the field-marshal reported that his formations were 3,500 officers and 115,000 men short of establishment, while the efficiency of the reinforcements, including those of the Himmler trained *Volksgrenadier* divisions, was poor 'because the training period had been too short'. The men were, he said, for the most part reliable and determined, but the enemy superiority in equipment could not be ignored and this had had a depressing effect on the German soldier.

On 15 December the Führer told Model 'that he had received his last order' and that all commands were to be carried out unconditionally to the last detail and at the lowest level. That same evening Model confirmed that the Führer's orders had been passed on to Dietrich 'word for word'. At 05.30 the next day the grand Ardennes counter-offensive began.

The two panzer armies numbered sixteen divisions, half of them panzer, and the two supporting armies on the flanks (15 and 7) totalled another fifteen divisions of which about a third came into action. The reserve amounted to three panzer and three infantry divisions, and 1,500 fighters had been promised by the *Luftwaffe* for the close support of the offensive. Complete surprise was achieved and the bad flying weather aided the progress of the attackers against the relatively few and inexperienced American troops that were holding what Bradley had regarded as a quiet sector of the front. Dietrich's 6 Panzer Army was, however, soon brought to a halt by the determined resistance of troops of 1 (US) Army south of Aachen, on the northern shoulder of the break-in. Von Manteuffel's 5 Panzer Army, on the other hand, continued to make ground rapidly and, bypassing Bastogne, struck towards the Meuse. By the third day, however, it became obvious that the offensive could never reach Antwerp and Student's attack was thereupon cancelled. By the seventh day von Manteuffel was halted and it was doubtful whether he could even reach the Meuse, hardly fifty miles from his starting point. By Christmas Day, only ten days after the start of the offensive, when Patton's 3 Army had begun biting into von Manteuffel's southern flank towards the besieged pocket at Bastogne, the whole offensive had already failed.

The attacks had inflicted on the enemy 75,000 casualties, nearly all of them American. On the other hand the *Wehrmacht* losses had totalled 100,000 men, 800 tanks and 1,000 aircraft. The American losses could be easily made up; the German casualties were irreplaceable. And so Hitler had lost what was in effect his last strategic reserve and the backbone of the western front had been broken. Even then, the Führer made light of his defeat, trying to insist that von Rundstedt should hold on to the ground inside the bulge; and throughout the remainder of the winter the dictator pretended to his military and political circle that his offensive had achieved 'an enormous relaxing of the [Anglo-American] pressure'.

Whether at Rastenburg or at Ziegenberg, Hitler and Jodl both lived in a world divorced from reality. Jodl had little interest in the war in the east and much of his time would appear to have been spent in trying to thwart any attempt by Guderian to persuade the Führer to transfer troops from west to east.* His adversary

* At about this period Goebbels wrote of Jodl how 'pitiable' it was to see him 'making a song and dance about the trivial matter of the right of entry into air raid shelters, as if it were a question of world historical importance'. According to the same source, the Führer thought Jodl a 'worn out fuddy-duddy'. Kesselring, on the other hand, regarded Jodl as one of the ablest and most helpful members of the OKW: no man, said Kesselring, could have done better in that impossible situation.

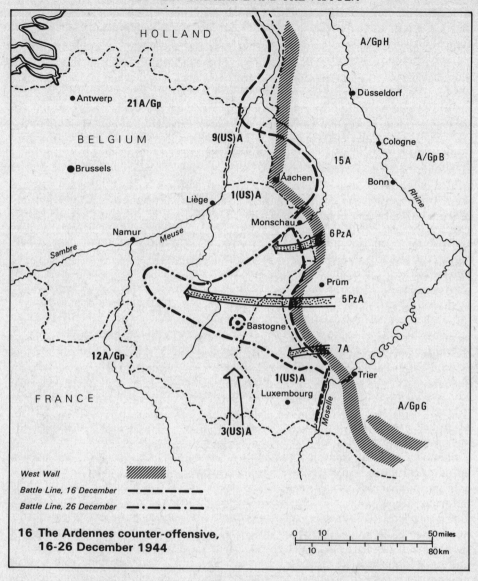

West Wall ▨

Battle Line, 16 December − − − − −

Battle Line, 26 December −·−·−·−·

16 The Ardennes counter-offensive, 16-26 December 1944

Guderian, shorn of authority, was no less blinkered than Jodl.* Guderian was convinced that it was preferable to lose territory to the western allies rather than to the Red Army, but he did not appear to realize that the war had for long been irretrievably lost and that the shuffling of divisions from west to east and back again could make no difference to the outcome. Taking his cue from the Führer, whose buoyant 'patch of bad luck' theme had changed to a dismal 'nothing ever went right now', Guderian was to explain away the lack of success in 'that Germany no longer had the commanders and troops of the 1940 quality': after the war was

---

* Of Guderian Hitler said at this time that 'he lacked stolidity of temperament and was nervous and excitable'.

166

ended, he blamed the Führer. Hitler meanwhile was telling his political cronies that Guderian himself was responsible for Germany's defeats. It was, as the cynical Goebbels noted at the time, so typically German that the officers should try to blame the party while the political leaders should lay the responsibility on the *Wehrmacht*.

The real reason for the rapid disintegration of Fortress Europe was that the world military situation had entirely changed. Germany's enemies of 1944 were battle experienced, powerful and superbly equipped. The German Army that had been Hitler's pride in 1941 was, in 1944, obsolete, poorly organized and inadequately trained; with little air or artillery support, it was almost crippled for want of mechanization and motor fuel. It was little wonder that Germany was fast losing the war.

Gehlen's *Fremde Heere Ost* had forecast the imminence of a Soviet offensive against East Prussia and the German held line of the Vistula, with a Russian superiority over the defenders of eleven to one in infantry, seven to one in tanks and twenty to one in guns. On Christmas Eve Guderian took these figures with him to the western command post in Ziegenberg near Bad Nauheim, to warn the Führer of the great danger in the east. This, however, availed him nothing for he was rewarded by an outright rejection of his appreciation and proposals. Mesmerized by divisional titles and numbers, Hitler had for long been raising new formations rather than reinforcing existing ones. German infantry divisions had been reduced to six battalions and some of the newest *Volksgrenadier* divisions numbered at full strength little more than 6,000 officers and men. Many of the divisions in the east retained their divisional titles partly for the purpose of deceiving the Soviet enemy. The German order of battle had become a pretence in which battalions were called brigades and regiments were called divisions, and the time was shortly to come when what were called mobile tank destroyer units were in reality companies of cyclists armed with anti-tank grenades. Hitler had become convinced that the enemy was trying a similar deception on him, and after the stormy Christmas Eve Ziegenberg meeting attended by Keitel, Jodl and the new military secretary and adjutant Burgdorf, Guderian was sent back to Zossen.*

Guderian had asked in vain that the German divisions returning from Finland (a former OKW theatre) be made over to the eastern front, and that Army Group North be evacuated by sea from Kurland where it was now besieged yet again; and he suggested that the Ardennes offensive should be broken off and that the troops there be sent eastwards to form a reserve to cover Brandenburg. On 31 December, and on 9 January, according to his own post-war account, he tried to bring the urgency and the seriousness of the situation in the east to the dictator's attention once more.

Hitler had lived, however, too long in his own shadowy world and, still convinced of his genius, he was pathologically suspicious of his military subordinates, who, he was sure, wrecked his plans by failing to obey his orders in the minutest detail. The responsibility for losing the war was theirs. Commanders and staffs, and this was to include Guderian's immediate deputy, continued to be arrested by the Gestapo. At the end of November Hitler had issued an order which was to be made known to every soldier, in which it was actually decreed that the commander of any fortress, garrison or post should, before retiring or breaking out from his

* Burgdorf had replaced Schmundt, who had died of wounds from the 20 July bomb explosion.

defences, offer his command to anyone willing to take it. Any officer or soldier who thought that he could continue the defence should then be given the full command, regardless of his rank, and the battle should go on.

The enemy's capabilities or likely intentions rarely had any place in the Führer's appreciations. Although, by stopping up his eyes and ears, he had usually refused to take any account of the Soviet threat during 1944, this resulting in the repeated disastrous defeats for Germany during that year, Hitler had learned nothing, for he again took the view that any further Soviet offensive in strength was most improbable. The only area in the east in which he considered himself at all concerned was in the defence of Budapest and the Hungarian oilfields. It was still easier, he thought, to give up territory in the east rather than in the west, where the Ruhr and German soil were directly threatened.

In the middle of January, after the great Soviet offensive predicted by Guderian and Gehlen had started and the eastern defences had already been torn apart, Hitler was sure that the leaders in the field were retreating through cowardice or lack of will-power, and he issued a Führer order that was remarkable even by the German standards of the time. No commander of any formation from division upwards was to attack, or counter-attack, or withdraw, without first notifying his intention through the normal military channels to the high command, in sufficient time to allow the Führer's intervention. The Führer's intervention usually meant a countermand. Hitler was now ready to conduct *his* war game from the bunker, like a champion chess player facing opponents on a dozen or more boards, the master of every move.

The population of the eastern territories, including the many evacuees from the bombed areas of Western Germany, were under no illusions as to their fate should they be caught up in a Soviet invasion, and, gripped with terror, most of them wanted to quit their homesteads and flee to the west. The army commanders, knowing that the flight of civilian refugees after the Soviet offensive had started would impede their operations, urged that forward areas be cleared of German civilians immediately. This proposal was denounced by Hitler as another example of defeatism, and the *Gauleiter* were ordered to see that the population remained firmly in place.* This order was to have terrible consequences in the early months of 1945. Since the war was about to be fought on German soil, the depth of the combat zone for an army group in which the German Army held powers of requisition and command over the civil administration was reduced to six miles, hardly sufficient to deploy a division. Behind this line, operations and even deployment were subject to interference by the party and by the state administrative machine.

In early October the German position in the Baltic States and East Prussia had deteriorated further. Schörner had been forced out of Estonia back to Riga when another thrust from Bagramian's 1 Baltic Front, crossing into the border areas of East Prussia, had driven westwards reaching the Baltic coast north of Memel. The whole of Army Group North in Kurland had again been enveloped and had finally been isolated from the remainder of the eastern front. The Führer's *Wolfsschanze* near the East Prussian frontier closed down in that November never to reopen. Hitler, as he later admitted, thereafter became a prey to his own conscience, for he had seriously debated with himself whether he should remain and die there when the Russians overran his headquarters.

---

* A police permit was required for such travel.

At the beginning of January the German forces in the east were made up of five army groups, although Schörner's encircled two armies of Army Group North henceforth played little part in the war. Reinhardt's Army Group Centre of three armies held East Prussia and Northern Poland as far south as Warsaw. Harpe's Army Group A (formerly North Ukraine) of four armies ran from Warsaw due south along the middle Vistula to the Carpathians and Czechoslovakia; Wöhler, who had replaced Friessner in command of Army Group South (formerly South Ukraine), was in Hungary, and von Weichs's Army Group F still held the far southern flank in Northern Yugoslavia. The new Soviet winter offensive that was to take the Red Army in one great bound from the middle Vistula to the Oder, not sixty miles from Berlin, was to fall on the seventy divisions of Reinhardt's Army Group Centre and Harpe's Army Group A.

During the month of November Stalin and his staff were already preparing the plans for the winter offensive. Cherniakhovsky's 3 Belorussian Front was to strike for Königsberg, the capital of East Prussia; Rokossovsky's 2 Belorussian Front was to make two blows, one at Marienburg to envelop the whole of East Prussia from the south and the other at Allenstein to assist Cherniakhovsky; Zhukov's 1 Belorussian Front was to bypass Warsaw and advance firstly on Poznan and then on the Oder. Konev's 1 Ukrainian and Petrov's 4 Ukrainian Fronts were to take Cracow in the initial offensive and then move into the industrial area of Silesia and the Upper Oder. Malinovsky's 2 and Tolbukhin's 3 Ukrainian Fronts were to clear Hungary and enter Austria. Konev's 1 Ukrainian and Zhukov's 1 Belorussian Fronts each had ten armies, including two tank armies, and their joint strength was said to number 163 divisions, 6,400 tanks, 4,700 aircraft and over two million men.

Although preparations for a Soviet offensive had been completed by the beginning of December, the Red Army lay inactive, and in the OKW the erroneous political view was expressed, possibly initiated by Hitler, that no military action need be feared for the moment since the Kremlin was trying to blackmail its western allies to recognize the Lublin Poles as the *de jure* government of Poland. Without this recognition, the Soviet ally would hold back and let the western powers absorb all the pressure in the Ardennes. In truth Moscow was unwilling to begin an offensive in the heavy mud and poor visibility, since these would make it impossible to exploit the Soviet fire, armoured and mechanized superiority. As early as 14 December Stalin had told Harriman, the United States Ambassador, that he was awaiting a spell of fine weather before starting any major action. The fact that the Red Army had long been ready and was waiting for clear and frosty weather had been noted in German army group war diary entries at the time.

On 6 January Churchill sent a personal message to Stalin asking whether a renewal of the Vistula offensive could be counted upon during January, the Ardennes battle being, in Churchill's words 'very heavy'. Then, on 8 January, there were meteorological forecasts of a clear cold spell, and although this in fact was to last only nine days, it was sufficient to harden the ground and take the Red Army right to the Oder. When, on 15 January, Tedder, Eisenhower's deputy commander, met Stalin in Moscow, Stalin told him that the offensive had already started three days before.

On 12 January Konev's 1 Ukrainian Front had begun the offensive from the Baranow bridge-head over the Vistula, against Graeser's 4 Panzer Army, part of Harpe's Army Group A. The forward German corps were powerless to move since they were pinned by Hitler's orders; the lack of any reaction by the defenders was so striking that even Konev was obliged to admit that, under this latest system of Führer control, the German tactical defence was paralysed. Five days later Soviet troops were in open country and across the Warthe, having advanced over 100 miles on a 160 mile front. German communications had broken down, and surrounded German corps, left like islands in the torrent of the break-through, were miles behind. On 14 January Zhukov's front had in its turn gone over to the offensive, this time against Reinhardt's Army Group Centre. Heinrici's 9 Army near Warsaw was almost shattered, and in the next two days the Pilica was forced and Radom fell. On 15 January the *Luftwaffe* flew forty-two sorties against 3,400 by the Red Air Force. Two days later Warsaw was evacuated by the Germans.

Hitler, still at Ziegenberg and attempting to control the Ardennes operation and mount an attack into Alsace at the same time, could do nothing to remedy the situation, but on 15 January he resorted to his usual strategy of robbing one sector to reinforce another. This frequently resulted in two sectors going without, while the reserves were shunted about in railway sidings.

On 16 January Hitler returned to Berlin, having at last ordered Dietrich's 6 Panzer Army out of the Ardennes. Undeterred by the ruin of Army Group A and the plight of Army Group Centre, with its frightening consequences for scores of millions of Germans, he sent Dietrich's force to Hungary to protect the oilfields and refineries. The evacuation of Warsaw against his orders fed the flames of the Führer's fury, and he busied himself over the next few days in conducting an inquiry and ordering the arrest of a number of general staff officers who appeared blameworthy. Harpe was removed and replaced by Schörner from the surrounded and idle Army Group North, Schörner's place being taken by Rendulic from 20 Army. Schörner, however, could do nothing to influence the battle situation. Such reinforcements as he received from Himmler's Replacement Army were a few poorly trained and half-equipped *Volksgrenadier* divisions, the staffs and students of military schools, and some police and SS. Meanwhile the troops of 1 Ukrainian and 1 Belorussian Fronts poured westwards, and the advance continued by day and by night, the tanks moving along the roads in great columns against negligible resistance. On 19 January, only seven days after the start of the offensive, the Red Army crossed the 1938 Polish-Silesian frontier to the east of Breslau into the old pre-war Reich. Of Schörner's new command, only Schulz's 17 Army, which had not been closely engaged, had managed to retire in some semblance of order, giving up Cracow and falling back into Silesia: elements of 4 Panzer and 9 Armies were miles behind in slow moving pockets desperately trying to reach the safety of the Oder.

Reinhardt, commanding Army Group Centre in East Prussia, had three armies, supported by a motley German force of police and *Volkssturm*, estimated to number about 200,000 men. Reinhardt felt himself to be in the greatest of danger and had advised Guderian that Rendulic's Army Group North should be brought by sea out of Kurland back to the main defensive front, and that Hossbach's 4 Army should be withdrawn from its exposed position in the south-east near Suwalki.

On 13 January Reinhardt was attacked by Cherniakhovsky and, the following day, Rokossovsky's front began its offensive. Then, on 15 January, Reinhardt was forced by Hitler to give up to Army Group A the panzer corps *Grossdeutschland*, whence it was lost in the maze of railways. By then East Prussia was under heavy attack from the east and south, the two Hitler designated fortresses of Mlawa and Modlin being lost; Tilsit fell on 18 January and Tannenberg three days later. Raus's 3 Panzer Army, although under heavy pressure, continued to present an unbroken front, and Hossbach's 4 Army, in the exposed salient forward of the Masurian Lakes, had not yet come under attack: Weiss's 2 Army, on the other hand, stood in the path of Rokossovsky's offensive and was in danger of disintegration; some strong points, when in danger of being surrounded, did not fight on, and some of the commanders of these garrisons were shot for their failure. By 26 January Rokossovsky's forces had advanced 125 miles in twelve days, Thorn and Marienburg had been taken, and 3 Panzer Army, 4 Army and part of 2 Army had been enveloped and isolated in East Prussia. The German war diarist noted that the Soviet troops made good use of maps and bypassed all centres of resistance, and German commanders had noted in particular the unexpected flexibility of the Red Army leadership.

Hitler was still sending out a torrent of orders aimed at patching the broken front and trying to hold everywhere. Reinhardt, on the other hand, was convinced that he must fight his way out westward, taking with him as many of the East Prussian population that could move, in a bid to rejoin the main German positions at the mouth of the Vistula to the west of Danzig: Hossbach, commanding 4 Army that had been facing south-east, agreed with him, and, in defiance of Hitler's orders, retired on Heilsberg preparatory to mounting an attack to the west. On 26 January, the Führer began to rage against both Reinhardt and Hossbach and ordered their immediate replacement by Rendulic and Müller, Rendulic being expressly ordered to hold Königsberg to the very end since Hitler feared that the Russians would set up a puppet German government in this historic capital of the Prussian kings.

On the same day, 26 January, Hitler reorganized and redesignated his army groups once more. The surrounded Army Group North, temporarily under von Vietinghoff, became Army Group Kurland: Army Group Centre, also cut off from the Reich by Rokossovsky's offensive, became the new Army Group North: Army Group A became Army Group Centre. A new Army Group Vistula had been formed covering Danzig and Pomerania, this taking under command the western part of Weiss's 2 Army and Busse's 9 Army, mainly made up of part formations and detachments. Himmler, fresh from what was held to be his success on the Upper Rhine, was given this military command, in addition to his many other posts, since Hitler believed that loyalty, reliability and fanaticism outweighed military ability and experience. Of these two latter qualities Himmler had none.

Since Army Groups Kurland and North were already cut off from the Reich, the defence in the east was to depend on Himmler's Army Group Vistula covering the approaches to North Germany and Brandenburg, while Schörner's Army Group Centre covered Saxony, Sudetenland and the whole of Czechoslovakia. Wöhler's Army Group South was still battling furiously in Hungary while von Weichs's Army Group F maintained its precarious hold on the northern part of Yugoslavia. Kesselring had, for the time being at least, stabilized his Italian front south of the valley of the Po. Twenty-six German divisions had been cut off in Kurland and twenty-seven in East Prussia, but Hitler still maintained that it was essential that they should stay there 'to protect the deep water U-boat training grounds in the Gulf of Danzig'.

The battle for East Prussia was almost at an end, although Rendulic was to hold on grimly to the city of Königsberg and Samland for some months to come. Meanwhile the battle for Pomerania was about to begin, since Stalin had decided to remove this German 'balcony' on the Baltic coast that might threaten from the flank his subsequent operations westwards into Brandenburg and Berlin. Part of Zhukov's 1 Belorussian Front was diverted to the north to assist Rokossovsky in overrunning Pomerania and closing up to the lower Oder and the Mecklenburg border.

The Ardennes offensive had failed and a powerless Germany was shortly to be submerged by its enemies flooding in from east and west. Yet the whole atmosphere in the O K W and O K H was so divorced from reality that the Führer and the O K H had begun to plan another grand counter-offensive, this time in the east, an offensive in which Guderian had the highest of hopes, for the acting Chief of the Army General Staff was hardly more of a realist than the dictator. Raus's 3 Panzer Army headquarters was brought back from East Prussia to Pomerania and added to the skeleton 11 Army to prepare for this new Hitler-Himmler offensive that was to drive southwards from Stargard into Zhukov's northern flank. But Raus's command was in fact only a motley force, much of it made up of engineers, *Luftwaffe, Marine* and *Volkssturm*, without air support, artillery, anti-tank guns, signals, transport, or supply services. Raus, far from having confidence in the new offensive, doubted that Pomerania could be held, but Himmler actually told him that he (Himmler) and the Führer were convinced that the success of the Stargard offensive would decide the whole war in favour of Germany. The Stargard operation, which began on 15 February, was a dismal failure and was halted almost immediately by the Soviet defence.*

On 20 February, to all Germans except the Führer and his immediate circle, the situation appeared to be very serious. Speer repeatedly, though somewhat belatedly, affirmed that the war was lost, but the dictator had for some time past refused to give him an audience. Even Guderian had been so bold as to tell von Ribbentrop that 'an armistice must be sought on at least one front'. To the more enlightened and critical the German position seemed hopeless.

On 21 February Hitler had issued another series of unrealistic orders: 17 Army in Upper Silesia was to counter-attack the left flank of 1 Ukrainian Front; the Oder-Neisse line was to be defended; the Pomeranian railway from Stettin to Danzig, so necessary, according to Hitler, for the German Navy in the Baltic, was to be held at all costs. Meanwhile, however, Rokossovsky's and Zhukov's fronts began to tear Army Group Vistula to pieces, reaching Köslin near the Pomeranian coast and fanning out towards Kolberg and Gdynia. The Führer's reaction was predictable. Kolberg became a fortress and he made a clarion call for the reconquest of Pomerania. Five motorized divisions were ordered up from Army Group Centre to Stettin; all moves had, however, to be made by rail and the shortage of vehicle fuels was such that barely sufficient remained for battle; by the time the divisions eventually arrived in Stettin they were needed to defend the mouth of the Oder and were swallowed up in the defence of Mecklenburg.

---

* As late as 5 March, when the German defenders of Pomerania were being thrown into the sea, Guderian told Goebbels that he was still of the opinion that 'we can succeed in clearing up | the enemy there| by counter-attacks'.

In Kolberg the *Volkssturm* fought on desperately until 18 March covering the evacuation by sea of the wounded and refugees. On 20 March Himmler, suffering from a heart complaint, retired to a sanatorium near Hohenlychen where he remained for the rest of the war, having given up the command of Army Group Vistula to Heinrici. By then the campaign in Pomerania was nearly over. Gdynia fell on 28 March and Danzig two days later, 2 Belorussian Front claiming the capture of forty-five U-boats. The German troops defending Gdynia and Danzig had risen up, taking with them the great mass of refugees who clung to them for protection, and moved eastwards into the delta of the Vistula where they held out between that river and the Nogat until after the end of the war.

All this time hordes of refugees from the Baltic States, East Prussia and Pomerania, mainly women and children, the young and the very old, blocked all roads and tracks as they made their way westwards with farm carts and on foot through the bitter weather away from the Soviet and the Polish terror. Under frequent attack from the air, they tramped in the wake of prisoners and slave labourers who were being moved under escort from the east to the west. The Latvian and French SS Divisions, which had become separated from 2 Army during the break-out to the west, flooded back, many of them in panic-stricken flight, and their conduct threatened to demoralize the hitherto staunch *Volkssturm*. Enemy soldiers, disguised as Baltic or Polish refugees, hid their weapons in carts and joined the wagon trek into the rear, so that they might occupy communication centres by *coup de main* attack. In the areas overrun by the Red Army there was an orgy of murder, looting and rape.

To the German Army's failure in Pomerania there was added yet another in Hungary. In December, at the time of launching of the Ardennes offensive, Hitler had demanded not only that Budapest should be defended house by house but that new German attacks should be mounted between the area of Lake Balaton and Velencze south-east to the line of the Danube.

At this time Friessner was still in command of Army Group South, and Friessner objected to being told not only where and how he was to attack but also *when* he was to mount his offensive, since the marshy ground was quite unfit for movement. The Hungarian front was by now an OKH responsibility and Friessner came under continuous and heavy pressure from Guderian, talking for the Führer, to begin the 3 Panzer Corps operation to the south of Budapest immediately. Guderian was so persistent that the exchanges became heated and, on 18 December, Friessner flew to Zossen to explain personally why the offensive must wait the coming of the frost. Friessner disagreed, too, with any attempt to hold Budapest, since he had insufficient troops to do it and a proper defence would require the removal of the civilian population.

Guderian appeared satisfied with Friessner's explanations and promised to put the case to the Führer. But when Friessner returned to Hungary he found that he had made his journey for nothing, for Hitler, aided by Guderian and the OKH, took over the personal command of the tactical battle, this in addition to fighting the Ardennes offensive nearly 800 miles to the west. Breith's 3 Panzer Corps, to the south of Budapest, was ordered to leave its armour and vehicles behind, so that the dismounted infantry, separated from its tanks, vehicles and gun support, was to be committed to the north of the capital against Kravchenko's tank army, this remarkable order coming, as Friessner said, by word of mouth of Guderian, the expert on armoured warfare. So it came about that when Tolbukhin attacked

173

17 The Eastern Front, January – April 1945

A/Gp Kurland

16A LATVIA

2 Baltic Front

SWEDEN

LITHUANIA

BALTIC SEA

Memel 1 Baltic Front

Tilsit

3 Pz A

Königsberg 3 Belorussian Front

Gdynia EAST

Danzig PRUSSIA

Kolberg Köslin Marienburg 4 A

3 Pz A Pomerania A/Gp Centre/North

Stettin 1 Belorussian 2 Belorussian Front 2 A 2 Belorussian Front

A/Gp Vistula Front

Brandenburg

Berlin 9 A Küstrin

Frankfurt Poznan Warsaw

9 A 1 Belorussian Front

Cottbus POLAND

4 Pz A A/Gp A

GERMANY Breslau Lublin

Saxony Dresden 4 Pz A

A/Gp Centre 1 Ukrainian Front

Prague 17 A Cracow Lvov

CZECHOSLOVAKIA

Brno 1 Pz A 1 Pz A

6 SS Pz A 8 A 8 A 4 Ukrainian Front

A/Gp South Vienna

Bratislava

6 A 2 Ukrainian Front

AUSTRIA 6 A 6 SS Pz A Budapest Debrecen

HUNGARY

L.Balaton

3 Ukrainian Front

2 Pz A

Trieste Zagreb

YUGOSLAVIA

Army E

A/Gp F

Battle Line, January 1945

Battle Line, mid-April 1945

0   50   100   200 miles

50   100   300 km

the armoured rump of 3 Panzer Corps south of Budapest some days afterwards, using large numbers of infantry formations to cross the marshy and ditch-intercoursed ground that would not bear the weight of tanks, he had no difficulty in bypassing Breith's divisions. Breith, without infantry, could not stop the advancing Red Army troops. Hitler's first Hungarian offensive was thus still-born. On 21 December Friessner and Fretter-Pico (the Commander of 6 Army) were removed from their appointments and were replaced by Wöhler and Balck.

On 26 December four German divisions were surrounded in Budapest. The Führer ordered Gille's 4 SS Panzer Corps down from Army Group Centre to retake the capital, and this fought its way to within twelve miles of the encircled garrison. If the garrison had been ordered to do so it could have broken out, but this solution was of no interest to Hitler who wanted only the recapture of the capital. By the end of January Gille's force had spent its strength and began to give ground westwards. The German troops remaining in Budapest were thereafter doomed to annihilation or capture.

At this time there were 135 skeleton divisions on the eastern front and seventy-seven disorganized and ill-equipped cadres on the Rhine. Hitler, undeterred by the Soviet forces massing on the Oder preparatory for the attack on Berlin, prepared yet a further offensive on the distant southern flank, his intention being to envelop part of Tolbukhin's 3 Ukrainian Front between the Danube and the Drava and, capturing new bridge-heads over the Danube, retake Budapest and eastern Hungary. His aims, so he persuaded himself, were mainly economic since the Hungarian and Austrian oilfields were together producing eighty per cent of the oil remaining to Germany. Dietrich's 6 SS Panzer Army was pulled out of the Ardennes and sent to Wöhler's command.*

Wöhler's Army Group South, when it undertook this second offensive, was made up of Balck's 6 Army and Dietrich's 6 SS Panzer Army, having in all ten panzer and five infantry divisions, and these were to attack between Balaton and Velencze, supported on the right flank by four infantry divisions of Angelis's 2 Panzer Army and further diversionary attacks by Löhr's Army E across the Drava in the far south. Kreysing's 8 Army, to the north of Budapest, was to remain on the defensive. The German attacks began on the night of 5 March and made ground slowly, four miles in the first two days and sixteen miles after four days, the casualties being heavy on both sides. On the Soviet side the situation appeared serious so that, on 10 March, Tolbukhin, a prey to anxiety, asked Stalin to release to him further reserves that were standing by in Hungary ready to envelop Wöhler's army group. This request was refused as, by 13 March, the German offensive was fast losing its momentum.** On 16 March Stalin ordered Timoshenko, who was co-ordinating the operations of Malinovsky's 2 Ukrainian and Tolbukhin's 3 Ukrainian Fronts, to start the Soviet two front offensive designed to destroy both Balck's and Dietrich's armies. A few days later Wöhler's army group, under heavy pressure, began its rapid withdrawal out of Hungary into Austria. On 25 March Wöhler was removed from his appointment and replaced by the Austrian Rendulic, considered by Hitler to be, like Model, 'an expert on defence'.

Rendulic did not arrive at his new post until the second week in April, and on

* The 6 Panzer Army had been redesignated 6 SS Panzer Army.

** It is of interest to note that when Tolbukhin reported to Moscow the presence of 6 SS Panzer Army in Hungary, he was at first disbelieved, since Moscow could see no rhyme or reason in Dietrich's troops appearing in a secondary theatre.

6 April, *en route* from Kurland to Austria, he was seen by the Führer to receive his orders: he has since described how he motored through the ruined Berlin streets to the gutted Chancellery, below which Hitler now lived and worked in the deep underground bunker in the Chancellery garden.* The dictator personally briefed his new army group commander on the battle situation. He had changed much since Rendulic had last seen him three months before; he was bent and stooping, dragged his left leg while continually holding his left arm with his right, and yet, Rendulic maintained, the deterioration of his body had not affected his state of mind. His speech, his eye and his manner appeared, said Rendulic, as clear and purposeful as ever. The Führer said that, since it appeared impossible to bring the Russians to a halt in Hungary, Rendulic's task was to hold Vienna and prevent the enemy getting further north up the Danube valley. The main enemy, Hitler had now decided, was the Russian; The Anglo-American forces were merely to be held back or delayed. The German Oder line defences, the Führer was convinced, were very strong, and he said that he was supremely confident that they would hold. Rendulic, suspecting that the quiet on the Oder was the lull before the storm, would have liked to have known more about the factors on which this optimism was based, but Hitler volunteered nothing. When Rendulic looked questioningly at Jodl, Jodl merely shrugged.

So Rendulic went on his way, while the Führer returned to poring over his out-of-date battle maps. The new army group commander soon found that he was to be allowed no freedom of command — not even to demolish the Danube bridges — without the express authority of the Führer; and the detail and reason for every action and troop movement within the city of Vienna were to be repeatedly questioned from Berlin.

Meanwhile Goebbels, during that March, was recording the daily happenings in his diary and trying to reconcile in his own mind the contradictions around him.** Guderian talked confidently of driving the Red Army from Pomerania while Schörner said that he expected to liberate the besieged Breslau in a few weeks time; the Führer gave 'an extraordinarily assured and resolute impression' and said that the whole military position was vastly improved. Meanwhile the air terror raged 'uninterruptedly, making people thoroughly despondent, . . . impotent', seeing no way out of the dilemma. Hitler had told Goebbels that he pinned certain hope on the new fighters and bombers under construction, but Goebbels confided to his diary that 'we have heard it so often before that we can no longer bring ourselves to place much hope in such statements'. The whole situation, said Goebbels, was due to the enemy air superiority, for German industry was largely demolished and the people's hope for victory had totally vanished. Each successive O K W bulletin gave the public an enormous shock and the heavy blows made the people fatalistic — not fanatical. The man in the street did not know what to think, but he was already disregarding German news and propaganda; Anglo-American

* The bunker was in use during air raids and particularly at night. During the day, if there was no raid alarm, Hitler used a relatively undamaged wing of the Chancellery.

**For the following paragraphs see in particular *The Final Entries 1945 — The Diaries of Joseph Goebbels.* Since 21 July 1944 Goebbels had been the 'Commissioner for Total Mobilization of Resources'.

leaflets were no longer carelessly thrown aside but were read attentively while the BBC had a grateful audience. The German public, continued Goebbels, was openly questioning why Göring and his *Luftwaffe* staff had not been shot for their failure, when those army officers held responsible for the loss of the undemolished Remagen bridge over the Rhine *had* been executed; and, to cap it all, said the Propaganda Minister, marvelling at their temerity, these critics made no bones about including their full names and addresses with their criticism.

The little minister was nursing a spiteful rancour against Göring and he urged the Führer not only to dismiss him but to bring him to account for his failure. Among some of his more radical suggestions were that the command of the *Luftwaffe* should be given to Dönitz or to Kammler of the SS, or that what remained of the *Luftwaffe* should be shared out between the army and the navy.* Once again Goebbels wanted Hitler to make a public address to the German people, but he noted on 30 March that the Führer had no great inclination to give the speech before 'the extraordinarily large scale measures' that he was about to initiate in the west had taken effect. These measures existed only in the dictator's imagination.

Yet Goebbels was reluctantly forced to believe that 'neither the civil population nor the troops had the necessary morale to continue the fight'. The troops certainly did fight, both in the east and in the west, since failure to do so meant a summary trial that was no trial at all and shooting or hanging within two hours of sentence, punishments that could be visited also on the victim's relatives. In the east the population lived in terror of a Soviet occupation; in the west they dreaded the allied bombing.** The Anglo-American troops, said Goebbels, were not feared by the German people, in fact many were pleased to see them come; although none dared speak of capitulation, everyone in West Germany was hoping that the war would blast its way over them as quickly as possible so that they might get relief from the bombing and be certain of allied protection against the Red Army.

Hitler had described to Goebbels the generals on his staff, whom he of course had chosen, as feeble and characterless, as indeed many of them were. Goebbels thought so too. But Goebbels could well appreciate the consequences of the ridiculous situation where every military decision had to be referred to the Führer and he asked Hitler why he did not appoint better men. According to the dictator, better men could not be found: his field commanders, too, he said, were poor, and only Schörner, Hube and Dietl had had stamina and talent, and the last two were dead. Model, said Hitler, was an excellent commander, but too intellectual and too impetuous and impulsive. Model and Rendulic, like Schörner, were approved of by the party since they were ardent Nazi supporters and did not shrink from 'fairly brutal methods'. The rest, however, were apparently of little use. Rundstedt was too old and too inflexible, and, said Hitler, his leadership was definitely bad; Guderian was hysterical and had, according to Hitler, largely messed up the situation in the east so that the dictator had had to send him on indefinite leave. In the German Army, said the Führer, there was treachery everywhere, and 'the same army [7 Army] that had failed at Avranches had failed at Trier'. Nor had the *Waffen SS* thrown up any commander of any operational talent, for neither

* We know from Boldt that Hitler threatened Göring at the *Führerlage* briefing session that he would do this.

** According to Goebbels, 353,000 civilians had been killed and 457,000 had been injured in air raids by the end of 1944.

Hausser nor Dietrich, according to the dictator, had any real ability. While Hitler was raging against Dietrich's conduct of the Hungarian offensive, Dietrich himself, according to Goebbels, was quite openly criticizing the Führer's actions in interfering with subordinate detail. And the Führer's decision 'to make an example of the SS formations in Hungary' by removing their armband insignia was not one that would be easily forgiven, even by the *Waffen SS*. By the Führer's order, *SS Gruppenführer* Reinefarth had been arrested for withdrawing from Küstrin. Himmler himself was in disgrace for the failure of the campaign in Pomerania and, so Goebbels recorded, had 'temporarily forfeited his promotion to Commander-in-Chief of the German Army'.*

In 1934 Hitler had smashed the power of the brownshirted SA using the German Army and SS. Between 1937 and 1941 the dictator had broken the German Army so that, by the end of July 1944, its leaders were, for the most part, terrified remnants of a *Generalität* that had long since ceased to be master in its own house; the real control of the army was exercised by the Führer through the SS and the party. By 1945 there were all the indications that the *Luftwaffe*, staunch supporter of Nazism though it had always been, might shortly go the same way as the German Army. Then, by March of that year, Hitler had turned against the SS. For, as Goebbels noted in his diary, the Führer was increasingly in conflict with those about him, and Goebbels himself began to wonder 'where all this would end'.

By 31 January 1945 the German military losses in the war had risen to 1.8 million dead (of which 1.1 million were casualties in the east) and 1.9 million missing (of which a million were reported on the eastern front). In all, 3.7 million men had been entirely lost to Germany.**

---

* According to Goebbels's diary Reinefarth was arrested; Boldt, however, said that no action was taken against the SS for this failure. Goebbels, too, appears to be the only source that Himmler had been earmarked for the post of C-in-C of the German Army.

** The numbers wounded stood at 4.4 million.

CHAPTER TEN

The Citadel

The Anglo-American air offensive was continuing without pause notwithstanding the divergences of opinions and aims, not only between allies but also between the governments and their military staffs and between the air commanders themselves. In general, the Americans tended to seek out industrial targets, among them oil, and gave a high priority to the disruption of communications. The British air staff's priorities also rated communications and oil high on the list, but in practice Bomber Command allotted the greater part of its effort to the area bombing of cities and towns so that industrial targets and enemy communications became subsidiary aims. In addition, both air forces carried out a wide variety of other offensive tasks that included the destruction of the *Luftwaffe* and its supporting ground organization, the bombing of the German Navy afloat and ashore, reconnaissance of all types and the air support of the allied ground forces.

As far as the *Luftwaffe* was concerned the effect of the joint offensive was total in that it became almost impossible for German aircraft to operate by day in the west or over a large part of the Reich. After the Ardennes offensive the *Luftwaffe* rarely attempted to interfere with Anglo-American air operations except that a small night-fighter force was kept in being, and a few score jet fighters, dispersed over eighteen airfields, took to the air each day in a forlorn effort to combat the incoming air armadas. The allied air supremacy was such that these jet fighters were often unable to get off the ground since the dust raised by their engines immediately brought down on them the swarms of enemy fighters circling overhead.

What remained of the flying arm of the *Luftwaffe* was mainly employed on the eastern front, where the air situation was very different. From early in the war until 1943 the *Luftwaffe* had enjoyed air superiority over the whole of the eastern theatre, yet it had never managed to drive the Red Air Force from the sky. During 1944 the situation had been reversed, for the Red Air Force had superiority everywhere but the *Luftwaffe* could still fly in some strength in areas of particular importance. Whereas in the west the *Luftwaffe* was lucky if it could put in much more than 100 sorties a day, in the east it might on occasions, even as late as March 1945, still field as many as 1,700 sorties. As against this the Red Air Force might fly 5,000 sorties, but the more usual figure for daily operations was nearer 2,000 — 3,000 for the Red Air Force and 300 — 400 sorties for the *Luftwaffe*. The *Luftwaffe* air losses for the month of December 1944, that month in which it had made its last effort over the Ardennes, show 1,400 aircraft destroyed in the west and over the Reich, but only 173 over the eastern front. Sperrle had been retired in September and his 3 Air Fleet headquarters withdrawn; von Rundstedt's air support, such as it was, was henceforth to be found by the Reich Air Command.

Otherwise there had been little change in the German high command and in the German deployment in the west. On the Biscay coast some of the garrisons were still holding out. In Holland and on the lower Rhine Student's Army Group H continued to hold its ground, with 25 Army near the coast, while further south the formations of Schlemm's 1 Parachute Army were still putting up a most obstinate resistance. Model's Army Group B held the centre, but was now reduced to 15 Army, 5 Panzer Army (under Harpe) and 7 Army, while Army Group G, now under *SS Obergruppenführer* Hausser, defended the south with 1 Army and 19 Army, the latter recently returned to him from Himmler's disbanded Upper Rhine Command.

On 11 March von Rundstedt, the Commander-in-Chief West, was finally retired and replaced by Kesselring, whose command in Italy had been taken by von Vietinghoff. Von Rundstedt had, according to Hitler, done badly, and it took all Goebbels's urging to ensure that the field-marshal was relieved of his post 'in a dignified manner' with the award of the Swords to the Oak Leaves of the Knight's Cross. If Blumentritt is to be believed, Hitler, the military usurper, respected von Rundstedt, the general of the old school, who was the holder of 'legitimate military authority'. This opinion has to be compared with Goebbels's assessment of 'a highly respectable officer who has done us great service, particularly in the liquidation [of the army officer conspirators] of 20 July'. That, and the fact that von Rundstedt could generally be relied upon to do anything that he was told, so cloaking the dictator's military actions with an aura of respectability, exemplified his use to the Führer and the party. Meanwhile the hangings, the shootings and the imprisonment of officers continued on the western front as elsewhere, not merely for what was said to be conspiracy, but for failure or for indiscipline, that is to say the expression of views contrary to those issued from the Berlin bunker. For, as Goebbels said, the Führer was rooting out the increasing indiscipline among the generals in the west by instituting itinerant courts-martial and having recalcitrant generals condemned and shot within two hours. One general who, said Goebbels, refused to permit an NSFO (National Socialist Guidance Officer) to do his job, was to be brought to trial and 'probably condemned to death'. On 10 March — even before the arrival of the Führer-commissioned General Hübner travelling court-martial — a General von Bothmer shot himself, having just been sentenced to five years imprisonment and the loss of all rank 'for failing to hold Bonn'. Nor could any officer merely opt out by finding an excuse for release from the army, for, on 7 February 1945, Burgdorf's *Heerespersonalamt* had issued an order that officers were no longer to be permitted to leave the service but would, if necessary, be employed in any junior rank vacancy — and, in cases where they had incurred official displeasure (*Verschulden*) they would be re-employed as non-commissioned officers. These were the conditions for officers which the field-marshal of the old school appeared to condone.

In Italy, by the end of the year, the situation was one of stalemate, the line having remained virtually static from the area around Spezia in the west to that near Ravenna in the east. The German 14 and 10 Armies remained side by side opposing the American 5 Army and the British 8 Army, but since the Anglo-Americans had removed numbers of divisions to France, and were to continue to do so, the allied strength had been considerably reduced. Nothwithstanding this, the allied army group had, throughout 1944, pinned nearly forty German divisions in Italy and the Balkans, about a sixth of the total of the German ground forces, and would shortly resume its offensive against a force of 440,000 Germans and 160,000 Italians of Mussolini's Italian Republic.* Behind the German front Italian partisans were becoming increasingly active.

In the Balkans those German formations that had been permitted to withdraw had continued their thousand mile, four month long, march, during which they had been engaged by numerous partisan bands and by Bulgarian and Russian divisions. Some of the garrisons left behind on the coast had also tried to withdraw, presumably without orders, but they had, for the most part, been destroyed by partisans or by allied air and naval forces. During March, von Weichs's Army Group F headquarters handed over the command in the Balkans to Löhr's Army E, but before the end of the month Löhr was being forced northwards out of Sarajevo. In all, Löhr's command numbered five corps, about nine German divisions together with several brigades, a Cossack division and Croat elements.** The German garrisons that had been left behind were scattered from the east Aegean to Crete.

Hitler awaited the final assault against the homeland of the German Reich, the Citadel, all that was left of Fortress Europe, prepared, in the last extremity, to let it go down in the flames that would provide his own funeral pyre. On 19 March he had issued his *Verbrannte Erde* directive ordering that all German resources should be destroyed rather than let them fall into the hands of the enemy; and it was only after persuasion by Speer and others that he brought himself to amend the order, so restricting the destruction to industries, installations and supplies 'likely to be used by the enemy'.***

Regular reports were received in Berlin from *V-Mann* intelligence sources, reportedly in the United Kingdom, that a new invasion force was being assembled on the east coast of England ready for an air and sea-borne landing in Holland and the north German coast; these fed the Führer's obsession that such a landing was imminent. But since he had no reserves there was little that he could do about it, except to form two new operative coastal commands, one for the German Bight (*Nordküste*) under Busch and the other for the German Baltic coast under Lindemann.**** These new commands were later to be drawn into the fighting for the mainland.

On the night of 23 March Montgomery's 21 Army Group crossed the lower Rhine and began to move eastwards, while further to the south Bradley's 12 Army Group started to break out of its bridge-heads at Remagen and Mainz. A few days

---

* By the end of February the German forces in Italy totalled two armies and the *Armee Ligurian*, seven corps, twenty-four German divisions and one Russian PW (Turkoman) division.

**Löhr became once more the C-in-C South-East.

***These destruction orders were in fact largely disregarded by Speer's ministry and by the *Gauleiter*, for these did not suffer from the same inquisitorial organization and methods that were to be found in the armed services.

****A 1942 plan known as *Valkyrie* had been revived in 1944 for the forming of skeleton divisions from the 300,000 convalescents and leave men in the Reich. It was overtaken by *Goten-Bewegung*.

later the Anglo-American troops were advancing rapidly into Germany against a much weakened opposition.

On 27 March Hitler issued his last-stand *Goten-Bewegung* order, some erring mind likening it to the historic movement of the Goths, although there was in fact no parallel. The troops inside the Reich making up garrisons, installations and depots were earmarked to form, in name, about ten field divisions; the military schools and the permanent staff of the Labour Service formed yet another six divisions. Forty-three trains were assembled and 96,000 men, the East Goths, set off by march route to the Oder, while the 72,000 West Goths began the march towards the Rhine. Except for the *Volkssturm*, these sixteen and seventeen year old youths, formed up as paper formations with imposing historical or regional designations and equipped with small-arms, but usually without artillery, signal or logistic support, represented the Citadel's very last reserve. The shortage of weapons, even of small-arms, was such that, on 14 March, Hitler had caused Bormann to send instructions to all *Gauleiter* that the *Volkssturm* must hand over its weapons to the regular forces, except where, as in the border areas, the *Volkssturm* had been permanently embodied and incorporated into the field army. Similar orders were given to the Labour Service and to the Hitler Youth.

During that late winter the western allies had suffered 96,000 casualties in crossing the two to three mile belt of the West Wall and in closing up to the Rhine, but they had taken 280,000 prisoners in doing so. At the time of the Rhine crossing Eisenhower had at his disposal ninety-four allied divisions, of which twenty were British and eleven were French, and about 10,000 aircraft. The German strength in the west was seventy-three divisions and less than 1,000 aircraft, many of which were unfit for flight.

Except for Schlemm's 1 Parachute Army, the fighting value of the German formations was by now indifferent, the officers having no faith in their ability to hold back the invaders and the men being apathetic. Those *Gauleiter* whose districts had already been overrun, having removed themselves to a place of safety, defended themselves by letters of excuses to the Führer and to Goebbels. The army's defeatism, some said, had infected the people; others protested conversely that the German people in the west undermined the morale of the troops in that they encouraged the men to withdraw or to give up, some civilians actually giving refuge to deserters. But the party officials themselves, Goebbels noted, came out of the business very badly, for they were the first to flee and the people had lost all confidence in them. Meanwhile the military staffs and diarists stressed in their reports, what was not by any means true (particularly after the Rhine crossing), 'the skill of the commanders and staffs and the outstanding heroism of the defenders' who were fighting, according to the compilers, 'to the last man and the last round'. This increasing emphasis on the steadfastness and loyalty of the German Army was, in the main, a defensive measure to protect the army from the terror of a Führer directed Gestapo investigation.

The Commander-in-Chief West had assumed that the western allies would drive across the North German plain in a compact group towards Berlin, and he was surprised to note that, after the Rhine had been crossed, it was only 21 Army Group that was advancing on a narrow front and then on a north-easterly axis; the Americans, on the other hand, were fanning out rapidly on a broad front with axes both to the east and, what was more significant, to the south-east. Although Hitler was not to know it, Eisenhower had already made his totally unexpected decision to ignore Berlin as an objective and direct his main axis south-east on Erfurt, Leipzig and Dresden; and he had, on his own responsibility and to the chagrin of the British, sent a telegram to Stalin on 28 March announcing this intention. Stalin, in reply, told the American mission in Moscow that he agreed with Eisenhower that 'Berlin no longer had its former strategic significance' and said that the main effort of the Red Army would likewise be directed south-westwards towards Dresden to form a junction with the United States forces there. The Soviet offensive, said Stalin, 'would begin in the second half of May, although this date might be subject to alteration'.

This answer was intended to mislead Eisenhower and to disguise the true Soviet intention. For immediately after the western ambassadors and missions had left, Stalin sent for Zhukov, who arrived in the capital from 1 Belorussian Front on 29 March. Stalin told him that the German defence in the west had collapsed and the possibility existed that the Germans might let the Anglo-Americans through to Berlin; 'as for Churchill', Stalin is reputed to have said, 'he might do anything'. Zhukov and Konev were required to launch their offensive *directly against Berlin* and to begin operations within a fortnight.

Meanwhile the rapid enemy advance in the west gave rise to another regrouping of the German high command. Montgomery's thrust was splitting Army Group H from Army Group B, so that part of Army Group H was isolated in Holland while the other part, mainly Schlemm's 1 Parachute Army, was being driven back towards the German Bight. Student took over this new sector covering the valley of the Ems, with only Schlemm under his command, while Blaskowitz reappeared once more, this time in command of Army Group H, made up of 25 Army and garrison troops and henceforth to be known as *Festung Holland*.

The threat to the German defence on the right flank of 21 Army Group was even greater when 9 and 1 American Armies, one to the north and the other to the south of the Ruhr, began the rapid double envelopment that ended on 1 April with the encirclement of the greater part of Model's Army Group B inside the Ruhr, 325,000 men being surrounded in a great eighty-mile pocket. Schlemm, to the north of the area of the breakthrough, had earlier been warned from Berlin in unmistakable terms that he would be personally answerable for holding a bridge-head west of the lower Rhine; 'not one bridge was to be lost and not one fit man or one piece of fighting equipment was to be taken back east of the river'.

Again a rapid command reorganization was necessary and Berlin ordered that 7 Army, outside the pocket, should be transferred from Model to Hausser's Army Group G. But as Hausser meanwhile had shown himself to be unable to hold Bradley's and Devers's thrusts in the centre and the south, he was removed from his appointment on 2 April and replaced by Schulz. These rapid reorganizations and changes of command became increasingly confusing the nearer the end was in sight; at first they damaged even further the remaining cohesion of the defence, and then, finally, ceased to have any significance for the men on the spot, for the western theatre was rapidly disintegrating. For those in the highest command, however, it was a time fraught with the greatest of personal danger, for the Commander-in-Chief in the bunker saw treachery everywhere and his orders and threats were becoming wilder day by day; the Gestapo and the SS were increasing their daily rate of shootings of arrested generals, apparently in order that none might survive the holocaust. None in the OKW had any doubts that the enemy intended to dismember Germany totally, for, on 11 April, a British memorandum for *Eclipse* had been captured, showing the Reich divided up into occupation zones, with Berlin and Bremen as separate enclaves.

A *Luftwaffe* attempt had been made to supply Model's army group by air, but this was, of course, insignificant; ten sorties only were flown, for example, on the night of 10 April. The end came very rapidly when, less than a week later, Army Group B went into captivity.* Model shot himself in Duisburg.

Meanwhile the Anglo-Americans were rapidly advancing into the centre of Germany, Simpson's 9 Army reaching Hildesheim on 8 April and the Elbe, only fifty-three miles south-west of Berlin, on 11 April. There appears to be little doubt that Bradley could have reached Berlin quickly, and probably without many casualties, if it had been Eisenhower's intention that he should have done so, for Simpson had covered fifty-seven miles in the twenty-four hours before he had been brought to a halt on 11 April. But Simpson was forbidden to move from the line of the Elbe and that is where he remained. On Simpson's right, 1 (US) Army, having dispersed the German remnants in the Harz, drove almost unopposed to the Mulde and seized two bridges intact. There that army, too, was ordered to halt. Further to the south the bulk of the American forces had veered south-eastwards towards Saxony and Bohemia, separating Kesselring's Army Command West from Group Student and *Festung Holland*, so that Kesselring was left with only 7, 1 and 19 Armies of Army Group G facing Patton and Devers. By 15 April Patton, too, had reached the stop line on the upper Mulde. On that day Simpson of 9 Army once again pressed Bradley that he be allowed to expand the Elbe bridge-head near Magdeburg and drive straight for Berlin, and again Bradley and Eisenhower refused. The British were at Uelzen moving north-east towards the Baltic while the Canadians were pressing in on *Festung Holland*.

The American thrusts indicated clearly to the OKW that Germany was about to be cut in two and the Führer made such arrangements as were necessary to enable the struggle to be continued from both the north and the south. As Kesselring was being driven back into Austria, Field-Marshal Busch's *Führungsstab Nordküste* was formed into Army Command North-West, taking under its command Blaskowitz's *Festung Holland*, Group Student and a newly raised Army Blumentritt.

It has been said, mainly by Soviet historians, that Hitler at this time began to voice the opinions that had been pressed on him in vain by Guderian during the previous year, and that he had now determined to transfer all available forces to the east against the Russians. But it was in any case too late for this. The forces in the west for which Guderian had argued with Jodl had been destroyed. Further afield, good divisions, many of them battle experienced, lay idle or committed to lost ventures from the Channel Islands to Sarajevo and from Narvik to Crete, in Norway, Kurland, Italy and the Balkans, while the defence of German soil was entrusted to civilians who were old men or children. The Führer was sensitive to any hint of criticism on this score and he denied to Jodl that this was the true position; but, for a long time past, Hitler had been unable to face facts or order priorities and his ideas had become totally illusory. The German people as a whole, ignorant that Germany had, in any case, already been partitioned at Yalta,

---

* Twenty-one divisions of 5 Panzer Army, 15 Army and elements of 1 Parachute Army ceased to exist: 320,000 prisoners were taken, including thirty general officers.

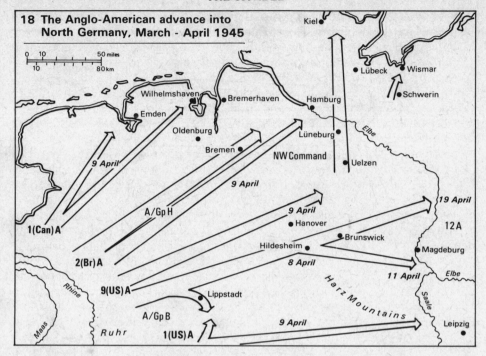

18 The Anglo-American advance into North Germany, March - April 1945

realized only too well that an occupation by the western allies was not to be compared with the terror of the Soviet régime and the dreadful barbarities that were already being perpetrated in the eastern territories. Yet it is certain that considerations of humanity did not, for one moment, enter Hitler's mind, for instead of bolstering up the eastern front (which, except for East Prussia, in any event lay dormant) at the expense of the west, he raised at the end of March a new 12 Army under Wenck, made up of eight divisions thrown together, 'in order to relieve Model's Army Group B and throw the Anglo-Americans back across the Rhine'.

Wenck's 12 Army had, of course, little fighting value. It had, admittedly, been allocated four experienced corps headquarters, but two of these were not able to operate because of a lack of transport and radio. Some of the newly raised divisions were called panzer and panzer grenadier, and had been given factory new tanks, assault guns, armoured personnel carriers and artillery, together with such stirring and resonant names as *Scharnhorst, Potsdam* and *Clausewitz*. Their ranks, however, were filled largely by recruits and members of the Labour Service. Many of the formations and units did contain cadres of experienced officers and non-commissioned officers, and to these were due such minor success that attended Wenck's efforts.

Since by then Model's army group had already been destroyed, Wenck was ordered south-west to relieve the beleaguered troops in the area of the Harz. Wenck left the Elbe behind him as he moved westwards with two of his best equipped panzer divisions in the van, one of these, *Scharnhorst*, brushing with the 15 Scottish Division near Uelzen on 14 April. Wenck was then counter-attacked by both British and Americans and shortly afterwards both of his panzer divisions

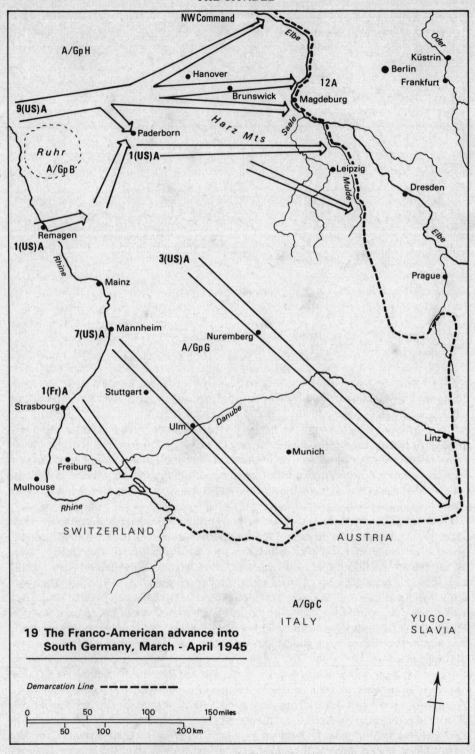

19 **The Franco-American advance into South Germany, March - April 1945**

Demarcation Line ▬ ▬ ▬

were almost destroyed. Wenck then fell back behind the line of the Elbe and the Mulde where, somewhat to his surprise, he found himself free from allied air attack. The American forces showed no inclination to follow him up across the river and there Wenck remained.

The final destruction of the German troops in encircled East Prussia, defended by Weiss's Army Group North, had been entrusted by Stalin to Vasilevsky, the former Chief of the Red Army General Staff, who had taken over the field command of 3 Belorussian Front from Cherniakhovsky, killed by enemy action at Mehlsack. Bagramian's 1 Baltic Front was also subordinated to Vasilevsky and redesignated as the Red Army Samland Group.

Vasilevsky's offensive had begun in mid March and was directed in the first instance against Heiligenbeil in the centre, held by Müller's 4 Army. The German troops there fought most stubbornly but, by 19 March, they had been forced back to a bridge-head only six miles deep. A representative of 6 German Corps was then sent back to the Führer to request permission to evacuate the beaches by sea; this was refused. On 26 March, however, Hitler sanctioned the withdrawal 'after all the artillery, tanks and vehicles had been shipped off'. By then it was too late even to save all the troops and their personal weapons. Many did escape across the Frisches Haff to the Frische Nehrung and Pillau, but Vasilevsky claimed to have captured 46,000 prisoners, 600 tanks and assault guns and inflicted 93,000 casualties. Vasilevsky then turned to what was left of East Prussia, that is to say the capital Königsberg and Samland.

Meanwhile the position inside Königsberg appeared to be without any vestige of hope. Headquarters Army Group North had been removed from East Prussian soil and the overall command had been given to Müller, the Commander of 4 Army. This officer who, after the war, was to meet his death before a Greek firing squad, arrived in Königsberg on 2 April on a one day visit, and there was an immediate and a heated exchange between him and Lasch, the commander of the Königsberg fortress; Müller threatened to report Lasch to the Führer on account of his pessimism. Müller then addressed all formation commanders and party leaders in the cellar of the university in the most buoyant tones, assuring them that not only would Königsberg be held, but that he, Müller, would drive the enemy out of East Prussia.

Lasch had four skeleton divisions and eight battalions of *Volkssturm*, in all about 35,000 men; *Luftwaffe* air support was virtually non-existent. The Red Army by this time was making good use of its Free Germany Committee organization, and was tapping telephone conversations inside the city and sending in numerous German spies dressed as soldiers or as civilians. Inside Königsberg treachery was suspected everywhere. In the 100,000 strong civilian population there was a feeling of great terror, and the presence of so many civilians can only have reduced the efficiency and morale of the defending troops. Koch, the *Gauleiter* of East Prussia, had carried out the Führer's instructions faithfully in that he had prevented any evacuation. These city dwellers, lacking even farm transport, had, in any event, been unable to disobey him.

After heavy air and artillery preparation the Soviet assault began at midday on 6 April and, by evening, Red Army infantry had fought their way into the town.

Lasch asked Müller's permission to withdraw from the city to Samland: this was refused. The next day, however, when the city was already cut off from Group Samland, Müller ordered Lasch to break out, presumably having put the position to Hitler, by which time a break-out was no longer possible. On 9 April the wounded Lasch asked in vain for permission to surrender, and the next day did so on his own authority. On 12 April an angry Führer had Lasch sentenced to death in his absence and without trial; his wife and daughters were imprisoned and his son-in-law, at that time commanding a battalion at the front, was arrested; all were fortunate to have remained alive at the end of the war.* Müller, too, lost his command. At about the time when *Gauleiter* Koch was fleeing to the safety of Denmark on an ice-breaker, the city of Königsberg was entered by the Red Army and became the scene of the most fearful barbarity and atrocity.

On the morning of 13 April began the final stage of the attack against the German Group Samland. The German force, reckoned at eight infantry divisions and one panzer division with a strength of about 65,000 men, began to fall back the next day on the Fischhausen — Pillau peninsula to prevent a Soviet penetration, and about 20,000 men managed to reach Pillau where they organized a hasty defence. The resistance there was fanatically desperate and took six days to overcome. Meanwhile the German Navy continued to withdraw numbers of the troops together with a great mass of civilians, most of the civilians from the Baltic coast being carried to Denmark. Between 13 and 26 April 3 Belorussian Front claimed to have taken a further 30,000 prisoners, by which time the fighting was at an end.

The campaign in East Prussia had lasted 105 days and the endurance of Army Group North and its German Navy supporters had been remarkable. Soviet casualties had been particularly heavy, for 3 Belorussian Front had lost twenty-two and 2 Belorussian Front fifteen per cent of their strength in the four weeks before 10 February.

Meanwhile in Silesia events had not stood still. The fanatical Schörner had taken over Army Group Centre (formerly Army Group A) on 20 January at a time when his major formations were retreating in disorder before Konev's 1 Ukrainian Front, and when 1 Hungarian Army on Schörner's flank had disbanded itself, following the signing of the 21 January armistice at Debrecen between Soviet and Hungarian representatives. But by 'fairly brutal methods', among them, according to the approving Goebbels, the hanging of deserters on trees displaying placards that read 'I am a deserter and have declined to defend German women and children', Schörner had managed to restore some cohesion to his front.

In the second week in February Konev's 1 Ukrainian Front had taken up the offensive once more, the Soviet intention being to occupy Silesia west of the Oder and close up on the line of the Neisse in Brandenburg, in order to bring Konev up alongside Zhukov, ready for the final assault on Berlin. As a result 18,000 German troops were encircled in Glogau and another 35,000 in Breslau, the railway between Berlin and Silesia being cut on 3 March. On 15 March Konev moved yet again and

---

* Shortly afterward two German officers who had escaped from Königsberg brought word to the OKW that Lasch had not surrendered until his headquarters had been overrun. In recording this the OKW diarist added, on what authority we know not, 'this is false!'.

by the end of the month had occupied the whole of Upper Silesia.

The Red Army approach and entry into Silesia caused a mass exodus of the German population, for of the 4,700,000 inhabitants listed in February 1944 only 620,000 remained in occupied Silesia by mid-April of the next year.

Breslau, like Glogau and Neisse, had been designated a fortress; it was to be defended by 609 Infantry Division, a formation that was a division only in name since it had been raised in Dresden only a few weeks before, its troops being thrown together from schools, detachments and stragglers, together with a hastily formed SS regiment and a *Luftwaffe* regiment of ground staffs. The fortress artillery consisted of thirty-two batteries of German, Soviet, Polish, Yugoslav and Italian guns; there were no tanks in the garrison except for a company of fifteen assault guns. This ill-assorted force was supported by thirty-eight *Volkssturm* battalions, each about 400 strong.

This most unpromising material continued to defend Breslau against all attack until the end of the war and it laid down its weapons only after the remainder of Germany had capitulated. The city fought desperately, buoyed by propaganda and rumour and encouraged by Hitler, Goebbels and the *Gauleiter* Hanke, the garrison purposely being fed with false news by the German propaganda machine. Convinced that Breslau was like a bulwark or breakwater in a Red Sea, and that help would eventually come, the soldiers and inhabitants repulsed all attacks. Some still pinned their faith on the Führer, others on the new wonder weapons on which Hitler said that he placed such hopes. Rumours were rife. Some of the defenders expected to be relieved by German troops, others by American forces fighting the Russians once the enemy coalition had broken down. The 17 Army main front between Striegau and Strehlen remained static for some weeks and the Breslau garrison could nightly see the flash and hear the distant rumble of artillery fire, and this, not unnaturally, kept up their spirits. The Kaiserstrasse on the north bank of the river was cleared and used as an airstrip to bring in supplies, and part of two parachute battalions were flown in. So the Breslau defenders fought on for nearly three months. Of the garrison of 35,000 troops and 15,000 *Volkssturm*, 29,000 are said to have become casualties; about half of the 80,000 inhabitants, according to the post-war official source, lost their lives.

By 1 April the remaining German troops in Pomerania had been virtually destroyed except for an isolated pocket near the mouth of the Vistula; the Soviet occupation of this Baltic coastal area finally removed, as Shtemenko said, any danger of the Soviet offensive against Berlin 'being wrecked by attacks from the flank or rear'. The German Kurland army group of 16 and 18 Armies still remained in being, but this could be safely ignored by the Russians, as they moved westwards, since it was too far to the rear and since, in spite of its twenty-four divisions, Group Kurland lacked the offensive power that could only have been given it by a strong air and tank arm.

At the beginning of the month Stalin summoned Zhukov, Konev, Antonov, the new Chief of General Staff, and Shtemenko to a Politburo meeting. Antonov first gave an introduction presenting the known situation on all German fronts, both in the east and in the west; Stalin then told those present that the intention was 'to take Berlin before the western allies did'. The new offensive into Brandenburg, he continued, would have to start by 16 April and be completed within fifteen days.

Zhukov and Konev in turn presented their plans to the Politburo, these having already been agreed with the general staff and Stalin so that the plans were new only to the other Politburo members. Zhukov's 1 Belorussian Front was to make a frontal attack due westwards on the Küstrin-Berlin axis, except that its two tank armies were to outflank the capital from the north. Konev's 1 Ukrainian Front was to move north-westwards on the centre line Spremberg-Beelitz (near Potsdam about twenty miles south-west of Berlin). The interfront boundary between Zhukov's and Konev's forces had been decided by Stalin and ran from Gross Gastrose on the Oder to Gross Michendorf twenty miles south of Berlin.

Konev had earlier remonstrated angrily with the general staff about this boundary line since it would stop his troops from entering the German capital, and at the Politburo meeting of 1 April Antonov had been so bold as to point this out to Stalin. Konev, whose orders with regard to his right flank had up to this time been by no means clear, also spoke up in favour of directing his tank armies into Berlin from the south-east.

Stalin would not readily give up his idea that Zhukov should take Berlin; nor would he at first accept the general staff's and Konev's view that 1 Ukrainian Front should share the victory. And so he apparently determined to leave the matter open, and, taking a pencil, he silently crossed out the interfront boundary, leaving only that part that ran from Gross Gastrose to Lübben, a distance of about twenty-five miles from the start line. The dictator gave no explanation and made no further comment at the time, but he later told the general staff that Berlin should be taken by whoever broke in first.

On 6 April, Rokossovsky was called to Moscow to be briefed by Stalin on his part in the new offensive, the advance into Mecklenburg to cover Zhukov's right. The troops of 2 Belorussian Front were still 150 miles away, having, only a few days before, cleared the enemy in the areas of Gdynia and Danzig; Rokossovsky argued that it was physically impossible to close his troops up to the lower Oder until 20 April, and in the end he persuaded a grudging Stalin that 2 Belorussian Front could only join the main offensive four days after Zhukov and Konev had begun their attacks.

In the reply that Stalin had sent to Eisenhower and to the western allies on 28 March, he had said that the Soviet attack would be made against Dresden and Leipzig, probably not before mid May. It was not until the end of the second week in April that the western allies became aware of the imminence of the Soviet offensive and then only through monitoring the German radio in the east: in answer to questions from the United States Embassy in Moscow, Stalin still insisted, even at this late hour, that the main thrust was to be made on Leipzig.

Guderian, the acting Chief of the Army General Staff, had been bundled off on indefinite sick leave, the occasion chosen for Guderian's dismissal being the failure of five divisions of Busse's 9 Army to destroy the Zhukov held bridge-head on the west bank of the Oder near Küstrin. This check was all the more galling to the Führer since, in mid March when at 9 Army on one of his very rare visits to a headquarters in the field, he had hinted at an ambitious—and a most unrealistic—plan to mount a counter-offensive from Frankfurt-on-Oder into the rear of 1 Belorussian

Front, for which the destruction of the Küstrin bridge-head was an essential preliminary. This of course was only one of the projected offensives that occupied the Führer's waking hours, the others including Wenck's drive to the west in conjunction with an operational sortie made by Bayerlein from the Ruhr, a flank thrust by Schulz from Thuringia, and a movement southwards by Student to take Hamm. These offensives, which were nothing more than a few general staff jottings committed to paper at the Führer's dictation, were rarely attempted and were shortly to exist only in Hitler's imagination.

On 28 March Guderian and Busse had appeared in the Reich Chancellery at Hitler's summons, where Busse was, according to a witness, subjected to a torrent of personal abuse directed not only at himself but against all under his command. Guderian, who had continued to serve when his immediate deputy, von Bonin, the head of the operations department, had some time before been arrested by Hitler's order, spoke out in Busse's favour, vehemently, like a man possessed, for, in truth, he was at the limit of his mental and nervous resources. This was the end of Guderian, and his staff were surprised and thankful that he had escaped joining von Bonin in a concentration camp.*

Guderian's recent chief of operations had been Krebs, a genial officer not long before transferred from Model's army group where he had been chief of staff. Krebs was a friend and drinking companion of Burgdorf. Burgdorf had already been admitted into the tight little circle about Hitler, together with Bormann and Fegelein, Himmler's SS representative with the Führer; Burgdorf was now much closer to the Führer than Keitel had ever been. Since Guderian was held by Hitler to be responsible for nearly all of the Führer's failures, the dictator making no bones about telling everyone so, it was inevitable that both Hitler and Burgdorf should be looking about them for a successor for the acting Chief of the Army General Staff. Krebs, having worked with Guderian for several weeks, was already *au fait* with current operational matters, and his personality was such that Hitler saw in him an obedient and malleable executive. Just as Zeitzler, the close friend of Schmundt, had been brought in by Schmundt to oust Halder, so did Krebs, through the prompting of Burgdorf, displace Guderian.

By the second week in April Fortress Europe had taken the form, as Goebbels said, of a small strip of territory from Norway to Italy, a gigantic elongated hour-glass with a waist restricted to a hundred mile land-bridge between the Elbe and the Oder, with Berlin in the narrowest part midway between the two rivers.

The disposition of the German troops on the eastern front had undergone but little change. On the lower Oder Himmler had given way to Heinrici and retired to Hohenlychen, and the SS element of his Army Group Vistula headquarters had been replaced by army reinforcements from von Weichs's disbanded headquarters Army Group F. Heinrici had under his command von Manteuffel's 3 Panzer Army in Mecklenburg, opposite Rokossovsky, and Busse's 9 Army in East Brandenburg facing Zhukov.** Further to the south against Konev, was Graeser's 4 Panzer

---

* It was not only the German Army that was subjected to such treatment. That spring Hitler had insulted Göring in front of junior officers, saying that the *Luftwaffe* was rotten to the core and should be disbanded; and he threatened to send Göring to the front as a private soldier. Knipfer, the head of civil defence within the *Luftwaffe* ministry, had already been sent to a concentration camp.

** Heinrici also commanded the rump of 2 Army encircled in the delta of the Vistula and a headquarters, under a corps commander *SS Obergruppenführer* Steiner, known variously as 11 Army, 11 Panzer Army and Group Steiner. It had no formations.

Army, but this formed part of the left wing of Schörner's Army Group Centre. Behind von Manteuffel and Busse stood Weidling's 56 Panzer Corps in army group reserve, but this had only tactical significance as it was already split between von Manteuffel and Busse. The German regular troops covering Mecklenburg and Brandenburg between the Baltic and Görlitz totalled about forty-five field divisions of which five were panzer, although this strength could be increased in that Schörner could, and did, allot further divisions to Graeser during the battle. Roughly then, there were fifty weak divisions facing a force, said, by Soviet historians, to total 193 divisions. This Soviet figure, like those of Red Army guns and tanks, is, however, to be treated with some reserve; moreover numbers by themselves meant little, for the mass of the Red Army infantry, like the German, was in a very wretched condition, the Soviet high command relying for its victories on the excellence of its tank arm and mechanized forces.

The Führer was sure, once again on the basis of intuition, that the main Soviet offensive when it came would not be directed against Berlin at all but would be made in the south into Czechoslovakia. On 6 April, the same day that he interviewed Rendulic in the ruined Chancellery, assuring Rendulic of his supreme confidence that the Oder front would hold, the dictator had removed three panzer grenadier divisions from Heinrici and sent them to the south. Heinrici's protests against the weakening of his sector were countered with the well-worn retort that the Red Army was at the end of its resources and that its troops consisted of nothing more than released prisoners of war and peasants rounded up from the reoccupied territories at the point of the bayonet. The Führer made promises of replacements, offering Heinrici 137,000 armed men from the SS, *Luftwaffe* and Navy. About 30,000 were eventually produced.*

Between January and March there had been a further induction of sixteen- and seventeen-year-old youths into the army, and these formed a substantial part of all reinforcements and of the newly raised formations. In addition to the regular divisions on the Oder and the Neisse there was a great patchwork of detachments and makeshift formations, together with more than a hundred *Volkssturm* battalions. Whereas the *Volkssturm* in the west had proved to be of negligible military value, this was not entirely true in the east, for many of those moved to the Oder realized the consequences of surrender, both for themselves and for their womenfolk. Although its armament was very poor, it had short-range anti-tank weapons in abundance and often had sufficient determination to use them at close quarters. The *Volkssturm* remaining in Berlin, on the other hand, tended to regard all as lost by the time the Russians reached the capital. In addition to the *Volkssturm* battalions there were armed police units and a large number of Hitler Youth detachments, hastily collected and commanded by SS or SA officers. Whether motivated by fear or by devotion to duty, these youths, who were mostly in their early teens, proved far more dangerous to the enemy than the Berlin *Volkssturm*.

Torgelow, Stettin, Gartz, Batzlow, Seelow, Frankfurt, Guben, Cottbus, Forst, Muskau, Zossen and Spremberg had been declared by the Führer to be fortresses

---

* Heinrici met Hitler in the Chancellery on 30 March for the first time in his life. Heinrici, a quiet and sober officer of some strength of character, was determined to have two of his divisions out of Frankfurt-on-Oder, designated by the Führer as a fortress. Suddenly, to his surprise and consternation, he was cut short by a violent outburst of abuse by Hitler directed against him and his officers. Boldt, who was present, said: 'Even today I can still see Heinrici's stupefied face. Thunderstruck he looked questioningly from one bystander to another. But none of the military, chosen as they were by Hitler and constantly in his presence, were prepared to take Heinrici's part.'

or strongpoints, irrespective of whether or not fortifications were in existence or the localities could be defended. In fact the field defences on the Oder itself had been well constructed by the use of civilian volunteers; but, although these earthworks had some tactical depth, they were linear, running from north to south parallel to the river and they therefore lacked operative or strategic depth. In addition, a few poorly developed peripheral defences had been thrown up in the outskirts of Berlin. There were no mobile or panzer forces capable of destroying, or even checking, the enemy tank armies once they had forced a break-through; nor was there in existence any plan of defence for the capital. German artillery was inadequate although, as usual, *Luftwaffe* 88 mm anti-aircraft guns were used in a close support and an anti-tank role; in the air barely 300 aircraft remained to Army Group Vistula.

On 15 April, the day before the Soviet offensive, Hitler issued his last order of the day. It foretold to the fighters on the eastern front the fate in store for their families if they lost this battle and the Bolsheviks overran Germany. Old people and children would be murdered, women and girls would become barrack-room whores and everybody else would be marched off to Siberia. Hitler promised the support of massive artillery he did not possess and assured his troops that the Red Army would be destroyed in front of the capital, choking in a bath of blood. All ranks were warned against obeying orders of unknown German officers, a precaution necessary in view of the previous Soviet activity of this type in Pomerania and East Prussia.* The order was issued too late, however, to reach the troops for whom it was intended.

Zhukov's 1 Belorussian Front began its offensive before dawn on 16 April against Busse's 9 German Army; the war diarist of that headquarters recorded that the army sector came under the fire that day of 2,500 guns and 450 tanks, a figure much at variance with the Soviet post-war official account that described the deployment of 41,000 guns and mortars and 6,200 tanks among the three fronts. The main German resistance was centred on the Seelow position, against which the Soviet frontal attacks proved so costly that they had to be abandoned. Thereafter the Red Army troops were broken up into small detachments so that they might infiltrate into the German rear; on 17 April, after a heavy bombing attack and concentric armoured thrusts, Seelow was taken; then, on 18 April, the second German defensive line was breached. The staunch resolution of the German defenders, many of them *Luftwaffe* and *Volkssturm*, had come as a surprise to the Soviet command, and Zhukov was already two days late in his ordered programme. Some of the flanking Red Army formations had hardly advanced a step.

Further to the south, however, Konev's Ukrainian Front was making excellent progress. By 17 April both of his tank armies were clear of the Neisse, and Konev had soon driven a great wedge between Heinrici and Schörner in spite of some fierce counter-attacks from 4 Panzer Army, commanded by Graeser, the one-legged veteran regarded by Goebbels as 'of the old school but a splendid fellow withal'. 1 Ukrainian Front could not take Cottbus or Spremberg, and these were bypassed. Konev was by now well into the German rear and, after a radio talk with Stalin in the Kremlin, 1 Ukrainian Front was ordered to turn both of its tank armies to the north, one on Potsdam to encircle the capital and the other to enter the

---

* The order ended: 'At this moment. when Fate has removed from the earth the greatest criminal of all time [Roosevelt], the turning point of this war will be decided.' Both Hitler and Goebbels imagined that the death of Roosevelt would be followed by a break-down in the enemy alliance.

Berlin suburbs from the south through Zossen. Meanwhile, on the night of 19 April, Zhukov had, at last, gained open country and he began his outflanking movement of Berlin from the north, at the same time entering the outskirts of the city at Ladeburg and Zepernick.

Busse's 9 German Army defenders had contained the heavy weight of the offensive for three days before Zhukov's Soviet tank forces had broken through to the north of Berlin and separated them from von Manteuffel's 3 Panzer Army. To the south they had already been isolated from much of 4 Panzer Army by Konev's thrusts that cut across Busse's lines of communication. Busse could no longer defend Berlin; nor could he possibly restore the line of his broken positions. The war, as even Jodl was forced yet again to admit, 'was finally lost'. It only remained to withdraw the remnants of the troops and save them from the Soviet concentration camps: most of the German commanders came to this conclusion.*

This, however, was not the Führer's appreciation of the situation, and he acted not as though the war was lost but rather as if the tempo of the battle was rising to a crescendo and approaching its critical point. On 20 April Hitler refused to permit the withdrawal of 9 Army and he committed it to remain on the Oder. Heinrici therefore moved Group Steiner, which consisted of little more than a corps, to the area of Eberswalde, due north of Berlin, to take command of a number of detachments there, and so secure von Manteuffel's and the army group's exposed southern flank. But when, on 21 April, the existence of this little formation came to Hitler's ears, he ordered Group Steiner, which he magnified to the size of an army, to take command of elements of a panzer grenadier and two infantry divisions and attack south-eastwards to seal off the great gap through which Zhukov's right wing was pouring, and so establish contact with Weidling's 56 Panzer Corps to the east of Berlin.** The troops that had been allocated to Steiner were either not available or were divisons only in name and, at the most, Steiner had about 15,000 men without heavy weapons under his command. Führer orders had gone out to both Busse's 9 Army and Graeser's 4 Panzer Army ordering them to close the gap in the south through which Konev's troops had already passed.

Hitler's mind at this time swung rapidly to and fro from euphoria to the deepest depression. How much of his optimism was self-deception it is impossible to say. What is more remarkable is the personal magnetism and uncanny power of suggestion that he continued to exercise on his commanders and on his personal staff. On 29 December, when at the Adlerhorst, he had told General Thomale, the Chief of Staff of the Inspectorate of Panzer Troops, that 'without the exercise of an iron will the war could not be won' and he blamed the general staff for the spread of pessimism. Even as he said this, the hopelessness of the situation was in reality well known to him, for he afterwards reproached himself for not having ended his life in Rastenburg that November. Yet such a course would have been

* A chief of staff of one of the principal formations covering a great sector of the eastern front told the author that he and his commander were of opinion that April that it was vital to prepare to withdraw westwards. The chief of staff of the next higher formation, although in agreement with them, was so fearful of Hitler that he preferred to remain in ignorance of their plans.

** Hitler then telephoned Koller, the Chief of the Air Staff, who was at Wildpark-Werder, to order him to annihilate the Russian heavy guns that, for the first time, were firing into the city centre; he also ordered every *Luftwaffe* man to the north of Berlin to go out and help Steiner. Then, every five minutes, followed a new or a rescinding order. Finally, just before midnight, the Führer came on the phone again to promise that 'the Russian was about to suffer the most bloody defeat in his history right before the gates of Berlin'.

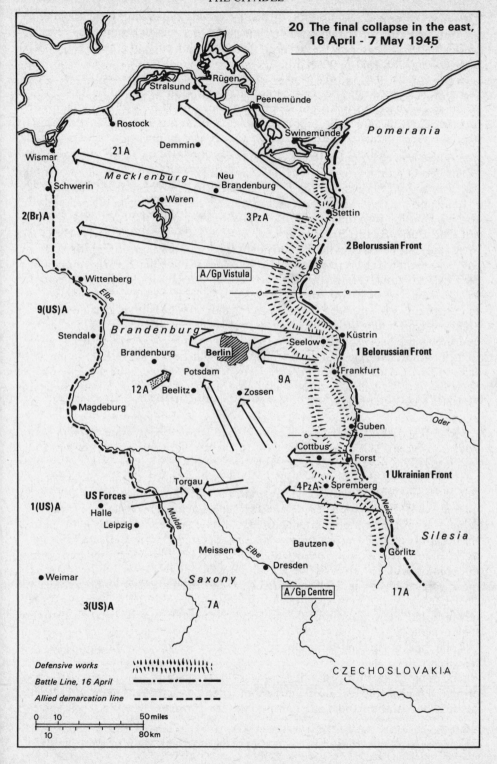

20 The final collapse in the east, 16 April – 7 May 1945

Pomerania

Rügen

Stralsund

Peenemünde

Rostock

Swinemünde

Demmin

21 A

Wismar

Mecklenburg

Neu Brandenburg

Schwerin

Waren

3 Pz A

Stettin

2(Br) A

2 Belorussian Front

Wittenberg

Oder

A/Gp Vistula

9(US) A

Brandenburg

Stendal

Küstrin

Seelow

1 Belorussian Front

Brandenburg

Berlin

Potsdam

Frankfurt

12 A   Beelitz

Zossen

9 A

Magdeburg

Guben

Oder

Cottbus

Forst

1 Ukrainian Front

Torgau

Spremberg

US Forces

4 Pz A

1(US) A

Halle

Mulde

Leipzig

Neisse

Silesia

Meissen

Bautzen

Görlitz

Elbe

Dresden

Weimar

Saxony

3(US) A

7 A

A/Gp Centre

17 A

CZECHOSLOVAKIA

Defensive works

Battle Line, 16 April

Allied demarcation line

0   10   50 miles

10   80 km

foreign to the man, for, hoping against hope and grasping at straws, he would continue with maniacal fanaticism to the very end, as long as there was a German whom he could persuade, or force, to fight for him.* He had surrounded himself with people who told him what he wanted to hear, reflecting and repeating his own grotesque views. Schmundt, Burgdorf, Keitel, Jodl, Krebs, Schörner, Rendulic, von Rundstedt and Model, had all had absolute faith in him, or, for reasons of their own, pretended that they had. Speer was in disgrace, but his deputy Saur had the dictator's ear, telling him that he *hoped* to produce 1,500 tanks a month, this at a time when the German armament industry was at the point of collapse due to the loss of Upper Silesia and the remaining sources of oil. On 23 January Hitler had said that without the Hungarian and Austrian oil a continuation of the war was no longer possible; but when he had lost these he still carried on.

Long ago, in 1925, Hitler had said in *Mein Kampf* that if the government was leading a nation into defeat then 'rebellion was not only the right of that people but their duty'. By the 20 July 1944 his views had changed. Similarly, Hitler had once said that it was the duty of the government, in the event of fighting a losing war, to safeguard the German people 'from a heroic end', that is to say annihilation. By 18 March, however, the dictator, according to Speer, took an entirely opposite view, saying that 'when the war is lost the people are lost, so that it is not necessary to ensure that resources are kept, even for them to eke out an existence'; on the contrary, continued Hitler, *it was better to destroy everything.* For, 'if the Germans had shown themselves to be weaker than their enemies, then the future belonged to the peoples of the east [of the Soviet Union]'. Those Germans that remained, he said, were of no account, for the best were dead. These were the judgements of a dictator who bent history and situations to suit himself, a man who, believing himself to be infallible, could easily absolve himself from all responsibility and blame.

Jodl subsequently said that he knew that Hitler had serious though secret doubts, even in 1943, as to the outcome of the war; according to Schramm, Hitler told his O K W circle that 'the war could no longer be won if the Anglo-American landings succeeded in Western Europe'. Yet at the same time this megalomaniac, this charlatan with something of the genius about him, continued to lead by the nose not only the German people but the vast majority of his colleagues and staffs, some of whom were highly intelligent men, buoying them up with the promise of the certainty of final victory, however long and hazardous the path might be. And, as Schramm has said, the generals and the general staff, though they had nothing in common with Hitler in origin, education, training or ideals, continued for the most part to have the highest respect for the man and his ability; some, the uncritical, placed him on a pinnacle; the others, in spite of his mistakes and his newly found-out reputation for unreliability, thought him to be on a distinctly higher plane than themselves. Only at the twelfth hour when the war was finally lost and the Russian was in the Chancellery, was this usurper condemned for what he was.

The senior German generals could not have been in ignorance of the total disregard for law, justice and decency about them, or of the existence and activities of the concentration and death camps; but they chose to close their eyes and ears

---

* That spring Hitler had begun to devote an inordinate amount of time to the design of new medals, promising ribbon and iron to anyone who destroyed six enemy tanks with close-quarter weapons.

since neither they nor their kith and kin were involved. By 1944, however, the situation was changing. Those few generals who first began to doubt the dictator's sense of direction were some of those who were in close contact with him. Halder, one of the first, was in a concentration camp. Rommel, formerly a firm supporter of Hitler and the party, said, not long before his end, that he sometimes doubted whether the dictator was normal. Zeitzler was another Nazi enthusiast who had modified his views. Guderian and Keitel changed theirs only after the war was truly lost. Jodl permitted himself to be critical after his master's death but then recanted when he felt the hangman's noose around his neck.*

Boldt has described how in the final weeks the dictator had lost his decisiveness and mental energy, his vacillation becoming such that three times he had instructed Boldt to have the Elbe bridges blown and twice had retracted the order immediately before the charges were fired. Yet Hitler was still telling the *Gauleiter* and his military chiefs, apparently with great confidence and assurance, that all would come right in the end, and many of them believed him. Even Goebbels continued to be taken in, for at the beginning of April the Führer told him, and Goebbels appears to have accepted it, that he had put out peace feelers to a receptive Russia, but the matter was hanging fire, as the Russian price, the cession of East Prussia, was reckoned to be too high. But side by side with these highflown essays in cloud-cuckoo-land were other more sombre indicators. Between 14 and 26 February the Führer had been dictating to Bormann, for the sake of posterity, his own misleading version of his policies and actions. At the end of March when the *Luftwaffe* General Kammhuber told the Führer that the war was finally lost, Hitler, without emphasis or emotion, had replied simply, '*I* know that! *(Das weiss ich selbst!)*'. On 18 April, when the Russians were already on the motor road from the Oder to Berlin, the Führer, after listening to a depressing dissertation by Hilpert, the Commander of Army Group Kurland, had leaned back in his chair and said: 'If the German people lose this war, then they have shown themselves to be unworthy of me!' In reporting this conversation to his war diarist, Hilpert said that it had made cold shivers run down his back.

The last Anglo-American air raid to be made on Berlin was a massive one lasting two hours from midday on 20 April, and the city lay thereafter heavily ruined and quiet. Electricity, gas and sanitation had broken down and the only water supply was provided by street fire hydrants. Little food could be obtained and that only by long hours of queueing.**

The 20 April was the Führer's birthday, the day on which Hitler had planned to leave Berlin for Obersalzberg; ten days earlier his personal servants and part of the OKW had already left for Bavaria. Almost all his former comrades appeared again to congratulate him, including Göring, Himmler, Speer and the heads of the

---

* Jodl added a postscript to his account of Hitler, after he had learned that he was to be executed: 'Let others who wish to, condemn him: I cannot.

** Among the draconian punishments meted out to the Berlin civil population in the event of disorders was the beheading of men and women in April for looting a Rahnsdorf bakery. Yet it was probably the fear of a Red Army occupation that kept the inhabitants docilely supporting the *Gauleiter* Goebbels, in spite of the fact that they wanted peace, almost at any price. The acting Chief of the Army General Staff was not so fortunate, however, for bystanders in the Berlin streets shouted 'Vampire' after his car.

armed services. Hitler seemed to be undecided whether he would leave Berlin or not, but he did order the implementation of the previously agreed plan whereby Dönitz should take over the command in the north, while it was assumed, but not confirmed, that Kesselring would command in the south. Göring then left for Bavaria while Himmler returned to Hohenlychen. The next day Schörner arrived in the bunker for a private meeting and restored the Führer to good spirits and such a pitch of breezy optimism that even Keitel and Jodl were surprised.

On 22 April the last war conference was held in the Chancellery. When it was reported that Rokossovsky was advancing deep into Mecklenburg, Hitler asked where Steiner and his attacking forces were, and the truth then came out that the grandiose attacks ordered by the dictator on 21 April had never even begun. Hitler leapt up and began to rant and rave, screaming about disloyalty, cowardice, treachery and insubordination, reproaching both the army and the S S. He would, he said, stay in the capital—all who wanted could leave him and Berlin. Then sinking back in his chair he started to sob, saying: 'It is all over. The war is lost. I shall shoot myself'.

Those present stood watching him, said Boldt, in bewildered silence. Jodl was the first to speak, telling the dictator of his duties towards the people. Others tried to comfort him, reminding him of the areas in the north and south not yet overrun. All tried, in vain, to persuade him to leave the ill-fated capital. Jodl pointed out the possibilities of a combined attack by 9 and 12 Armies and proposed that all O K W divisions should be returned from their distant theatres to defend Berlin. According to Keitel, Hitler's face was yellow, his twitching was accentuated, he was extremely nervous and his mind kept wandering.

That night the remainder of the Führer's circle left Berlin, except for Goebbels, Bormann, Burgdorf and Krebs. Göring had sent the Führer a telegram asking for confirmation that he (Göring) should assume plenipotentiary powers in accordance with a Führer conversation recounted to him second-hand by Koller; the answer, prompted by Bormann, came swiftly, removing Göring from all his posts and placing him under S S arrest.* Keitel had left the capital in search of Wenck's 12 Army on the Elbe to turn it eastwards to relieve Berlin, while Jodl went to Krampnitz in search of Steiner and von Manteuffel. By 25 April the Russians had completely encircled the capital. Wenck, who had turned his army about, could get no nearer than Potsdam, about twelve miles to the south-west, and there he awaited the remnants of Busse's 9 Army that were moving slowly westwards.

By 29 April 9 Army lay beween Beelitz and Luckenwalde due south of Berlin, being unable to make further movement by day because of attacks by Soviet aircraft and tanks. In the following two nights, troops, variously estimated to number between 3,000 and 30,000 together with a mass of civilians that clung to them for protection, infiltrated through by night to reach Wenck's 12 Army. Except for elements of 56 Panzer Corps in Berlin, Busse's 9 Army had ceased to exist. On 1 May Wenck, with the wounded and a great horde of refugees, prepared to fall back on the Elbe, where one of his corps commanders was attempting to negotiate with the Americans the terms of the surrender of 12 Army.

To the north of Berlin Heinrici wanted to take Steiner back under his own command together with Corps Holste, detached from Wenck, in order to cover the withdrawal of his troops westwards through Mecklenburg, an attack on Berlin

---

* Bormann, Goebbels and Himmler, even at this late hour, were fighting for power with their eyes on Hitler's succession.

from the north being by then entirely out of the question. Keitel, who had just arrived in the area, began, in the best Führer fashion, to cry treason. For the first time in seven years Keitel was free from the dominating presence of Hitler. Inexperienced in field command, he rushed about the countryside, quizzing the troops and threatening the commanders, and was horrified to find that Heinrici had begun an orderly withdrawal without obtaining the permission of the Führer or of himself. On 28 April Jodl informed Hitler of this fact by radio and Army Group Vistula was forbidden to retreat further. Later that night Heinrici came on the telephone to say that, in spite of the Führer order, he was going to continue to withdraw. For this both he and his chief of staff were removed from their posts and Student was appointed by Keitel as Heinrici's successor. Von Tippelskirch, the commander of a newly raised 21 Army in Mecklenburg, was ordered, very much against his will, to assume the temporary command of the army group.

That done, Keitel and Jodl left the scene of operations for Dobbin, where they joined Himmler, who gave them a radio message from the Führer, dated 28 April and addressed to Keitel, asking for the location of Wenck's, Busse's and Holste's spearheads in the breakthrough to Berlin. On that night of 29 April Keitel replied by radio that a break-in was no longer possible and he advised the Führer 'to break out or fly out'. Hitler did not deign to reply. Keitel and Jodl, *en route* to Schleswig-Holstein and Dönitz, continued their rituals of the daily *Führerlage* in which they solemnly briefed each other.

On 28 April Hitler was informed of a Reuter report concerning Himmler's attempted negotiations with the western powers, and this threw him into a great rage, for he saw in the report a deep-seated SS conspiracy between Himmler, Fegelein and Steiner. Fegelein, who was Eva Braun's brother-in-law, had been found in civilian clothes at his home in Charlottenburg and was under suspicion of trying to escape. Brought to the bunker, he was immediately shot by Hitler's order. Himmler, who was safely out of the Führer's reach, was disowned, although Bormann, on 30 April, was to send a radio signal to Dönitz ordering, in the Führer's name, instant and ruthless action against the *Reichsführer SS*. Ritter von Greim, who had been wounded flying into the city merely to be informed that he was appointed Göring's successor and promoted field-marshal, was thereupon ordered to fly out again to ensure that Himmler was in fact arrested.*

The Berlin population had for weeks past hoped against hope that the Americans would reach the city before the Russians. Now, surrounded and under heavy Red Army fire, they awaited relief by German forces. The approach of Wenck had been used by Goebbels as a call to arms to unite the defenders of Berlin and spur them on to new endeavours. But as the hours ran out it became obvious that no help could be expected from Wenck, Steiner or Busse. On the morning of 29 April, at four o'clock, Adolf Hitler, having finally resolved to take his own life, signed his last will and testament.** This was witnessed by Bormann and Burgdorf, two of the closely knit group about him; the third member of the trio, Fegelein, lay

---

* Immediately after he had flown out from Berlin, von Greim, 'enthusiastic and inspired by his talk with the Führer', told Koller that 'the most important thing was not to lose faith [in victory], for all could still turn out very well': the Führer's surprising strength of character had, he said, given him extraordinary energy: it was in truth a complete rejuvenation: the Führer, continued von Greim, no longer reproached the *Luftwaffe* with anything, for it had all been Göring's fault!

** When earlier the Führer had been told of the suicide of Germans in positions of responsibility he had condemned their deaths as cowardly.

dead outside. The other two signatories were Goebbels and Krebs.

In this testament for posterity the Führer disclaimed all responsibility for the starting of the Second World War and made an oblique condemnation of the officers of the German Army; Göring and Himmler were condemned as traitors. Dönitz was to be President and Commander-in-Chief of the Armed Forces. Hitler continued to interfere from the grave when he appointed the members of the new Dönitz government to include Goebbels, Bormann, Hanke, Seyss-Inquart, Schörner, von Greim and von Krosigk.

On the afternoon of 30 April, Hitler, together with Eva Braun, his newly wedded wife, committed suicide. And so ended the short-lived Third Reich that, according to the dead Führer's boast, was to have endured for a thousand years.

CHAPTER ELEVEN

Epilogue

In the Berlin bunker Bormann and Goebbels saw themselves, individually or jointly, as Hitler's successor as the true government of Germany, irrespective of what the dictator might have willed. Göring was under S S arrest, partly as a result of their machinations. Bormann had wanted Göring killed and he had seen to it that orders had gone out for the arrest and the liquidation of Himmler. There were no other rivals' for power, for, in their view, Dönitz was of little account and they intended to use him merely as their tool. Although the pair had informed the admiral of the terms of the Führer's testament—that he should succeed Hitler after the dictator's death—they had not in fact told him, or the world, that Hitler was already dead. Their immediate aim was to get themselves out of Berlin and take over the Dönitz government in North Germany, and this could be done only by hoodwinking both Dönitz and the Russians. Goebbels had now allied himself with his former enemy Bormann, ditching his old colleagues Göring and Himmler—friends they had never been. The determination to fight to the last disappeared with Hitler's dying breath.*

On the evening of 30 April, within a few hours of Hitler's death, a German officer was sent under cover of a white flag from the S S Division *Nordland* sector in the capital to the forward defended localities of Chuikov's 8 Guards Army, asking whether Krebs might be permitted to cross the line. Then, shortly before 4 a.m., the last Chief of General Staff of the Army, accompanied by a staff officer of 56 Panzer Corps and a Russian speaking Latvian lieutenant in the German service, appeared at Chuikov's headquarters. Speaking on behalf of Goebbels and Bormann, Krebs asked for a truce, and his requests were relayed by telephone from Chuikov to Zhukov and then on to Moscow. According to the Soviet account, Krebs told the Russians of Hitler's death and said that he had been commissioned to negotiate an armistice that would permit *the new German government* (as appointed by the dictator) to assemble, presumably in North Germany, and then to enter into peace negotiations. There followed a protracted argument as to which was to come first, the cease-fire before the surrender or the surrender followed by the cease-fire. After midday Krebs returned to the Chancellery without having achieved any agreement at all, and the Soviet troops began their final assault on the Tiergarten and the government buildings immediately to the east and south-east.

---

* The tragedy for Germany was that the government and military communication system functioned efficiently to the very end.

The conspirators had obviously wanted to arrive at Dönitz's headquarters before he was aware that he was, for the time being at least, the *de jure* head of state, and had been so since the previous day. But because the Russians now knew of Hitler's death and might at any moment broadcast it to the world, Goebbels and Bormann thought it politic to inform Dönitz that 'the testament was in force' without telling him, however, that the Führer was dead. At three o'clock in the afternoon, after Krebs had returned and they knew that Stalin did not intend that the Berlin rump should escape the capital, they realized that the game was up and that the grand admiral must be told the truth. For themselves, all hope had gone. Goebbels and his wife murdered their children before committing suicide. Burgdorf, hated and despised even by the German Army, and the amiable and compliant Krebs shot themselves. Bormann and the remainder of the Führer's court attempted to escape from the Chancellery through the Soviet lines; and, as far as is known, Bormann died by his own hand somewhere near the north limits of the city.

Just after midnight on 2 May, Weidling, the Commander of 56 Panzer Corps and of all German forces in Berlin, surrendered to the Russians and called on all German troops to cease resistance.

Elsewhere, other members of the Hitler-appointed government took whatever steps they could to join Dönitz. Hanke, the Breslau *Gauleiter*, left the doomed garrison by a light plane and was not heard of thereafter. Schörner, the Commander of Army Group Centre, also left to take over his new post, and eventually turned up in his home city of Munich where he was promptly arrested by the American military authorities and handed over to the Russians. Others of Hitler's men, the old military guard, including von Bock (the elderly field-marshal dismissed and unemployed since 1942), thought they had something to offer and sought appointment and power, and hurried northwards to place themselves at Dönitz's disposal.

Meanwhile the real rulers of Germany had been making their own arrangements for the disposal of the Third Reich. Bormann's call for the arrest of Himmler had gone unheeded and the *Reichsführer SS* had for some time been telling his immediate circle 'that there was no one left of sufficient stature, other than himself, with whom the western allies would be willing to negotiate'. His subordinates, Kaltenbrunner of the RSHA, the main SS and German State security organization, and Wolff, 'the Highest SS and Police Commander in Italy' who had formerly been Fegelein's predecessor at the OKW, were both attempting to contact the allies. Von Ribbentrop was trying to do the same. Meanwhile the whole of the Reich, the armed forces and civilian administration, were under the rigid control of the SS.

The first approach for a German surrender had come as early as February, in Italy, the German initiative being made by the SS general Wolff, who had the agreement of von Vietinghoff and the two army commanders that a capitulation was inevitable and urgent. By the end of March German casualties in Italy had totalled 420,000 (against an allied loss of 300,000), and although the Army Group C field strength of 600,000 was almost as great as the joint field strength of 5 (US) and 8 (British) Armies, the allied naval, air and logistic support brought the Anglo-American theatre total to about one and a half million men. The allied might was overwhelming. Since the fall of Rome, the Germans had held on desperately to the Appenine defensive positions, fighting for every mountainous foot of territory. By now, however, the Italian partisans, and in particular the communists, were gaining the upper hand in many of the rearward areas.

By April, North Italy was already in turmoil and German troops were making their way northwards as fast as they were able to escape capture by the allies or destruction at the hands of the partisans who controlled many of the main routes out of the country. On one such route Mussolini, in the garb of a German soldier, had been removed by the partisans from the German convoy taking him northwards, and on 28 April the former Italian dictator was executed by the irregulars who had captured him.

The capitulation of the Axis forces in North Italy was signed at Caserta on 29 April. Kesselring meanwhile, however, had been made responsible for all German army groups in the south so that Army Groups D, G and C were now under his command.* When Kesselring was briefed as to the signing of the surrender, he was so fearful of the possible consequences that he refused to countenance it, ordering the immediate replacement of von Vietinghoff by Schulz from Army Group G. Wolff, however, arrested Schulz and his chief of staff when they arrived in the theatre, and prepared contingency plans to engage Löhr's Army E forces retreating from the Balkans in case these should attempt to take punitive action against the German command in North Italy.

Kesselring tried to safeguard his own position by reporting Wolff's action to Kaltenbrunner; Kaltenbrunner was himself in a conspiracy to contact the allies. But the public announcement of Hitler's death, at 11 p.m. on 1 May, more than twenty-four hours after it happened, released Kesselring from his oath of allegiance and lessened any possibility of retribution. Army Group C in Italy then laid down its arms and Army Group G, immediately to the north, approached Devers's 6 Army Group to capitulate.

Hitler's Fortress Europe and his SS Reich had been in a state of disorder and lawlessness, that had grown worse after 20 July 1944, with the German people and its own armed forces terrorized by Hitler's SS henchmen. For months before the end SS patrols were hanging or shooting officers and soldiers out of hand. By April, Göring, the Commander-in-Chief of the *Luftwaffe*, the Führer's deputy and earlier nominated successor, together with his wife, were in SS hands and fearful for their lives. Koller, the Chief of the Air Staff, was also arrested by the SS. Field-Marshal Busch, the overall commander in the North-West, was ready to surrender Hamburg and the Jutland peninsula to Montgomery but dared not do so until the British had sealed off Denmark and reached the Baltic, because he feared that, without the protection of his former enemies, the *Waffen SS* might move in to liquidate him and his headquarters. Dönitz, the newly appointed commander in the north and shortly to be both the temporary head of state and *Wehrmacht* Commander-in-Chief, was speedily providing himself with a strong naval bodyguard from U-boat crews to protect himself against arrest or elimination by Himmler or one of his SS deputies. Dornberger and von Braun with the V-2 development teams and staff organization had taken refuge in South Germany when the Russians had overrun Peenemünde; but they soon came to the conclusion that there was a very real danger that what they called their SS supervisors' '*Totale* complex', might encourage the SS to destroy the V-2 plans and equipment and murder the

* Army Group D being his own OB West headquarters.

German military and civilian staff so that the secrets should not fall into allied hands. On Dornberger's orders they therefore gave the S S the slip and, hiding the records, put as great a distance as possible between themselves and their black-uniformed guards.

On 23 April, when Hitler was of course still alive, Himmler had met the Swede Bernadotte, asking him to transmit a message through Sweden that Himmler 'was ready to surrender in the west to enable the Anglo-Americans to advance rapidly eastwards'. The allied reply of 27 April, demanding unconditional surrender to all its enemies, was released to the world press on the following day and the news report was taken by Goebbels to Hitler, this causing the final breach between the dictator and the *Reichsführer S S*.

Dönitz, the new head of government, had instructed all German troops in Western Europe to surrender to the British and Americans and had ordered all U-boats back to port. Army Groups C, G and North-West were already laying down their arms. On 5 May he sent von Friedeburg, the Naval Commander-in-Chief, to Eisenhower at Rheims, and the next day Friedeburg was joined by Jodl. Eisenhower, sensing that Jodl was playing for time while the troops on the eastern front withdrew towards the west, threatened the sealing of the Anglo-American front against all line-crossers unless an immediate and unconditional surrender was signed. This was done by Jodl on 7 May and two days later a second surrender document ratifying the first was signed by Keitel in Berlin.

Meanwhile the mass movement westwards of German troops and civilians continued. Whether or not they were permitted to cross the boundary between east and west appeared to vary according to the sector: in Mecklenburg troops and refugees.were admitted; in Brandenburg troops were allowed across the Elbe but not civilians; in Bohemia and the south, troops and civilians were halted at gunpoint and in some cases disarmed prisoners of war were handed back to the Red Army. With few exceptions German commanders on the eastern front, even though they knew that they had been listed by the USSR as war criminals, remained at their posts and went into captivity with their men.

With the final surrender of the citadel of Fortress Europe ended the greatest war in Germany's long history.

Göring, Himmler, Keitel and Jodl were unable to bring themselves to understand the conditions of the defeat and the determination of the Anglo-Americans to root out war criminals. For Göring and Himmler the realization came with arrest and suicide. Jodl meanwhile was at first busily employed at his desk, almost without a break, inserting a daily report in the O K W war diary as before, but this time for a different master—his former enemies—without, however, the same blind obedience with which he had served the dictator. For he seemed to have thought that he was dealing with a 1919 Allied Disarmament Commission that could be thwarted and deceived at every move. On 12 May he was instructing his O K W staff that 'the allied delegations [*sic*] must be overwhelmed with documents and memoranda'; and, although he himself had signed the instrument of unconditional surrender, he appeared to think that the German forces, collapsed, disarmed and thoroughly demoralized though they were, could actually be made ready, at his bidding, to continue the war, for he told his O K W representatives that the allies 'must be made to understand that we Germans love life, but do not fear death!' Such nonsensical posturings were, however, soon brought to an end, a few days later, with the allied arrest of Keitel, as Jodl expressed it, 'for giving out the order to liquidate English officers at the prisoner of war camp in Sagan Silesia'. Jodl was shortly to follow Keitel on trial for his life.

Keitel and Jodl were the courtiers in Hitler's military circle, the 'type of people' whom Rommel once condemned in that they 'waged a battle for power on the backs of the fighting troops'. Jodl passed his own judgement on himself when he said:

> For five years I have worked and obeyed and kept silent . . . regarding obedience as honourable and praiseworthy . . . and for Mexican gangster methods [of 20 July] I have only contempt. For five years I have been silent although I did not agree with my chief and although much of the nonsense that was ordered appeared impossible. And I knew that the war was lost in the spring of 1942.

The impossible position of the officer corps, and in particular of the higher field commanders, was described after the war by Jodl, and by no means incorrectly. The generals, said Jodl, were:

> fighting a war that they did not want under a Commander-in-Chief who did not trust them and whom they themselves did not fully trust, by methods contrary to their experience and accepted views, with troops and police that were not completely under their command.

On the other hand, it must be remembered, as Faber du Faur said, that the generals were happy enough at the time of the Führer's victories—it was his defeats that they did not like. For many German generals had two faces and two stories; one under the Third Reich and the other displayed and recounted to the Anglo-Americans, particularly to the writer and journalist and the avid seeker of good copy. Under Hitler, Germany's most senior generals were, or pretended to be, enthusiastic supporters of Nazism, an attitude that they shared with all ranking officials in the Third Reich. German generals later excused themselves by the plea of ignorance, by hiding behind the provisions of Hitler's Basic Order No. 1, that none should know more than was needed for the performance of his duties. Others professed to regard themselves as bound, come what may, by the personal oath of allegiance to the dictator.

It is of course easy to criticize these officers after the event. British generals and American generals, too, came in all shapes and sizes; the able and the inefficient, the courageous, the ambitious, the dishonest and the weak. But education and political conditions in the democracies were very different from those in the Third Reich, and, in consequence, western generals were not to be faced with the same dilemma.

It is probably more pertinent to compare Hitler's generals to Stalin's generals, where the repressive government and social system of the Soviet Union approximated to that of the Third Reich in the last year of the war, with concentration camps filled to overflowing, with purges, deportations, torture and mass killings, the ubiquitous secret police and centralized personal control; where families, friends and even acquaintances disappeared, together with the principal suspect; where no man, however trusted, could go abroad without leaving 'a tail'; where the families of prisoners of war could be, and were, incarcerated for the misfortune of their men-folk. The position of the Red Army general was little different from that of his German counterpart. His feared, and sometimes hated, commissar was his shadow, and he was reported upon by both the commissar and by the secret police special sections set to watch him. Mindful of the consequences of disobedience, he did what he was told, however barbarous or unlawful the orders.* The penalty even for remonstrance would have been a dire one. The Soviet NKVD troops approximated to the *Waffen SS*, and the Soviet general's loyalty and responsibility, like the German's, were to his superior and to the head of state, not to the men under his command.

Nor in the end were Hitler's and Stalin's military systems very different. During the twenties and the thirties Stalin controlled all senior Soviet military appointments and approved or vetoed military theory, organization and equipment. Stalin alone had been responsible for the purges that had destroyed the larger part of the command of the Red Army. Stalin's principal positive contribution (the one in which Hitler had so significantly failed) was a rearmament in breadth and in depth, the creation of a well-developed home industrial base responsible for the production of a great quantity of military equipment, much of it of modern design and good quality. Stalin's immediate failure in the opening days of the war, like Hitler's, was political, rather than military.

At the time of the invasion of the Soviet Union, however, Stalin's faults were military, and not political, for during the course of the whole war, when Hitler had renounced all diplomacy, Stalin, on the other hand, hardly put a political foot wrong.

Hitler's defeat in Russia was due to an over-ambitious strategy based on inadequate resources and a wilful underestimate of enemy potential, together with a failure to overcome the problems of movement and supply: *his world-wide failure* was an effect of his own folly, the abandonment of all diplomacy and a lack of any understanding of the heavy preponderance of allied resources over those of the Axis powers. By 1943, when Fortress Europe was taking shape in Hitler's mind, the balance was entirely weighted against Germany and from then onwards this was to show itself in an unbroken series of calamitous military disasters.

* Vasilevsky, the first deputy head of the operations department and later Chief of the Red Army General Staff, in closest touch with Stalin, has told how his aged father, a preceptor or choirmaster in a Russian church and therefore a Soviet undesirable, used to write to him. Vasilevsky did not dare to answer the letters but thought it safer to inform the responsible commissar on the Red Army General Staff and ask for advice whether or not he should reply to his own father. The commissar thought it wiser not to do so. One may well assume even from this little incident that neither Vasilevsky, nor Shaposhnikov, his predecessor, educated and humane though both were, would protest at the atrocities and barbarities that they saw about them.

Appendix A

The German Army Groups in the East (OKH) June 1943 — May 1945

	NORTH	CENTRE		SOUTH	A
1943					
June	v. Küchler	v. Kluge		v. Manstein	v. Kleist
Oct		Busch			
1944				NORTH UKRAINE	SOUTH UKRAINE
Jan	Model			Model	Schörner
March	Lindemann				
June		Model			
July	Friessner Schörner				Friessner
Aug		Reinhardt		A	SOUTH
Sept					
Dec	Rendulic			Harpe	Wöhler
1945	KURLAND	NORTH	VISTULA *(new)*	CENTRE	
Jan	v. Vietinghoff	Rendulic	Himmler	Schörner	
March	Rendulic	Weiss	Heinrici		
April	Hilpert	*disbanded*			Rendulic
May			Student		OSTMARK

Appendix B

The German Army Groups in the West (OKW) June 1943 – May 1945

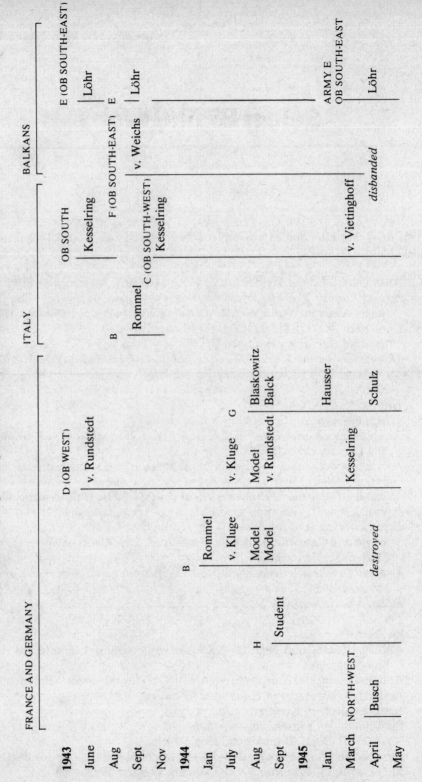

Select Bibliography

This list is not intended as a complete bibliography but merely to indicate the principal works to which reference has been made in writing this account.

I. Anthologies, Edited Works, Official and Semi-Official Publications
    Buying Aircraft Material Procurement for the Army Air Forces. The United States Army in World War II. (Holley) Department of the Army 1964.
    Camera at Sea. US Naval Institute, Annapolis 1978.
    Command Decisions. Harcourt Brace, New York 1959.
    Documents on the Expulsion of the Germans from Eastern-Central-Europe (Volume 1). Federal Ministry for Expellees, Refugees and War Victims, Bonn.
    Istoriia Velikoi Otechestvennoi Voiny Sovetskogo Soiuza (six volumes). Moscow 1961-5.
    Kriegstagebuch des Oberkommandos der Wehrmacht (four volumes). Bernard und Graefe, Frankfurt am Main.
    Nazi Conspiracy and Aggression (eight volumes). US Government Printing Office 1946-8.
    Ordnance Department Procurement and Supply. The United States Army in World War II. (Thompson and Mayo) Department of the Army 1960.
    Statistical Digest of the War. HMSO, London 1951.
    Strength and Casualties of the Armed Forces of the United Kingdom 1939-45. Cmd. 6832, HMSO, London.
    Velikaia Otechestvennaia Voina Sovetskogo Soiuza 1941-5 (Kratkaia Istoriia). Moscow 1965.
    50 Let Vooruzhennykh Sil SSSR. Moscow 1968.

II. Books
    Ahlfen, H. von, und Niehoff, H. *So Kämpfte Breslau.* Graefe und Unzer, München 1960.
    Ahlfen, H. von, *Der Kampf um Schlesien.* Graefe und Unzer, München 1961.
    Anders, W. *An Army in Exile.* Macmillan, London 1949.
    Beck, L. *Studien.* Koehler, Stuttgart 1955.
    Birkenfeld, W. *Geschichte der deutschen Wehr- und Rüstungswirtschaft (1918-45).* Boldt, Boppard am Rhein 1966.
    Birse, A. H. *Memoirs of an Interpreter.* Michael Joseph, London 1967.
    Blumentritt, G. *Von Rundstedt.* Odhams, London 1952.

Boldt, G. *Hitler's Last Days*. Barker, London 1973.

Bor-Komorowski, T. *The Secret Army*. Gollancz, London 1950.

Bradley, O. N. *A Soldier's Story*. Eyre and Spottiswoode, London 1951.

Bryant, A. *Triumph in the West*. Collins, London 1959.

Buchheit, G. *Hitler der Feldherr*. Grote, Baden 1958.

Butcher, H. C. B. *My Three Years with Eisenhower*. Simon and Schuster, New York 1946.

Butler, J. R. M. *Grand Strategy. History of the Second World War*. (Volumes 2 and 3 (2)). HMSO, London 1957 and 1964.

Choltitz, D. von. *Un Soldat parmi des Saldats*. Aubanel 1964.

Chuikov, V. I. *The End of the Third Reich*. Macgibbon and Kee, London 1967.

Churchill, W. S. *The Second World War* (six volumes). Cassell, London.

Ciano's Diaries 1939-43. Heinemann, London 1947.

Deakin, F. W. *The Brutal Friendship*. Weidenfeld and Nicolson, London 1962.

Deane, J. R. *The Strange Alliance*. Murray, London 1947.

Djilas, M. *Conversations with Stalin*. Rupert Hart-Davis, London 1962.

Dönitz, K. *Memoirs*. Weidenfeld and Nicolson, London 1959.

Eden, A. *Memoirs — The Reckoning*. Cassell, London 1965.

Eisenhower, D. D. *Crusade in Europe*. Heinemann, London 1948.

Ellis, L. F. *Victory in the West. History of the Second World War* (Volumes 2 and 3). HMSO, London 1962-8.

Erfurth, W. *Der Finnische Krieg 1941-4*. Limes Verlag, Wiesbaden 1950.

Faber du Faur, M. von. *Macht und Ohnmacht*. Günther Verlag, Stuttgart 1953.

Feis, H. *Churchill, Roosevelt, Stalin*. Princeton University Press, 1966.

Fretter-Pico, M. *Missbrauchte Infanterie*. Bernard und Graefe, Frankfurt am Main 1957.

Friessner, H. *Verratene Schlachten*. Holsten, Hamburg 1956.

Gareis, M. *Kampf und Ende der 98. Infanterie Division*. Gareis, Tegernsee 1956.

Gilbert, F. *Hitler Directs His War*. OUP, New York 1950.

Goebbels, J. *The Goebbels Diaries* (ed. Lochner). Hamish Hamilton London 1948.

Goebbels, J. *Final Entries 1945 — The Diaries of Joseph Goebbels* (ed. Trevor-Roper). Putnam, New York 1978.

Gorbatov, A. V. *Years off my Life*. Constable, London 1964.

Greiner, H. *Die Oberste Wehrmachtführung*. Limes Verlag, Wiesbaden 1951.

Guderian, H. *Panzer Leader*. Michael Joseph, London 1952.

Halder, F. *Kriegstagebuch* (three volumes). Kohlhammer, Stuttgart 1962.

Halder, F. *Hitler as War Lord*. Putnam, London 1950.

Heiber, H. von. *Hitlers Lagebesprechungen*. Deutsche Verlags-Anstalt, Stuttgart 1962.

Heidkämper, O. *Witebsk*. Vowinckel, Heidelberg 1954.

Hillgruber, A. *Hitlers Strategie*. Bernard und Graefe, Frankfurt am Main 1965.

Hillgruber, A. *Hitler Konig Carol und Marschall Antonescu*. Franz Steiner, Wiesbaden 1965.

Hillgruber, A. *Die Räumung der Krim 1944*. Mittler, Berlin/Frankfurt 1959.

Hitler, A. *Mein Kampf*. Hurst and Blackett, London 1939.

Hubatsch, W. *Hitlers Weisungen für die Kriegführung 1939-45.* Bernard und Graefe, Frankfurt am Main 1962.

Huzel, D. K. *Peenemunde to Canaveral.* Prentice-Hall, New Jersey 1962.

Ismay, H. L. *The Memoirs of General the Lord Ismay.* Heinemann, London 1960.

Jacobsen, H. A. *Der Zweite Weltkrieg in Chronik und Dokumenten.* Wehr- und Wissen Verlagsgesellschaft, Darmstadt 1961.

Janssen, G. *Das Ministerium Speer.* Ullstein, Berlin 1968.

Keilig, W. *Das Deutsche Heer 1939-45* (three volumes). Podzun, Bad Nauheim.

Keitel, W. *Memoirs. Kimber, London 1965.*

Kesselring, A. *Soldat bis zum letzten Tag.* Athenäum, Bonn 1953.

Kissel, H. *Die Katastrophe in Rumanien 1944.* Wehr- und Wissen Verlagsgesellschaft, Darmstadt 1964.

Kissel, H. *Der Deutsche Volkssturm 1944-5.* Mittler, Frankfurt am Main 1962.

Klink, W. *Das Gesetz des Handelns 'Zitadelle' 1943.* Deutsche Verlags Anstalt, Stuttgart 1966.

Konev, I. S. *Zapiski Komanduiushchego Frontom 1943-4.* Moscow 1972.

Kurowski, F. *Armee Wenck.* Vowinckel, Neckargemünd 1967.

Lange, W. *Korpsabteilung C.* Vowinckel, Neckargemünd 1961.

Lasch, O. *So Fiel Königsberg.* Graefe und Unzer, München 1959.

Leliushenko, D. D. *Moskva-Stalingrad-Berlin-Praga.* Moscow 1970.

Liddell-Hart, B. H. *The Rommel Papers.* Collins, London 1953.

Lossberg, B. von. *Im Wehrmachtführungsstab.* Nölke, Hamburg 1949.

Ludendorff, E. von. *Vom Feldherrn zum Weltrevolutionär und Wegbereiter Deutscher Volksschöpfung.* Ludendorff, München 1940.

Malinovsky, R. Ia. *Final.* Moscow 1966.

Malinovsky, R. Ia. *Budapesht-Vena-Praga.* Moscow 1969.

Mannerheim, C. G. *Memoirs.* Cassell, London 1953.

Manstein, E. von. *Lost Victories.* Methuen, London 1958.

Manstein, E. von. *Aus einem Soldatenleben.* Athenäum, Bonn 1958.

Mazulenko, W. A. *Die Zerschlagung der Heeresgruppe Südukraine.* Berlin 1959.

Medlicott, W. N. *The Economic Blockade. History of the Second World War* (Volumes 1 and 2). HMSO, London 1959.

Mellenthin, F. W. von. *Panzer Battles.* University of Oklahoma Press 1956.

Meretskov, K. A. *Na Sluzhbe Narodu.* Moscow 1970.

Milward, A. S. *The German Economy at War.* The Athlone Press, London 1965.

Moloney, C. J. C. *The Mediterranean and the Middle East. The Second World War.* HMSO, London 1973.

Montgomery, B. L. *Memoirs.* Collins, London 1958.

Moskalenko, K. S. *Na Iugo-Zapadnom Napravlenii 1943-5.* Moscow 1972.

Müller-Hillebrand, B. *Das Heer* (three volumes). Mittler, Frankfurt am Main.

Munzel, O. *Die Deutschen Gepanzerten Truppen bis 1945.* Maximilian, Herford 1965.

Nicholson, G. W. L. *The Canadians in Italy.* Clouter, Ottawa 1956.

Oesch, K. L. *Finnlands Entscheidungskampf 1944.* Huber, Frauenfeld 1964.

O'Neill, R. *The German Army and the Nazi Party.* Cassell, London 1966.

Picker, H. *Hitlers Tischgespräche.* Seewald, Stuttgart 1963.

Pickert, W. *Vom Kuban-Brückenkopf bis Sewastopol.* Vowinckel, Heidelberg 1955.

Platonov, S. P. *Vtoraia Mirovaia Voina.* Moscow 1958.

Pohlman, H. *Wolchow 1941-1944.* Podzun, Bad Nauheim 1962.

Rehm, W. *Jassy.* Vowinckel, Neckargemünd 1959.

Rendulic, L. *Gekämpft, Gesiegt, Geschlagen.* Welsermühl, Wels, München 1957.

Rokossovsky, K. K. *Soldatskii Dolg.* Moscow 1968.

Roskill, S. W. *The War at Sea. The Second World War* (Volumes 2 and 3). HMSO, London 1954-61.

Roskill, S. W. *The Navy at War 1939-1945.* Collins, London 1960.

Seeckt, H. von. *Thoughts of a Soldier.* Benn, London 1930.

Shtemenko, S. M. *General'nyi Shtab v Gody Voiny* (two volumes). Moscow 1968-73.

Speer, A. *Inside the Third Reich.* Weidenfeld and Nicolson, London 1970.

Speidel, H. *Invasion 1944.* Regnery, Chicago 1950.

Tedder, A. *With Prejudice.* Cassell, London 1966.

Tessin, G. *Verbände und Truppen der deutschen Wehrmacht und Waffen SS 1939-1945.* (Volumes 2 and 3). Mittler, Frankfurt am Main.

Tornau, G. und Kurowski, F. *Sturmartillerie Fels in der Brandung.* Maximilian, Herford und Bonn 1965.

Trevor-Roper, H. R. *The Last Days of Hitler.* Macmillan, London 1947.

Vasilevsky, A. M. *Delo Vsei Zhizni.* Moscow 1974.

Voronov, N. N. *Na Sluzhbe Voennoi.* Moscow 1963.

Vormann, N. von. *Tscherkassy.* Vowinckel, Heidelberg 1954.

Warlimont, W. *Inside Hitler's Headquarters.* Weidenfeld and Nicolson, London 1964.

Westphal, S. *The Fatal Decisions.* Michael Joseph, London 1965.

Wheeler-Bennett, J. W. *The Nemesis of Power.* Macmillan, London 1961.

Woodward, E. L. *British Foreign Policy. History of the Second World War.* HMSO, London 1962.

Wuorinen, J. H. *Finland and World War II 1939-1944.* The Ronald Press, New York 1948.

Zhukov, G. K. *Vospominaniia i Razmyshleniia.* Macdonald, London 1969.

Index

213

INDEX

INDEX